"I like Texas highways because, unlike
If you miss your exit, you can always
miles in the form of an easy turnaround. That's why I love this wonderful title and the equally heartening stories within. If you wonder if
you, or your   Christ
is the orig   IAN
                                                               hor

"Have yo   nd
with now   hap
out new   ew
book, Go

                                                              JER
                                                              ker

"Jesus tol   gal
son. Since   od
has been p   ng
and applar   ec-
ond chanc   Go
and sin no   er
tripped an

                                                              NI
                                                              st

ALLISON GAPPA BOTTKE
with CHERYLL HUTCHINGS and ELLEN REGAN

GOD
ALLOWS
U-TURNS

TRUE STORIES OF
HOPE AND HEALING

PROMISE
PRESS
An Imprint of Barbour Publishing

3261

Layout and typesetting by Robyn Martins and Gladys Dunlap

All Scripture quotations, unless otherwise indicated, are taken from the HOLY BIBLE, NEW INTERNATIONAL VERSION®. NIV®. Copyright © 1973, 1978, 1984 by International Bible Society. Used by permission of Zondervan Publishing House. All rights reserved.

Scripture quotations marked NRSV are taken from the New Revised Standard Version Bible, copyright © 1989. Division of Christian Education of the National Council of churches of Christ in the United States of America. Used by permission. All rights reserved.

Scripture quotations marked KJV are taken from the King James Version of the Bible.

Scripture quotations marked RSV are from the Revised Standard Version of the Bible, copyright 1946, 1952, 1971 by the Division of Christian Education of the National Council of the Churches of Christ in the USA. Used by permission.

Scripture quotations marked NLT are taken from the *Holy Bible,* New Living Translation, copyright © 1996. Used by permission of Tyndale House Publishers, Inc. Wheaton, Illinois 60189, U.S.A. All rights reserved.

Scripture quotations marked NKJV are taken from the New King James Version. Copyright © 1979, 1980, 1982 by Thomas Nelson, Inc. Used by permission. All rights reserved.

Published by Promise Press, an imprint of Barbour Publishing, Inc., P.O. Box 719, Uhrichsville, Ohio 44683, www.promisepress.com

Member of the
Evangelical Christian
Publishers Association

Printed in the United States of America.

*Through Jesus, therefore, let us continually offer to God a
sacrifice of praise—the fruit of lips that confess his name.
And do not forget to do good and to share with others,
for with such sacrifices God is pleased.*
HEBREWS 13:15–16

FOR OUR CONTRIBUTORS AND READERS

This book is dedicated to our brothers and sisters in Christ who sent us stories and to our readers around the world who will come to depend upon this and future volumes of *God Allows U-Turns* to uplift and encourage them in their personal walk of faith.

It is our prayer that God will be pleased with the fruit of sharing offered by the contributors whose true stories appear in this first volume of *God Allows U-Turns*. We were overwhelmed by the thousand plus stories we received, stories that openly praised and confessed how God is at work every day in every life.

May these slice-of-life stories touch your emotions and warm your heart. May they bring you to a better understanding of God's love for us all. God's peace and protection to you always.

ALLISON

FOR MY DEAREST LOVED ONES

Kevin K. Bottke
Who taught me about unconditional love and commitment.
Thank you for writing to me.
Christopher John Smith
Who taught me that our greatest gifts are our children
and how vital it is to pray for them.
Dolores B. Gappa
Who taught me all about love, survival, loyalty, and forgiveness.

God has richly blessed me.
I love you all.

CONTENTS

ACKNOWLEDGMENTS

The phrase *God Allows U-Turns* pretty much sums up my life. As a former "prodigal daughter," I can now see clearly how many times my heavenly Father was there to rescue me, guide me, and give me the wisdom to turn around in my tracks and retreat from ways destined to bring me to destruction. Today, I cannot imagine my life without God's love, without the knowledge that Jesus Christ died for me. I am a living, breathing example of how a life can be drastically changed. . . with God's help.

When I started writing my personal testimony over a decade ago and titled it *God Allows U-Turns,* I had no idea how the Lord would change my life; how He would work in me to share with others the vital message of salvation and forgiveness through this book series.

The inspiration to turn my personal testimony book into a collection of true short stories came to me in late 1999. As we ushered in the new millennium, God was at work, opening one door after another to make this dream a reality. Within two months, we had a web site and the God Allows U-Turns Project was born. Virtually overnight, stories began to come in from around the world. Soon, I was joined by two coeditors whose talents I could not have done without. By April, we had one of the best literary agencies in the country believing in the book series, and by November we had acquired an international publisher whose vision matched our own in reaching the world. The volume you now hold in your hands took almost two years from inception to publication to write, compile, edit, and produce. It is, we pray, the first in a series of short story collections that will encourage and uplift people around the world.

There are many people to acknowledge for their contributions, without which this book could never have been created.

To the thousands of authors/contributors whose stories made us laugh, cry, and praise the Lord with joyful alleluias: You are gems beyond value. May God continue to shine His light on your lives.

Reading Group members who spent hours reading first, second, third, and final story drafts. Your input was more valuable than you could ever know.

Tammy Thorpe and Lisa Copen for being Internet angels sent by

God Himself. Each version of our evolving web site has been made richer by your individual talents.

Chip MacGregor at ALIVE Communications, Inc. I thank God for you daily!

Susan Schlabach at Barbour Publishing, Inc., for seeking us out from the very beginning and never losing sight of the fact that you wanted this series at your house. Your support and direction have made such a difference.

Cheryll Hutchings, who is always there with a kind word of encouragement and sisterly advice. Your editing skills were apparent to me years ago, and it is such a blessing to work with you as this project grows. May the Lord do mighty things in your life.

Ellen Regan, who spent countless hours editing stories, and whose commitment kept me sane and mellow through the last weeks of editing the final manuscript for volume one. How I love your Irish wit and east coast accent! You are truly my sister in Christ.

To my "California family." The Lord used the years I spent with you to teach me many important lessons. I give thanks to Him for bringing you all into my life. A special thanks to Sharon Esterley Rubino whose talents and teachings helped me to become a fun-loving, organized perfectionist. . .much of who I am is thanks to you. And to Don Laffoon whose strength and love helped my son and me through many difficult times. I love you both.

During the early years of my Christian walk, the Lord sent special people into my life to guide me, to give me encouragement, and to share their wisdom with me. I hold a special place in my heart for Pastor Victor Constein who was instrumental in lighting the flame that quickly grew. To the Reverend Robert Schuller for giving me the encouragement to follow my dreams. And to Chuck Colson, whom I have never met, but whose book, *Born Again,* touched me profoundly and set me on a course of sharing my testimony with those who will listen.

To my mother, Dolores Gappa, who is responsible for praying me back into the fold. Always my strongest supporter even when my actions did not deserve it, you never gave up on me. I owe so much to the person you are. Thanks for always being there for me. I love you, Mom. You are one in a million.

Much love to my brothers Greg and Art. . .the first men in my life I could look up to.

To my son Christopher John Smith who has been here through it all. You saw the person I was before I opened my heart and life to the healing power of the Holy Spirit, and you see my life now. I pray you will one day come to understand that no one can fill the empty place in our souls except Jesus. I love you, Son. Jesus loves you, too.

To all of my children, Christopher, Mandy, Kermit, and Kyle. Never forget that God is at work in each of your lives. May each of you grow in your faith to become all that God intends you to be. I love you.

And to my dearest husband, Kevin, . . .thank you for believing in me. Your incredible sense of humor makes me laugh even when I don't want to. Being with you has opened my heart and mind to become all that God intended me to be. I love you more each day and am so blessed to call you not only my husband, but my most treasured friend. Growing old with you will be an honor.

Last but by no means least, I give praise and thanks to my holy Father. The Lord alone turned me around and set my path straight. Thank You, my most holy Lord, for giving me the wisdom to understand not only that God allows U-turns, but that no matter what I have done I can continue to turn my heart and mind toward You. You will always forgive me, always love me, and always bring me the peace I need. Because it is so very true. . .God allows U-turns!

INTRODUCTION

It is sometimes difficult to see that God is paying even the slightest attention to us when our lives are a mess. I mean, where is He, exactly, when you really need Him? This is one of the prime arguments voiced by non-Christians. The "God is great," "God is good," and all the other "God is terrific" stuff is hard to find during times of turmoil and tragedy.

I know I did not think God was so "great" when my now ex-husband was dragging me up a flight of stairs by my hair, often leaving bald and bloody patches where chunks of hair had been ripped out of my scalp. No way was God "good" when my bones ached from punches and kicks, my skin shrieked from cuts and scrapes, and my eyes burned from hot tears of despair and fear. God did not seem so "terrific" when I stared into the hate-filled eyes of my husband as he held a knife to my throat or a gun to my head and sneered, "If you scream one more time, I will kill you."

I had given up on God long before I ran away at the age of fifteen to marry the eighteen-year-old man who in one year went from being the love of my life to my abuser, jailer, kidnapper, rapist, and attempted murderer. No, by the time I was "sweet sixteen," there was no doubt in my mind—if God existed it was certainly not in my world.

It had not always been that way, however. As a little girl, during summer vacation I loved attending daily vacation Bible school at the Madison Avenue Baptist Church in Cleveland, Ohio. We did not attend church on a regular basis. Ours was not a Christian home in the sense that God was an active part of our upbringing. But we knew the Ten Commandments, and Mom exhibited the values of a Christian woman by the example she set for her three children, children confused by the divorce of their parents and the accompanying difficulties of living as welfare recipients on the edge of poverty.

A brutal experience at the hands of a temporary foster parent, during a time when my mother had been hospitalized for a serious illness, left me catatonic for months, with a debilitating fear of the dark that would last until adulthood. The children's prayer "Now I lay me down to sleep" saw me through many a sleepless night in my early years as I struggled through the devastating effects of that early childhood molestation. It was a trauma that would color who I became and how I related to virtually everyone in my adult life.

As a teenager, I felt apart from girls my own age, and I rebelled strongly against any and all authority. It was no surprise that I chose to run away and get married when I met "Mr. Right." Except he wasn't. The horrific year I spent married to a man whose physical and emotional abuse almost killed me dispelled any remaining vestiges of my belief in a higher power watching over me.

After the birth of my son and my divorce, both at the age of sixteen, there was no room in my life for anything but the here and now. Practical things consumed me, like going back to school, working, child care, housekeeping, paying bills, and learning how to be a mother. I vowed to be the best I could be at all of these things and was determined that my head, not my heart, would get me through what I now call my "Decade of Destruction." I was so very lost.

My poor son never had the opportunity to be a child. There was no time for that. He also never had the opportunity to have a normal mother. I was anything but. I filled my days with busy take-charge tasks, always on the move, always on a schedule, always following a list. I filled my nights with alcohol, drugs, promiscuity, and self-destruction. I filled my soul with empty promises and emptier pursuits. By the time I reached my late twenties, a time when many of us are just beginning our families and settling down, I had a teenaged son who had, in his turn, become the out-of-control rebel, causing me to slip further into an abyss of guilt and despair. The rapid succession of yet another marriage and divorce, several broken engagements, more than one abortion, and frequent extreme weight gains and losses left me even more emotionally crippled.

Why couldn't I find happiness? Why did it seem as though nothing I did worked out? Why did I feel so worthless? The feelings of utter helplessness and despair overwhelmed me. My spirit broken, I was an angry, lonely young woman when I hit bottom the first time, swallowing dozens of pills only to be foiled by a well-meaning friend who stopped by unannounced.

How we come through times of struggle often depends on our level of faith and hope, and at that time I had neither. As a nonbeliever, there was no room in my life for a higher power greater than myself. It took me years to discover that while I was attempting to fill the void in my soul, I was, as the song says, "looking for love in all the wrong places." Never in my wildest dreams would I have thought to find it in the spirit of Christ Jesus. I now know there is a place only God can fill. This, however, is a lesson we must each learn and come to believe in our own time, or in His time—whichever comes first.

The Lord knew it would take a pretty miraculous scenario to catch my attention, and He did not let me down. He must have known how stubborn I was, how I would continue to keep walking the same dead-end paths if He didn't step in and move me.

And move me He did.

It was the summer of 1989, and I was not actively questioning my faith at the time. Frankly, I did not understand the depth of the spiritual void in my life the evening that I found myself taking a walk in my neighborhood. I was contemplating what steps I would need to take now that another engagement had been broken. I had to move from the home we had shared. Added to that were thoughts of my stressful job and how I would cope with its increasing responsibility and time demands. Topping it all off was the anguish of having my son incarcerated in yet another juvenile detention facility. I was at a loss as to what I should do or where I should turn first. Drugs and alcohol would get me through the night, numbing the feelings of loss and loneliness, and I knew somehow I would survive. I always did, even if each transgression left me emptier than before. *Soon, there will be nothing left of my heart,* I thought sadly.

Then I noticed people getting out of cars nearby, crossing the street in front of me. It was Wednesday night, about 6:45, and they were going into the neighborhood church, a lovely red brick building with an impressive bell tower. I had often stopped what I was doing to listen to the bells chime strangely familiar hymns from my childhood days in Bible school. *Must be a funeral or meeting or something,* I recall thinking, never imagining a church would have a midweek evening service.

I crossed the street, reading the sign on the wall, "Wednesday Evening Service, 7:00 P.M." Could I go inside if I was not a member? Would they let me in? The church in Orange, California, was called St. John's Lutheran. Was that Catholic? What was a Lutheran? I felt so ignorant. Then, as my mind shifted into gear, telling me all the reasons I should not go inside, my legs developed a mind of their own, virtually propelling me up the steps and through the doors. A sign with an arrow pointing to the balcony beckoned me, and as I walked up the steps I worried, *Will someone come and throw me out, knowing I do not belong here?* I had no idea what I was doing, where I was going, or what to expect. I was quite literally not in control of my actions.

There is a feeling you get when you step from an air-conditioned car or building out into the warm summer air that takes your breath away. A "whoosh" seems to envelop you, leaving you a little weak, a little disoriented. That is how I felt as I walked under the arched doorway and into a sanctuary straight out of a picture book. There was no one else in the balcony, which allowed me to gasp in awe at the immense arched ceiling with gold leaf edging, gleaming dark woodwork and pews, and breathtaking stained glass windows. This building was a work of art, and I could appreciate the majesty of it all. Being alone also allowed me to fall back into one of the pews as I looked toward the pulpit and saw the statue of Jesus with outstretched hands, looking right at me. Hot tears fell down my cheeks as emotions I could not explain filled my heart and soul. Deep sobs, leaving me gasping for air, racked my body.

What was wrong? What was happening to me? Why was I sitting in a strange church crying like a baby? *Thank God I am alone up here,* I thought, *or they would be carting me off to a loony bin.* Then it hit me. Yes. Thank God! That was why I was here. That was why He had led me up the steps and into my own private balcony, to acknowledge Him! To allow Him to touch a part of my soul and give me something I had for too long lacked—hope, faith, thankfulness, forgiveness.

When the pastor began to speak, it was as though his message was for me alone. A message of being lost, without direction, without hope, without faith—and how it did not have to be like that. He talked of how we needed only to ask the Lord Jesus Christ to come into our hearts and He would be there—just like that.

I literally could not see for the tears flowing nonstop from somewhere deep within my soul, but I could see in another way, more clearly than I had in a long, long time. Instead of looking through the eyes of one in fear, bondage, and sin, I was suddenly seeing from the wonderful vantage point of freedom and redemption. Isaiah 53:5–6 says, "But he was pierced for our transgressions, he was crushed for our iniquities; the punishment that brought us peace was upon him, and by his wounds we are healed. We all, like sheep, have gone astray, each of us has turned to his own way; and the LORD has laid on him the iniquity of us all."

My walk with the Lord started that day, a day that forever changed the course of my life. Suddenly, I wanted to know more about this relationship with Jesus of which the pastor spoke. I began to read the Bible, study the beliefs of different denominations, and research tales of spiritual conversion throughout time. I practically devoured contemporary Christian books written by authors like Billy Graham, Phillip Yancey,

Chuck Swindoll, Max Lucado, Gary Smalley, and Robert Schuller. I sifted through it all, searching for the meaning it had in my life. I took a lengthy series of church membership classes, and on April 8, 1990, was confirmed as an adult in St. John's Lutheran Church by the same pastor whom the Lord had used to speak to my heart that lonely evening many months before. Pastor Constein chose as my confirmation passage Psalm 27:1, "The LORD is my light and my salvation—whom shall I fear? The LORD is the stronghold of my life—of whom shall I be afraid?" It is a passage I cling to still.

Over the next decade (what I now call my "Decade of Discovery"), the world opened up to me in ways I could never have imagined. Seemingly out of the woodwork, good Christian people came into my life where previously there had been none. Opportunities, experiences, and spiritual illumination did not make my life perfect, but it was a life of healing and hope, a life of promise. Psalm 71:20 says, "Though you have made me see troubles, many and bitter, you will restore my life again; from the depths of the earth you will again bring me up."

And bring me up He did. I felt encouraged along the way to share my experiences with others, to use the gifts He gave me to bring others the message of peace and freedom He alone can provide. Being deeply touched by the spiritual conversion stories of Chuck Colson, C. S. Lewis, Stormie O'Martian, and others caused me to pen my own account of a troubled life, lost and without spiritual direction. When publishing that account looked dismal, the Lord sent yet another inspiration my way, "Open the door for others to share their faith," I heard Him say to me. Hence, the second version of *God Allows U-Turns* was born, and my story became one of hundreds coming together collectively to sing His praises and share His love and His peace.

This incredible love and peace is available to everyone, and my passion is to shout that fact from the lowest valley to the highest hilltop. I know that through Him all things are possible. The Scripture passage from 2 Corinthians 5:17 that sums it all up is printed on the stationery for the God Allows U-Turns Project. It says, "Therefore, if anyone is in Christ, he is a new creation; the old has gone, the new has come!" It is my prayer that *God Allows U-Turns* will grow from one book into a global ministry that will cross all boundaries, sharing with all who will listen that it is never too late to turn around. Hope, healing, joy, and love exist for all.

Jesus Christ took my broken spirit and my lost soul and turned me around, setting me on a new course. He filled the empty place in my soul that I was trying so desperately to fill with drugs, alcohol, relationships, material goods, work, and empty pursuits. He forgave the sins that weighed heavily on my heart and showed me I no longer had to carry the burden alone. He will do the same for you.

I did not "get religion." I made a spiritual connection that turned my life around. I "got a relationship"—a relationship with Jesus Christ. I know in my heart that no matter what we have done, no matter where we have been, it is never too late to fill that empty place in our hearts and souls. It is never too late to change direction, because God allows U-turns!

Those of us working on the God Allows U-Turns Project feel blessed as we see one door after another being opened to allow this new Christian inspirational book series to succeed. From the beginning, we have all felt the incredible power of the Holy Spirit weaving through every aspect, divinely inspiring every step we take. The Lord has delivered to us awesome web site designers and people willing to list our call for story submissions in their Internet publications. He brought us co-editors, a world-class literary agent, and an international publisher. He brought us just the right Scripture passages to open each chapter. And He brought us people like you. People willing to share their personal stories of faith and people eager to read them.

The stories you are about to read are as varied as the people who have written them. Some are beautifully simplistic in their message of faith, while others dig deeper, leaving us to ponder their meaning. Some will make you laugh; others will make you cry. All are guaranteed to touch you in a way that will make you think about your personal walk of faith. We pray that within these pages you will find a confirmation of faith that will instill in you a heartfelt desire to make God your guide and the Lord Jesus Christ your Savior.

Do not be conformed to this world,
but be transformed by the renewing of your minds,
so that you may discern what is the will of God—
what is good and acceptable and perfect.
Romans 12:2 NRSV

CHAPTER ONE

God's Love

We love because he first loved us.
1 John 4:19

IN GOD'S EYES

by Candace Carteen, Portland, Oregon

By the time I was ten, I was totally ashamed of my father. All my friends called him names: Quasi-Moto, hunchback, monster, little Franken-stein, the crooked little man with the crooked little cane. At first it hurt when they called him those things, but soon I found myself agreeing with them. He was ugly, and I knew it!

My father was born with something called parastremmatic dwarf-ism. The disease made him stop growing when he was about thirteen and caused his body to twist and turn into a grotesque shape. It wasn't too bad when he was a kid. I saw pictures of him when he was about my age. He was a little short but quite good-looking. Even when he met my mother and married her when he was nineteen, he still looked pretty normal. He was still short and walked with a slight limp, but he was able to do just about anything. Mother said, "He even used to be a great dancer."

Soon after my birth, things started getting worse. Another genetic disorder took over, and his left foot started turning out, almost backward. His head and neck shifted over to the right; his neck became rigid and he had to look over his left shoulder a bit. His right arm curled in and up, and his index finger almost touched his elbow. His spine warped to look something like a big, old roller coaster and it caused his torso to lie side-ways instead of straight up and down like a normal person. His walk be-came slow, awkward, and deliberate. He had to almost drag his left foot as he used his deformed right arm to balance his gait.

I hated to be seen with him. Everyone stared. They seemed to pity me. I knew he must have done something really bad to have God hate him that much.

By the time I was seventeen, I was blaming all my problems on my father. I didn't have the right boyfriends because of him. I didn't drive the right car because of him. I wasn't pretty enough because of him. I didn't have the right jobs because of him. I wasn't happy because of him.

Anything that was wrong with me, or my life, was because of him. If my father had been good-looking like Jane's father, or successful like

Paul's father, or worldly like Terry's father, I would be perfect! I knew that for sure.

The night of my senior prom came, and Father had to place one more nail in my coffin; he had volunteered to be one of the chaperones at the dance. My heart just sank when he told me. I stormed into my room, slammed the door, threw myself on the bed, and cried.

"Three more weeks and I'll be out of here!" I screamed into my pillow. "Three more weeks and I will have graduated and be moving away to college." I sat up and took a deep breath. "God, please make my father go away and leave me alone. He keeps sticking his big nose in everything I do. Just make him disappear, so that I can have a good time at the dance."

I got dressed, my date picked me up, and we went to the prom. Father followed in his car behind us. When we arrived, Father seemed to vanish into the pink chiffon drapes that hung everywhere in the auditorium. I thanked God that He had heard my prayer. At least now I could have some fun.

Midway through the dance, Father came out from behind the drapes and decided to embarrass me again. He started dancing with my girlfriends. One by one, he took their hand and led them to the dance floor. He then clumsily moved them in circles as the band played. Now I tried to vanish into the drapes.

After Jane had danced with him, she headed my way.

Oh, no! I thought. *She's going to tell me he stomped on her foot or something.*

"Grace," she called, "you have the greatest father."

My face fell. "What?"

She smiled at me and grabbed my shoulders. "Your father's just the best. He's funny, kind, and always finds the time to be where you need him. I wish my father was more like that."

For one of the first times in my life, I couldn't talk. Her words confused me.

"What do you mean?" I asked her.

Jane looked at me really strangely. "What do you mean, what do I mean? Your father's wonderful. I remember when we were kids, and I'd sleep over at your house. He'd always come into your room, sit down in the chair between the twin beds, and read us a book. I'm not sure my father can even read," she sighed, and then smiled. "Thanks for sharing him."

Then, Jane ran off to dance with her boyfriend.

I stood there in silence.

A few minutes later, Paul came to stand beside me.

"He's sure having a lot of fun."

"What? Who? Who is having a lot of fun?" I asked.

"Your father. He's having a ball."

"Yeah. I guess." I didn't know what else to say.

"You know, he's always been there," Paul said. "I remember when you and I were on the mixed-doubles soccer team. He tried out as the coach, but he couldn't run up and down the field, remember? So they picked Jackie's father instead. That didn't stop him. He showed up for every game and did whatever needed to be done. He was the team's biggest fan. I think he's the reason we won so many games. Without him, it just would have been Jackie's father running up and down the field yelling at us. Your father made it fun. I wish my father had been able to show up to at least one of our games. He was always too busy."

Paul's girlfriend came out of the restroom, and he went to her side, leaving me once again speechless.

My boyfriend came back with two glasses of punch and handed me one.

"Well, what do you think of my father?" I asked out of the blue.

Terry looked surprised. "I like him. I always have."

"Then why did you call him names when we were kids?"

"I don't know. Because he was different, and I was a dumb kid."

"When did you stop calling him names?" I asked, trying to search my own memory.

Terry didn't even have to think about the answer. "The day he sat down with me outside by the pool and held me while I cried about my mother and father's divorce. No one else would let me talk about it. I was hurting inside, and he could feel it. He cried with me that day. I thought you knew."

I looked at Terry and a tear rolled down my cheek as long-forgotten memories started cascading into my consciousness.

When I was three, my puppy got killed by another dog, and my father was there to hold me and teach me what happens when the pets we love die. When I was five, my father took me to my first day of school. I was so scared. So was he. We cried and held each other that first day. The next day he became teacher's helper. When I was eight, I just couldn't do math. Father sat down with me night after night, and we worked on math problems until math became easy for me. When I was ten, my father bought me a brand-new bike. When it was stolen, because I didn't lock it up like I was taught to do, my father gave me jobs to do around the house so I could make enough money to purchase another one. When I was thirteen and my first love broke up with me, my father was there to yell at, to blame, and to cry with. When I was fifteen and I got to be in the honor society, my father was there to see me get the accolade. Now, when I was seventeen, he put up with me no matter how nasty I became or how high my hormones raged.

As I looked at my father dancing gaily with my friends, a big toothy grin on his face, I suddenly saw him differently. The handicaps weren't his, they were mine! I had spent a great deal of my life hating the man who loved me. I had hated the exterior that I saw, and I had ignored the interior that contained his God-given heart. I suddenly felt very ashamed.

I asked Terry to take me home, too overcome with feelings to remain.

On graduation day, at my Christian high school, my name was called, and I stood behind the podium as the valedictorian of my class. As I looked out over the people in the audience, my gaze rested on my father in the front row sitting next to my mother. He sat there, in his one and only, specially made suit, holding my mother's hand and smiling.

Overcome with emotions, my prepared speech was to become a landmark in my life.

"Today I stand here as an honor student, able to graduate with a 4.0 average. Yes, I was in the honor society for three years and was elected class president for the last two years. I led our school to championship in the debate club, and yes, I even won a full scholarship to Kenton State University so that I can continue to study physics and someday become a college professor.

"What I'm here to tell you today, fellow graduates, is that I didn't do it alone. God was there, and I had a whole bunch of friends, teachers, and counselors who helped. Up until three weeks ago, I thought they were the only ones I would be thanking this evening. If I had thanked just them, I would have been leaving out the most important person in my life. My father."

I looked down at my father and at the look of complete shock that covered his face.

I stepped out from behind the podium and motioned for my father to join me onstage. He made his way slowly, awkwardly, and deliberately. He had to drag his left foot up the stairs as he used his deformed right arm to balance his gait. As he stood next to me at the podium, I took his small, crippled hand in mine and held it tight.

"Sometimes we only see the silhouette of the people around us," I said. "For years I was as shallow as the silhouettes I saw. For almost my entire life, I saw my father as someone to make fun of, someone to blame, and someone to be ashamed of. He wasn't perfect, like the fathers my friends had.

"Well, fellow graduates, what I found out three weeks ago is that while I was envying my friends' fathers, my friends were envying mine. That realization hit me hard and made me look at who I was and what I had become. I was brought up to pray to God and hold high principles for others and myself. What I've done most of my life is read between the lines of the Good Book so I could justify my hatred."

Then, I turned to look my father in the face.

"Father, I owe you a big apology. I based my love for you on what I saw and not what I felt. I forgot to look at the one part of you that meant the most, the big, big heart God gave you. As I move out of high school and into life, I want you to know I could not have had a better father. You were always there for me, and no matter how badly I hurt you, you still showed up. Thank you!"

I took off my mortar board and placed it on his head, moving the tassel just so.

"You are the reason I am standing here today. You deserve this honor, not me."

And as the audience applauded and cried with us, I felt God's light shining down upon me as I embraced my father more warmly than I ever had before, tears unashamedly falling down both our faces.

For the first time, I saw my father through God's eyes, and I felt honored to be seen with him.

SMILE, GOD LOVES YOU

by Michelle Matt, Sanford, Maine

During a particularly stressful point in my twenties, my car broke down. Unable to coax it back into operation, I called a towing company. The woman answering the phone responded to my request for a tow with about as much good humor as an old grizzly disturbed during hibernation.

"Hullo." She growled.

"Hello. Yes, my car won't start, and I need a tow—"

"Didja check the gas?" she interrupted.

"Yes. It's not out of gas—"

"Ya sure?"

"Yes, I'm sure. I'd like—"

"Whenz the last time ya filled it?"

"Uh, I don't remember offhand, but I know it's not out of gas—"

"Well, if you don't know when the last time ya filled it was, how do you know you're not out of gas?"

"I always make sure I have at least half a tank."

"Well, are ya really sure or are ya just guessin'?"

"It's not out of gas!" I tried to sound convincing.

"Did ya check the gas gauge?"

"It's not out of gas!" I insisted.

" 'Cause a lot of people only think they're broken down when they never even bother to fill their tank," she warned me.

"I'm sure it's not out of gas—"

"And then they call us. We go out of our way only to find out they're just out of gas."

Frustration welled up at the lack of progress I was making with this dispatcher.

"Could you just send a tow?"

A long, drawn-out sigh came from the other end of the phone. "Yup."

Finally! The answer I wanted to hear. I gave her directions to my stranded car and was told to wait at the pay phone for the towing man to call me. "I just hope you're not out of gas," was her parting shot.

My wait wasn't very long. The tow truck driver called within a few minutes.

"Where exactly is this car located?" barked a male, no-nonsense voice. I gave him the location of the car and asked him if he could pick me up at the pay phone. That was fine with him. "One last question," he said. "Did you check the gas?"

"It's NOT out of gas!" I fairly shrieked. The constant grilling left me rattled. I began to doubt myself. *I hope it does have gas,* I thought. *What if it doesn't? What if I've just broken some new law about calling tow companies, obviously busy people, with a needless request that is really my fault?*

I was beginning to feel as broken down as my car. It was one of those times when "life hassles" seemed to be bigger than my puny faith. Plus, paying for a tow would really put a crimp in my finances. There wasn't much left over at the end of each paycheck for even the slightest emergency. *Where is God in the mundane moments of life?* I wondered.

The tow truck pulled up next to me suddenly. It was without my car, however.

"Are you the one calling for the tow?" asked the same gruff voice from the phone. "The blue car parked on Bowden and Glidden?"

"Yes."

"Yeah. Well, I just drove by it. I wanted to check to make sure it's the right one." He looked at me with stern suspicion. I could tell his day wasn't going any better than mine at the moment. He put his truck in gear and then stopped, giving me one more scrutinizing stare. "Is it the car that says, 'Smile, God loves you'?"

"Yes," I answered, feeling a smile begin to reshape my face.

The gruff expression of this man softened instantly. In spite of himself, he smiled too. We just grinned at each other for a moment. Life's problems suddenly seemed to mean nothing compared to the vital truth that passed between us. He drove away, still smiling.

He towed my car free of charge.

I never saw that tow truck driver again. But I still smile when I think of that afternoon. In the midst of one of life's irritating problems, God had found a way to remind me, and a not-so-gruff tow truck driver, of His love and His presence.

He is with us at all times if we would just remember.

Oh, and just so you know, it wasn't out of gas.

LOVE'S POWER

by Harry Randles, Hot Springs Village, Arkansas

Does Mom hear that train whistle? Pam wondered. Her mother and grandmother were having a loud argument as they rode in the front seat of the car. Pam's mom had been cross all morning. *I'd better not say anything,* Pam thought.

As the noise got louder, Pam could see the locomotive fast approaching the crossing. Her mother was oblivious to the danger and hadn't even slowed. "Mom!" she cried, trying not to scream.

"In a minute," her mother snapped.

And then Pam did scream, "Mom, look!"

It was too late. The train careened into the car, cleanly shearing off the front seat. Pam and her sister were left unhurt in the backseat as mother and grandmother were ground beneath the train for a full quarter of a mile down the track.

The tragedy occurred in the summer between Pam's seventh- and eighth-grade years. The eighth-grader who returned to school that fall was not the same girl who had left. In the seventh grade, Pam had been a student that teachers enjoyed having in their classes. Bright and eager to learn, she'd never been a discipline problem and had always seemed to enjoy school. That Pam had ceased to exist. The Pam that came back to school in September was a sullen, angry, and inattentive person who was very difficult to have around. It became commonplace for her to be disciplined for her rudeness and disrespectful behavior. She was obviously a very troubled young lady.

As a guidance counselor, Rose was worried about Pam. Rose was usually successful at reaching troubled kids, but week after week went by, and her frustration grew. No less frustrated was Ken, Pam's science teacher. Great with kids of almost any age, Ken was disturbed by the fact that he couldn't get through Pam's shell. The three of us met frequently to discuss her. By November her behavior had worsened. All of us were worried but felt like our hands were tied. It's difficult in this day and age to reach out to a student without being accused of some indiscretion or outright perversion.

The week after Thanksgiving, Ken showed me a newspaper article and picture of his high school science teacher who was retiring. It was a long article which traced the life experiences of this man who had been Ken's mentor. Ken had enjoyed a very special relationship with this man who long ago had served as Ken's inspiration. In reading the article, Ken became determined to meet with Pam and discuss some personal feelings with her, regardless of the political incorrectness of doing so. "I can't help but think, Where would I be today if Mr. Smith hadn't reached out to me?" Ken fumed, "I am so sick of this walking on eggshells when kids need help!" We talked about it for a bit. Ultimately, Ken took Pam's school picture from her student file deciding to go ahead and hang the consequences of overstepping "politically correct" boundaries.

At the end of science class, Ken gave Pam a note for her study-hall teacher requesting that Pam come to see him that afternoon. Pam came in with a big chip securely fastened on her shoulder, expecting to be reprimanded for some new transgression. She slumped down in a seat in the first row with a sullen face. Ken moved a chair over next to her and opened his folder on the desk that they now shared.

The folder contained pictures. Pam didn't say anything and looked suspiciously at the desktop. "This," he said, "is my mother. I love her. She's always been there for me. I can't even imagine my life without her. It must be hard for you." When Pam just looked away, he moved on to the next picture, his mentor. He explained his affection for that man and told her how without that person in his life, he would not be who or what he was today. "He was a great teacher," Ken said. "He inspired me. I loved him, too. But it was a different kind of love than I have for my mom."

There were more pictures in the folder. One of Ken's two little girls and his wife, and one of Christ. The love he had for his family was easily expressed as he talked with Pam. The picture of Jesus prompted him to explain how he loved the Lord and how that love differed from any earthly love. Pointing to those pictures, he said, "All of these are people that I love."

The final picture in the file was of Pam herself. Holding her picture, he said very gently, "This is someone else I love. I haven't told you until now. I know it's awkward for a teacher to tell a student something like this. But I think you need to know. What happened last summer convinces me that you should know." Tears sparkled on Pam's lashes. "You're a terrific person. I love you for that. And I love you for your love of learning and many, many other things. And I love you unconditionally." The sullen look had been replaced by an expression of pain and hurt as tears streamed down her cheeks. It was the first time Ken had seen anything but anger from her in a long time. Ken retrieved a box of Kleenex from the front of the room and slid the box across to her. They just sat quietly until she seemed ready to leave.

The change in Pam began that afternoon. Day by day, week by week, she began to gain ground again. Rose, Ken, and I watched with delight as she progressed. By Easter she was doing very well. She was nearly the delightful girl she had been before that traumatic accident. I congratulated Ken on his success. I was convinced it was the power of Ken's love that inspired Pam's journey back to her former self.

Rose didn't agree with me. She believed it was the power of the Holy Spirit moving through Ken that inspired him to share his feelings with Pam and thus heal her. Only God knows for sure, as He smiles down on a living photo album of the children He loves.

This story first appeared in Connection *magazine, September 2000.*

A SIGN FROM GOD

by Sara Jordan, Canton, Ohio

It was black and white with simple lettering and read: "We need to talk. —God." I had to look twice to be sure I'd read it right. I was having one of those particularly frustrating days. I was stuck in traffic, raised my eyes to heaven and asked, "Why, Lord, why?" for the millionth time, when this billboard caught my attention. Normally, I don't pay attention to the countless billboards in the city, but this one was obviously different. A billboard from God?

I found it timely in the extreme.

I have spent my life trying to attain the patience of Job, the wisdom of Solomon, and the faith of Abraham, but all too often, I fall short, ending up the doubting Thomas. And at this point in my life, as I looked at that billboard, I thought with a tinge of bitterness, *Yes. Lord, You're right. We do need to talk.*

We need to talk about why, when I've prayed so hard and so long, You took our two babies through miscarriage. With so many unwanted, abused, and neglected children in the world, why were mine not given the chance to live? Why was I given Graves' disease at age twenty-two? Why are we still struggling even now to have children? Why, why, why?

I was at a particularly low point in my life. My faith had been shaken to its very foundation. I needed to reconnect with God, and that billboard spurred me to revisit my relationship with my creator. We "talked" for quite some time.

Through the rest of my week, I gave little thought to the billboard. It was still there with its simple, unadorned message. I wondered whose it was and what it was for. I could see no names or sponsors listed anywhere. Even so, I looked for ulterior motives, cynically assuming it was some church "advertising" for souls. It wasn't until that weekend, when I was in the car with my husband, David, that I had a change in attitude.

We were driving down the interstate at a good clip when I saw it. Again, it was a black billboard with simple white lettering that asked:

#3261

"Need directions?—God." I practically shouted, "Dave, look. Another sign from God!"

He was so startled, he nearly drove off the road. "For heaven's sake," he said, "don't do that!" He craned his neck to see what I was talking about. "Oh yeah. I see it. I was expecting the sky to open up and angels to appear when you said it was a sign from God!"

We laughed at the word play, discussed the possible origin of the sign, and then each became lost in our own thoughts again. I thought, maybe God does give us "signs" along the way. Maybe even in the form of billboards. Who knows? It could be His way of giving us a nudge in the right direction.

And, I thought, *I do need directions, Lord. Guide me.*

From then on, I began to consciously look for those "signs from God." I found seventeen in all. They were in locations of every description, from back country roads to busy highways. "Remember that love thy neighbor thing? I meant it." "If you keep taking my name in vain, I'll make rush hour longer." All of them signed—God.

Everywhere I went, the signs spoke to me when I seemed to need answers or encouragement the most. Maybe God has a hand in this, I acknowledged, and He's trying to tell me something.

That became apparent to me in the middle of a heated discussion between Dave and me. The loss of our children and the subsequent financial and emotional strain of infertility treatment had begun to take its toll on our relationship. I was disillusioned with prayer and with love altogether. We were arguing in the car when we passed a sign that was surely meant for us: "Loved the wedding. Now invite me to the marriage.—God."

It stopped us cold. It was a powerful reminder to us of where we should turn for strength and the faith to keep on going. God had brought us together and, for whatever reason, He was putting this grief in our lives. He would get us through it if we would just turn to Him. It was a pivotal moment for us. We were refocused by that simple reminder.

It is difficult to "let go and let God" when you want something with all of your heart. The hardest lesson I had to learn is that God's will is not always my will. Even now, I resist things that I don't understand because they don't make sense to me in my world. I know, though, that I can rest in the knowledge that God has a plan for me. I don't always have to understand right away what it might be. In His time, all will be revealed.

I never have learned who erected those billboards or for what purpose, but I'm sure it wasn't for personal gain. The signs are slowly being replaced with the usual billboard fare of radio stations, restaurants, and other commercial ads. I'm sorry to see them go. I hope someone else took as much from their messages as I did. Maybe other lives were as forever changed as mine. Now, whenever I'm discouraged or disgusted with life, I remember one sign in particular:

"I love you. . .
    "I love you. . .
        "I love you. . ."
          —God.

A FATHER'S LOVE

by Michael T. Powers, Janesville, Wisconsin

His name was Brian. He was a special education student at the small high school I attended. He was constantly searching for love and attention. It usually came for the wrong reasons, from students who wanted to have some "fun." He was the joke of the school and was "entertainment" for those who watched. Brian, who was looking for acceptance, didn't realize that they were laughing at him, not with him.

One day, I couldn't take it anymore. I had enough of their game and told them to knock it off. "Aw, come on, Mike! We are just having fun. Who do you think you are anyway!" The teasing didn't stop for long, but Brian latched onto me that day of my sophomore year. I had stuck up for him, and now he was my buddy. Thoughts of *What will people think of you if you are friends with Brian?* swirled in my head, but I forced them away as I realized that God wanted me to treat this young man as I would want to be treated.

Later that week, I invited him over to my house after school to play video games. We sat there playing Intellivision (this was the '80s) and drinking Tang. Pretty soon, he started asking me questions like, "Hey, Mike, where do you go to church?" I would politely answer his questions, then turn my concentration back to the video games. He kept asking me questions about God and why I was different from some of the kids at school.

Finally, my wonderfully perceptive girlfriend, Kristi, pulled me aside and said, "Michael, he needs to talk. How about you go down to your room where you can talk privately?" She had picked up on the cues better than I had.

As soon as we arrived in my room, Brian repeated, "Hey, Mike. How come you're not like some of the other kids at school?" I knew I needed to share with him the difference that God had made in my life. I got out my Bible and shared John 3:16 and some verses in Romans with him. I explained to him that God loved him just the way he was and that He sent Jesus down to earth to die on a cross for him. All the while, I did not know if he was comprehending anything I was telling him. When we were done, I asked Brian if he wanted to pray with me. He said he would like that.

We prayed together: "God, I know I am a sinner, and that even if I were the only person on earth, You still would have sent Your Son down to die on the cross for me and take my place. I accept the gift of salvation that You offer, and I ask that You come into my heart and take control. Thank You, Lord. Amen."

I looked at him and said, "Brian, if you meant those words you just prayed, where is Jesus right now?"

He pointed to his heart and said, "He is in here now."

Then he did something I will never forget, as long as I live. Brian hugged the Bible to his chest, lay down on the bed, and the tears flowed down his face. Brian was unearthly silent as the faucet behind his eyes let loose. Then he said to me, "Mike, the love that God has for me must be like the love a husband has for his wife." I was floored.

Here was someone who had trouble comprehending things in school, but who now understood one of eternity's great truths. I knew that he understood what I had shared with him.

About a week later, everything came into perspective for me. It was then that Brian really opened up to me. He explained that his dad had left him and his mom when he was five years old. Brian was standing on the porch the day his dad told him he was leaving. He told Brian he couldn't deal with having a son like him anymore, then he walked out of Brian's life and was never seen again. Brian told me that he had been looking for his dad ever since.

Now I knew why the tears kept flowing that day in my bedroom. His search was over. He found what he had been looking for since he was five years old. A Father's love.

He would never again be alone.

READY TO MEET THE RIDER

by Michelle Matt, Sanford, Maine

I thought my life was over the day my father died. At age fourteen, I was unprepared for the loss of a parent. After the shock of his death, I took a long time to heal.

I had a wonderful father. His commitment to fatherhood was evident in the open affection and love he lavished on his family.

It was Dad who often met us at the bus stop after school, taught me how to ride my bike without training wheels, and bravely ripped old Band-Aids off my skinned knees when I was too afraid to do it myself. He snuck quarters in our pockets when the tooth fairy forgot, made up funny stories, and attended school plays that I knew interrupted his workday. Often on his days off, he would join us in a game of hide-and-seek, finding creative and original places to hide my younger sister. I was certain the safest place in the world was in his strong arms. His hugs melted all of my fears.

Dad was a hard worker, usually holding down at least two jobs at a time. He was employed nights as an electrician and often took on day jobs as well. On our days off from school, my sister and I would often accompany Dad to his different job sites. Many afternoons were spent in musty basements skillfully directing flashlight beams to electric boxes. He did his best to keep us entertained while wiring a house at the same time. Not an easy task.

All in all, Dad did a lot of things right: praising us and building us up at every opportunity he could. He would write notes on the back of my artwork or school projects that would say such things as, "I love you more than you'll ever know," or "I'm so proud of you."

One day, though, he did something totally uncharacteristic. He bought a motorcycle, his lifelong dream.

"I used to have a bike when I was in the navy," he said. "I've waited years for another. This is all I've ever wanted!"

My father drove it every chance he could, often taking my sister or me out on the road, as well. He bought us helmets and took the time to teach us the rules of the road as they applied to motorcycle riding. I knew this was not just a passing phase with Dad. He sincerely enjoyed this motorcycle. He and the bike were a perfect fit. One day while we were on a road trip, he even confided to me that when his time came to die, he hoped it would be on his bike.

My dad dusted off his bike one spring and went for a ride. I never saw him alive again. He was killed instantly when a drunk driver collided with him.

The grief and terror of the following days were a blur. Many nights I would wake up and discover my pillow wet with tears I had wept while asleep. I was inconsolable. My heart sustained an immeasurable void. I was convinced I would never feel joy again.

The grieving time my family and I endured seemed endless. We passed each other in rote daily movements, yet we mysteriously held each other up at the same time.

On one difficult night, my mother shared with me a vision she used to console herself. "I saw your father taking that last trip on his bike down a beautiful country road that led straight into heaven. He never knew what happened to him."

That image was like a healing balm on my aching heart. I held that soothing thought in my mind and retrieved it whenever I felt insecure about losing him.

I was in my late twenties when I met John. He was in his early forties, the same age my father was when he died. John had warm eyes, a pony-tail, leather jacket, and, you guessed it, a motorcycle which he enjoyed just as my father had. John and I became friends through our shared faith in God. I never told him of my father's death. Secretly, I prayed for John's safety every time I saw him riding his bike.

After an absence of several months, John caught up with me at a church gathering, excited from a recent road trip. He looked healthy, and his eyes had an excited sparkle.

"Come with me. I have something to show you." He took my hand and led me out the door. I had no idea what he was up to. We walked past rows of cars and turned the corner of the building. There stood his huge, shiny motorcycle.

A sense of both terror and grief overcame me.

"Come closer and take a look at this." John was completely un-aware of the emotions I was fighting.

I took a deep breath and walked up to the bike. The leather seat, paneled instruments, and shiny chrome were all reminders of an inno-cent past. My heart began pounding wildly in my chest. Buried mem-ories of a cherished childhood surfaced in one bittersweet swell. How vividly I remembered traveling on a bike, my arms wrapped tightly around my father's waist, and my head buried in the back of his shoul-der as the sharp wind snapped against us. At John's urging, I walked closer to the bike and stopped. I couldn't believe my eyes.

"My son painted this," he said, his smile now spread across his face.

I saw a beautiful scene that was skillfully hand-painted on the upper body of the bike. It was a man riding a motorcycle down a beau-tiful country road that extended to heaven. The clouds held an image of Jesus with arms outstretched ready to meet the rider. It was an exact representation of the vision my mother had shared with me over a decade before.

"It's beautiful," I murmured to John.

I drank in the picture, not wanting to leave the image.

Thank You, God, I cried with overflowing eyes. *Thank You, God.*

The old grief and terror melted as I let my father ride to the wait-ing arms of Jesus. God graciously uprooted a deep sorrow and planted seeds of peace and acceptance in my soul.

THE NATIVITY SCENE AT EASTER

by Cindy Appel, Crestwood, Missouri

It was too beautiful to box up, so there it remained, proudly displayed on the top shelf of the living-room bookcase. My husband noticed it in mid-January. "Shouldn't you have put the nativity scene away with the other Christmas decorations?" he asked.

"Yes, I should have," I replied, "but I just couldn't stand the thought of wrapping those delicate porcelain figures in smelly newsprint and shoving them into an old shoe box."

"Yes, they are lovely. . .oh, well, nobody will notice them up there and think we're out of touch with the real world," he mumbled as he left the room.

But they were noticed. "Mom, you forgot to put the baby Jesus and His family away after Christmas," my nine-year-old daughter announced a few weeks later.

"Don't you think they look nice there on the shelf?" I asked her with a smile.

"Yes, but Christmas is over now. Shouldn't we be thinking of Easter decorations?"

"You're right—we will in about a month," I promised. So the stable and its occupants stayed, quietly witnessing the birth of the newborn king.

My youngest daughter loved it when I lifted her up to the top shelf to dust the china figurines. "Away in the manger, no crib for a bed," she sang as we dusted the baby Jesus. My husband and oldest daughter tried correcting her—it wasn't Christmas so she shouldn't be singing Christmas carols. "I am singing for baby Jesus," my four year old replied.

Easter came—and out came the Easter baskets and plastic eggs garnered from the previous year's Easter egg hunt. Out came the pictures of bunnies, ducks, and flowers they had drawn at school. Still, the nativity scene remained on the top shelf.

As we dyed eggs, we talked of Jesus' trial and crucifixion, death, and resurrection, and then we talked of Jesus' birth. "It must have been awfully cold when Jesus was born," my oldest daughter remarked.

"December is the beginning of winter." I told her that a lot of people think Jesus was probably born in the springtime—that's when the shepherds would have been out in the fields watching their flocks during the lambing season.

"Then Christmas and Easter could be on the same day! Two times the candy and presents!" she exclaimed.

"And two birthday parties!" my youngest daughter added.

"Birthday parties?" the nine year old wondered. "What birthday parties?"

"The one for baby Jesus—and the one for Jesus when He was growed-up and was born again out of the tomb," the four year old replied matter-of-factly.

I suddenly smiled. That was why I hadn't wanted to pack away our nativity this year! Jesus wasn't born on just one day. He is reborn every day in the hearts of those who believe in His powers of forgiveness and love and His conquest of death. The wood of the Christ child's nativity manger would one day be transformed into the wood of the cross upon which the adult Christ would carry out God's plan for our salvation—our own rebirth.

As Peter the Apostle proclaimed: "Praise be to the God and Father of our Lord Jesus Christ! In his great mercy he has given us new birth into a living hope through the resurrection of Jesus Christ from the dead" (1 Peter 1:3).

If every Sunday is a "mini-Easter," celebrating the day on which Christ rose from the dead as a "growed-up," then why can't we celebrate His birth as a child in a Bethlehem stable year-round as well? After all, spring is a time of renewal and rebirth. The symbols of birds hatching from eggs, butterflies awakening from their cocoons, and flowers bursting forth from the "dead" earth are all supposed to remind us of Jesus being born again from the death of the tomb. What better symbol of Easter rebirth than the newborn king lying in a manger?

Happy "birthdays," Jesus!

AN ENCOURAGING WORD

by Cheryl Norwood, Canton, Georgia

Usually when I get discouraged, doing a chore helps my mood. I guess that's because most of my discouragement comes from not being able to do something about a problem. I'm definitely a "doer," with all the associated strengths and weaknesses that entails. One of the hardest things about surrendering my life to Christ minute by minute, day by day, is giving up my right to fix things. Not that God doesn't ever let me do anything, but many times it's not what I want to do or how I would have fixed it. Or else He makes me wait as I chomp at the bit, anxious to get at it. And then there are those situations that have a big effect on my life about which I am able to do absolutely nothing.

I was pretty down that day as I began to do the laundry. Someone else's lousy attitude and bad decisions were really causing me a lot of grief. This wasn't a new problem. God and I had discussed it again and again and again—why I allowed the actions and attitudes of others to affect me so. I had prayed and fasted and prayed some more. And here I was again, back with the same request, the same pain.

Usually folding clean, sweet-smelling clothes into nice, neat little piles put a smile on my face, but not this time. All of a sudden it hit me—laundry and problems were exactly alike. Until you die, you'll always have both. It never ends. It's never over!

As I threw the next load into the washer, I was so caught up in my personal little pity party that I didn't bother to check pockets or turn shirts inside out or clip socks together. *Who cares? What's one load of wash in a lifetime? Let's see, this must be load number 30,746 of about 142,360, right? Big deal,* I thought.

It wasn't until I was unloading the washer and came across my windbreaker that I realized what I had done. I had worn that windbreaker over the weekend, and in the pocket, wrapped in a tissue, was a handmade seed bead necklace that I had taken off because it kept getting caught on branches as I walked. I checked the pocket, and yes, the necklace was there. It was tangled into a hundred knots with frayed thread between the beads and bits of torn tissue glued to the beads. It looked like a pile of turquoise spaghetti. What a mess—it was most certainly ruined.

This was not a priceless heirloom. It had probably only cost my husband a few dollars. He had bought it in the mountains of Mexico from a Christian lady, an Indian woman who made necklaces from the tiniest beads imaginable. This one had flowers beaded into the chain and a large cross. No, it wasn't the earthly value that made my heart break at its loss.

My husband, Mike, had been feeling that his relationship with the Lord had reached a dry spell and was looking for renewal. I had encouraged him to use his vacation for a short-term mission trip. Sometimes God has to get us away from our comfort zone and the things we think we need to get our attention. God had used the very same thing to speak to me about my relationship with Him, so I felt maybe that would work for Mike. He had been a little hesitant, but, after much prayer, had decided to go. At my urging, he had gone on a mission trip to Mexico to help build a school and church.

Mike bought the necklace as a thank-you gift for me and to remind us both that God meant for us to encourage each other in our walk with the Lord. It was also a reminder, he said, that every day in Mexico he thought of me. His mission trip was the first time we had been apart for more than one night, which was rough. There are only the two of us, and we are pretty dependent on each other. Whenever I wore that necklace, I always seemed to feel both Mike's love and God's love even stronger. Now, because of my foolishness, it was ruined. I cupped it in the palm of my hand and took it into the office to show Mike what I had done. I poked it with the index finger of my other hand, thinking that maybe, just maybe, I could salvage the cross part and put it on a chain.

Crying, I showed Mike the necklace, frayed thread, knots, tissue, and all. I could see the disappointment in his face. He sighed and mumbled something about it being all right, but I could hear the disapproval in his tone. I reached for the cross part with my free hand, to show him that I could probably save that part of the necklace. I grasped the cross with my thumb and index finder, to pull it loose, and then—the entire necklace began to uncoil itself, like a living snake, unknotting as I pulled the cross up, until it was fully extended. All that was left in my hand were scraps of wet tissue.

If Mike hadn't witnessed this, I would have thought I had gone crazy. We both just looked at each other and at the necklace. We had both seen the knots, but hanging from my hand was a perfectly fine, seed bead woven necklace!

We praised God together. We both knew God had done it. Once again, He had traded "beauty for ashes." His beauty, my ashes. He had taken my foolishness, my lack of care and returned His wisdom, His repair. God was still in the miracle business. He does care. He does listen. He does allow U-turns! And we can always bring Him our ruined treasures, our busted up dreams, our careless mistakes, and He can fix them.

That day was a turning point in my life. Just like laundry, there will always be challenges, there will always be challenging people. However, I do not have to allow the "tangled messes" of life to affect me adversely. Now, whenever I get discouraged about something, I find that little necklace, focus on the cross, and remember that God today is the same God who yesterday repaired that little necklace. Nothing is too messed up for Him to fix. He loves me that much!

A KNOCK AT HEART'S DOOR

by Candice Lee Wilber, Denver, Colorado

As a teenager, my life seemed to me a living hell. I had an abusive step-father whose rage, when I became old enough to try to ignore it, would lead to verbal, and sometimes physical, battles of will. My real daddy, whom I saw very little of, disappeared out of my life, leaving a false address and broken hearts in his wake. Nothing I did seemed to be worth the effort.

Thinking the solution to our problems was only a "sniff" away, my friends and I finished a bottle of 150-proof Ever-Clear, numbing the present pain, but replacing it with an emptiness far more agonizing. The day after that event, feeling so hungover and so sorry for myself that I could find no reason to stay alive, I took a bottle of morphine hoping to sleep forever. I woke up later, realizing I had failed again.

"God, I hate You!" I raged. I stormed over to my shelves and threw one book after another at my wall, cursing as I went along. I lifted out an old Bible and heaved it the hardest, taking out my bitterness against God and the life He had given me. As I stopped to catch my breath, out of the corner of my eye, I noticed that a page had fallen from the Bible during the crash. Time seemed to stop as I walked across the room, bent over, and picked up the torn page. I stared at it for a long time. The margins were filled with notes in an elegant hand, Jeannie's hand.

My thoughts flew back to a time over a year before; I had been sitting in my bedroom listening to the raucous beat of Metallica when someone knocked on my door. The knock was unlike my stepfather's raging bangs, unlike my mother's "Candice?" punctuated with tentative taps. My brother never knocked at all.

It was a frail, gentle knock, but insistent, as if knocking at heart's door, afraid of damaging its contents. I carelessly flipped off the stereo, opened the door, and found Jeannie, a widow who attended a Bible study group with my mother, standing in my doorway. I raised an eyebrow at her. Few sane people dared to enter this teenager's room, but she brushed aside magazines, clothing, and candy wrappers; sat down on the floor; and motioned for me to sit beside her. "I want to give this to you," she said quietly, handing me an expensive-looking, leather-bound book. She started to speak again but seemed to think better of it. Smiling at me, she picked up her long skirt and left, closing the door behind her.

Shrugging, I started to place the book on my shelf, but curiosity proved even stronger than teenage apathy. I carefully opened the thick book to the first page and found the title: The Holy Bible. New International Version. I laughed aloud and wondered what right that silly old lady had to give me a Bible! I closed it quickly, as if the pages had burnt my fingers, and placed it upon my shelf next to the other dust-covered classics that would be forgotten.

For the first time since that day, I realized the worth of this book to its former owner. With tears streaming down my face, I searched for tape to repair the page and thought about Jeannie: her kindness to strangers and animals; her quiet, gentle voice; her long, elegant hands that had knocked so gracefully on my door a year earlier.

What could have motivated her to give this treasure to an ungrateful teenager who had never taken the time to thank her, much less appreciate the gift? For the first time since the day I had received it, I opened Jeannie's Bible. I think I was looking for the Shepherd Psalm. What I found was Psalm 27:10, "Though my father and mother forsake me, the LORD will receive me."

I never found the Shepherd Psalm that day; sleep overtook me too quickly. But that day proved to be the U-turn which changed my life forever! Two weeks later, at the altar of Christ Episcopal Church, I found a God Who understood this frightened, misunderstood child, and Who loved me unconditionally. When I went home that evening, I never went to sleep. I read Jeannie's Bible into the early hours of the morning. Within its pages, I found the comfort and answers I had searched for in vain all of my life. It beckoned me to come to a heavenly Father Who would never leave, no matter what I had done. I wept as I read the story of the prodigal son, who spent his father's inheritance, but was, nevertheless, welcomed back home with open arms.

The transformation in my life was incredible. The drinking, swearing, and fistfights stopped, as well as enough outward changes to drop the jaws of my classmates the next school year. However, the inward qualities I learned, from daily quiet times reading the Scripture and spending time with its author, were far more remarkable. Characteristics I had never experienced before emerged: Love replaced hatred; joy replaced depression; hope replaced despair. Becoming a Christian did not solve all my hurts, but God's "peace which passes all understanding" was there like a gentle friend, like the love letter He had authored and sent to me through a weathered but faithful, gentle servant.

A LOVE NOT FORSAKEN

by Tammera Ayers, St. Mary's, Ohio

I was sitting in our kitchen writing in my journal, when I suddenly realized what I had been longing for had come to pass. It was a coming home for my heart at last.

It had been twelve years since I had given my heart to the Lord, but I struggled daily to try to make God more "real" to me. I knew in my mind that Christ died and rose again, but I would pray day after day, "God, I want to love You with all of my heart, but I don't feel it. I don't know how to feel it, and I think, Lord, it is because all my life, I have never felt loved."

Circumstances and situations I experienced as a child made it impossible for me to truly understand love. My basic needs were met and that sufficed for a time, but as I grew, a sense of emptiness and fear developed within my heart and soul.

I was sixteen when I gave my heart to the Lord, but by that time my ability to accept unconditional love was tainted. When you don't know what love is, you can't accept it. I couldn't understand that God loved me. I knew it in my mind, but I didn't feel it in my heart.

What I didn't know was that God recognized those voids that had developed during my childhood. Even before I gave my heart to Him, He gave everything so that He could carry me until I could gain the ability to understand His love. God knew I would have trouble comprehending His love, so He had to show me in a real-life way that I could personally see and understand.

He gave me a husband and children to help me experience first-hand a portion of what His love meant. Ever so slowly, with this first-hand experience and knowledge of the Scriptures, the voids in my life began to fill up and smooth over. The Lord brought me to a time and place of emotional understanding. I think He must have said, "Now you're ready. Here it is." A veil lifted that morning as I sat writing in my journal, and the understanding of God's love settled over me. At last I understood the truth. Scripture says in John 3:21, "But whoever lives by the truth comes into the light, so that it may be seen plainly that what he has done has been done through God."

Hosea 6:3 says, "Let us acknowledge the LORD; let us press on to acknowledge him. As surely as the sun rises, he will appear; he will come to us like the winter rains, like the spring rains that water the earth."

If we have faith, God's grace will hold us fast, because in time, if we allow it, He will bring us to emotional understanding. Some learn this lesson quickly. For others, like me, it takes awhile to understand that love is not an elusive feeling available to only a chosen few. Love is there for all of us, from the moment we are born until we leave this earth.

The lesson is quite simple. When we realize that God is love, our love will be complete, and there will be no fear in it.

THE BROKEN ANGEL

by Maxine Wright, Bremen, Georgia

I have a lot of angel figurines around my house. As I was dusting recently, I picked up one with a broken wing. My granddaughter, Jessica, had been looking at it and accidentally dropped it one day. She was heartbroken when she saw it had broken. She was also sure I would be upset. But I hugged her and told her not to worry about it. It was just a "thing." Things could always be replaced. I didn't throw it away, though. For some reason, I hesitated to do that. I had simply put it back on the shelf—where I'd just come across it again.

As I fingered the broken bits of plaster, I thought back over some mistakes and accidents in my own life. There were some bad judgments I had made. There were harsh words to my family that could never be taken back. There were definitely some paths I wished I'd never gone down. There were times that I had shut myself off from everyone and everything because I didn't want to be hurt. And it was always some-body else's fault, not mine.

Looking at that little angel, I realized how much I had grown. What-ever my past experience or circumstances, they couldn't be changed. Whether or not they should have happened was immaterial. What was important was that I had come to understand that I have a choice in regard to how I react to them. It took years of hard work and lots of love and support from my family to get me to this place of healing and recovery.

Standing there, holding the broken angel that I had decided not to throw away, I had a revelation. That is the same decision my heavenly

Father made in regard to me so many times! Times when I had failed, times when I had fallen, or turned my back on all that was good, He just picked up the pieces and put them on the shelf. He didn't throw them away. He gave me the time to work through my difficulties and then took all the pieces and put them back together in His way and time.

Because of God's love and patience, I can now look at each new day with hope and purpose. I can face life with a smile. I can serve Him. In doing that, I can teach others that their lives can also be changed. You can learn to see the beauty around you and be a vessel of the Lord. Why? Because He never throws the pieces of a broken vessel away.

Looking at my little broken angel, I decided to return it gently to the shelf. I wouldn't throw it away, either.

CHAPTER TWO

Tales of Triumph

I know what it is to be in need,
and I know what it is to have plenty.
I have learned the secret of being content in any and every situation,
whether well fed or hungry, whether living in plenty or in want.
I can do everything through him who gives me strength.
Philippians 4:12–13

THE WEDDING

by John P. Walker, New Cumberland, Pennsylvania

Jack and Jean were among our earliest friends when I began ministry in my very first church as a full-time pastor. Their friendly faces and warm smiles were a great encouragement to a young preacher with the Sunday morning pulpit jitters. Their smiles were genuine, which was a surprise to me, as they had been through more trials than almost anyone I had ever known.

Jack had been a chemist with a successful company. Over a period of ten years, a diagnosis of a severe form of rheumatoid arthritis took Jack from a healthy workingman to someone confined to a wheelchair and living on a disability pension. By the time I met him, he could move himself from the wheelchair only with great difficulty, and then, only to shift to another chair, or to stand for a moment. Pain and effort showed in his face when making these transitions, which were usually few and far between.

He and Jean got around well in a new van converted for the wheelchair. A small elevator installed in their townhouse moved Jack between the floors, and in spite of his misshapen, arthritis-bent fingers, Jack learned to use a computer and assisted us at the church with some of our financial work.

Through Jack and Jean, I also came to know their now adult daughters. When Susan, the eldest, arrived at my office to ask me to perform a wedding for her and her fiancé, Eric, it was no great surprise. Her father had hinted only a few weeks earlier that this might be coming.

The counseling and the planning of the ceremony seemed to go by very quickly, and soon it was almost time for the wedding. One day, Susan made an unscheduled stop at my office. From the look on her face, I knew that something was seriously wrong. She came straight to the point. "My dad wants to walk me down the aisle," she said, close to tears. "He really thinks he can do it. He absolutely insists on it."

"I'll practice until the wedding. I'm going to do this," he told me adamantly while sitting at his kitchen table drinking tea the next day. "Please pray for me!" I knew there was no changing his mind when he was determined to do something, and so I let the subject drop. I did, however, pray.

When the evening of the rehearsal arrived, we set up several scenarios that would allow Jack to "present" the bride. Only one of the three involved him walking down the aisle, and we included it only to please Jack. A brief experiment that evening seemed to deflate Jack's determination as he only took a few steps before he had to sit back down. From the platform, I watched sadly as he hung his head where he sat. Again, I prayed.

The day of the wedding arrived. Everything was going as planned. At the top of the hour, I found myself standing on the steps of the platform with groom and groomsmen, awaiting the bridal party.

The music began playing, and the bridesmaids proceeded down the aisle. Each paused and turned as she passed the front row of pews and took her place opposite the groomsmen. The maid of honor was last to walk, and as she turned in her appointed position, the music softly concluded.

After a brief pause, the organist played the dramatic opening notes of the wedding march. "Will you all please stand," I instructed.

I found myself thinking of Jack. He had been brought up the steps to the sanctuary in the lift earlier and now waited in the wheelchair by the door. With the struggles of the previous evening still in mind, Jack would not be walking the aisle today. I was disappointed for his sake, but I couldn't imagine his hurt. This had meant so much to him.

The doors to the church sanctuary opened to the side at the rear. This meant that the bride would have to walk behind the last row of pews before turning into the center aisle. I could just make out Susan's progress above the heads of the now standing congregation because of the puff of white taffeta that stood up from her veil.

I saw that puff of white stop, and then murmuring began near the back. A moment later, the beautiful bride made her turn into the main aisle. It took a second to realize what was happening. Susan was being escorted by her father, and he was walking!

Slowly, and painfully, Jack took a few steps and then paused to catch his breath. With a cane in his left hand and her arm on his right, father and daughter moved toward me. It seemed as if the entire congregation was holding its collective breath, all of us fearing that the next step would be the last. I believe, in that moment, we were all unified in prayer for Jack.

The organist looked at me with panic in her eyes as the music came close to its conclusion. I motioned for her to continue playing, and a few more minutes inched past before the bride and her father finally arrived at the front.

As the music concluded, I quickly gathered my thoughts. Still awestruck, I voiced a rather shaky introduction. I almost choked up when I asked, "Who presents this woman to be married to this man?"

Jack's voice came back clear and strong, and not without some measure of pride, "Her mother and I do."

As Susan hugged her father and then took her place alongside her soon-to-be husband, I noticed that her face was wet with tears. I noticed my own face was wet! In fact, it seemed like the whole congregation had been as deeply moved.

The wedding reception that followed was a wonderful affair. It was one of the grandest I had ever attended. But, whatever the charm or excitement of the postwedding celebration, the highlight of the day, in everyone's eyes, remained the miracle we had witnessed shortly before. The miracle of Jack, with determination born of love, and faith in the living God, escorting his daughter down the aisle on her wedding day!

No truer words express the miracle of that day as those written in Mark 10:27: "With man this is impossible, but not with God; all things are possible with God."

KEVIN

by Gerry Di Gesu, West Chatham, Massachusetts

My daughter, Nancy, hesitated as we walked up the broad steps into our church. "What's the matter, Mommy? You look sad." I smiled down at my seven year old, not surprised she sensed my mood. She was an intuitive and sensitive child. "Oh, nothing, Honey. I just feel a little nervous for Kevin." I felt a sick lump in my stomach and wished this night was over. Christopher, thirteen, and my husband, Roger, had already found seats for us in one of the first pews in the church so we would be able to see Kevin clearly.

Parishioners quickly filled the seats, eager to participate in the Lenten Holy Thursday services. Members of the senior Catholic Youth Organization (CYO) would each read a passage from the Bible, one for each station of the cross in remembrance of Christ's suffering. Kevin's reading was for the twelfth station of the cross—Christ dies. Socially immature and with few friends, he had at last found a small niche within the CYO group, which was led by an understanding and compassionate priest. Kev had been thrilled to invite many family friends and neighbors to join us for the service.

I was proud but upset that Kevin had volunteered. His childhood had been filled with emotional pain. A chronic asthmatic, he also experienced serious learning disabilities which made each day of school a trial for him. Awkward, and with poor coordination, he was considered a klutz by peers who didn't include him in sports activities or games. Labeled "retard" by classmates, he was a severe stutterer. Now fifteen, and a junior in high school, he saw a speech therapist weekly at school since his speech still became unintelligible when he was nervous or upset.

But Kevin also possessed a joy and zest for life I envied. His wonderful optimism helped him cope and compensate for problems he faced daily. We had adopted Kevin and brought him home when he was only a week old. Roger and I loved him like crazy and helped him in every way we could. But neither of us possessed Kevin's inherent accepting and nonjudgmental personality. He considered everyone he met a friend. Through the years, I often wished I could meet his birth parents to discover which of them (or perhaps both) enjoyed the joyous spirit they had passed on to our child.

The buzz of conversation quieted as Monsignor walked to the podium and greeted us warmly. He spoke softly, gently reminding us of what Christ had endured for us. All lights in the church clicked off with only the light over the lectern glowing on the Bible. One by one the CYO members, dressed in simple white robes, solemnly shared their readings. Some were nervous and read so quickly it was hard to understand them, and others, composed and confident, read slowly and deliberately. Finally, it was Kevin's turn.

He smiled as he opened the Bible to the passage he had practiced reading endlessly at home the last few weeks. My husband's hand closed over mine. Chris and Nancy looked at me for reassurance I was unable to provide. "The–the–the–," Kevin began. He stopped. His mouth twisted slowly as he tried painfully to say the next word. Nothing. We sat paralyzed in the quiet stillness. He wasn't stuttering; he was "blocked," unable to speak.

I looked away from him and tried not to cry. My family stared straight ahead. None of us could look at each other. Then, as we all waited in the soundless black church, I felt a tiny warm glow flicker inside of me. It grew slowly, until I felt consumed by its radiance. Moments later, I realized it had to be the prayers of everyone in the church forming a slow, single wave of hope directed toward Kevin, willing him to speak.

"Lord spoke." Two more words. Again his mouth contorted painfully, but at last he continued his reading, halting for endless minutes between many words. He took a deep breath, a breath from which he seemed to draw strength from parishioners, family, and friends. A smile crept into his eyes and over his face as he slowly and deliberately continued reading the exceptionally long passage. Finally he finished and stood there a moment. Unabashedly, he grinned broadly, gave a slight wave, and stepped down from the lectern.

Nancy gave me a big hug, and I had to grab Chris's hands to stop him from applauding. There were two more passages to be read. As the church lights clicked on one by one, it seemed as if I had been on a long journey and was now returning to reality. My family sat silently for a long time, each saying "thank you" in his own way before we went into the church hall to share refreshments with our church community.

I thought I might find Kevin upset or embarrassed but should have known better. God's wonderful gifts of optimism and joy hadn't let him down. He stood in the center of a large group, grinning broadly. "That was great, Kev. We all felt Jesus' pain when you were trying to speak." "Congratulations on a great job. You really hung in there. I would have flipped out." "Did you feel our prayers as we struggled with you?" "You really have guts." He laughed as more CYO members gathered around him, gently joshing and teasing. He was part of the group.

Father Charles, the CYO moderator, hugged Kevin tightly. "Well, Kevin. You are our hero tonight. I'm so proud of you. Every person here certainly could imagine the physical agony and mental suffering of Jesus when He hung on the cross as we watched you struggle. Your pain certainly showed how the Lord suffered before He died. You gave the word courage new meaning."

After the group drifted away, Kevin joined us for cake and punch. "Hey, Mom. I told you not to worry. I knew I could do it. At first I really got upset when I got stuck. But then I remembered what my speech therapist tells me every week. She says, 'Kev, when you have something to say and people care about you, they'll wait till you can finish.' And isn't it great? She was right."

A SHOT IN THE DARK

by Cory Ball as told to Joyce Larson, Phoenix, Arizona

I kept drifting in and out of consciousness, never quite grasping what was happening, but realizing I was in a hospital somewhere. I kept hearing people talking around me but could never quite make out what was being done or said. One day I was finally able to remain awake. I could not see, and since I couldn't lift my arms to touch my face, I assumed my eyes were bandaged. I could hear someone moving around the room and called out to them. They said they would get my doctor and promised to return shortly.

While I waited, I went over the last thing I remembered. It was almost midnight, April 15, 1995. I was out walking and listening to my cassette player when a motorist passed by yelling at me to get out of his way, even though I had moved aside and he had plenty of room to pass me. I yelled back that it was a free country. He responded, "Not while I'm in town," and drove away.

Apparently his anger, fueled by my cocky attitude and God only knows what else, brought him back. I heard the car behind me, and as I turned around, was stunned to see him reach up with a handgun and shoot me at point-blank range in the chest, then speed away never to be seen again.

I instinctively clasped my right hand over my left breast in a mock pledge of allegiance and let out a terrified scream for help as I staggered dazed toward my apartment. Those were the last visual memories I have of my prior life. I was twenty years old.

The story the doctor told me was unbelievable. The present day was June 9, 1995, almost two months after I had been shot. The damage to my body had been extensive. The bullet had entered through the left side of my chest, ricocheted off my left collarbone, and embedded itself in my right shoulder where it still lies to this day. Removing it might have caused paralysis in my right arm, therefore the surgeons felt it best to leave it alone. The bullet's trajectory severed the main artery to my heart and tore off the top lobe of my right lung. The lung damage was minuscule in comparison to the damage done by the severed artery. I lost all of my blood internally which caused full system shutdown, or what is called pulmonary edema and renal failure. This led to the loss of proper kidney function which, in turn, caused massive gangrene in my extremities.

My body had endured many exploratory surgeries, one extensive heart resuscitation, three open-heart surgeries, and five tracheotomies. I listened in amazement. I could recall none of this. However, the worst was yet to come as the doctor told me the severe gangrene had forced the surgeons to amputate both of my legs above the knees and my left arm above the elbow. I awakened to the shocking realization that the only limb remaining on my body was my right arm, the one the doctors were able to save by leaving the bullet intact. And the bandages on my eyes? There were none. The extensive blood loss and oxygen deprivation to the ocular center of my brain severely damaged my optical nerves, leaving me totally blind.

In my mind, one minute I'm walking on the street listening to my Walkman, and the next I'm phenomenally crippled and weak as a newborn kitten. I went from six feet seven inches and 215 pounds to four feet ten inches and 100 pounds.

After six and a half months in the hospital, I was released to my parents' home on October 26, two days before my twenty-first birthday and what we now refer to as the "Celebrate Life Festival." Physical therapy and vocational rehabilitation followed, but I soon abandoned modern prosthetic devises because my utter blindness made them so cumbersome.

As each day went by, I became increasingly bitter over the entire situation. I wasn't angry at God; I just didn't know how I was supposed to feel. One of my Christian friends told me that God was going to use what had happened to me in a great and powerful way for His glory, but I didn't understand what that could possibly be.

My main question to God was not "Why me?" because I knew in my heart all things happen for a reason, but instead I persisted to ask God simply, "Why?" I wanted to know why, and what it was He wanted me to do now.

On September 29, 1996, almost seventeen months after being shot, I discovered why. Before my life changed, I had searched many religions for happiness but found only empty philosophies. I tried seeking the thrill of gathering material objects and sexual pursuits for happiness, all to no avail. Throughout my early years I had caused grief for those who loved me with my wild ways, and like many young men my age, I had lived a sinful life. Even though I had been raised a Christian, I was not myself a disciple of Christ. I didn't know what that meant.

But because He died for me, I didn't have to keep dying from the memory of my sins. Christ wanted me to accept Him freely and willingly as my Savior. That was it. He wanted me to stop running from Him. That was when I began a personal relationship with God and with Jesus Christ. Astonishingly enough, I realized it only took one simple choice. One simple decision to say "yes" and my life was changed. I made my U-turn toward God. After this decision to accept Christ's forgiveness for my sinful acts, for my selfishness, and for my total disobedience of God's laws in my life, I received a most wonderful gift. It is that gift that changed my life, not the shooting, not the tragedy, not the disabilities I now faced.

It was the gift of utter peace. I was filled to overflowing with a breathtaking peace that was totally new to me. And with that peace came a forgiveness for myself and for others that freed my soul. I was able to completely forgive the man who shot me, as well as come to terms with all the other variables that played a role in my current situation. It is a peace that now causes me to look at everything in a different light. God did not punish me. This is just what it took for me to acknowledge Him, to ask Him into my life.

Less than one week after my U-turn toward God, I was at the table with my parents, sharing my newfound exuberance, when my mother, who was completely dumbfounded at the turn my life had so quickly taken said, "How is it, that after twenty-two years of trying to get you to understand God's plan for your life, it has only just now become clear to you?"

That's when I responded with a smile, "I can't explain it, Mom. That's just the power of God. We all know how much He likes doing things in His own time."

Published in Virtue *magazine, April 1999*

MIRACLE IN THE RAIN

by Jan Coleman, Auburn, California

My husband, Carl, and I inched our way to the hospital, driving through the streams that gushed over the roadway. We had been given no details of my daughter's accident other than the information that she had been speeding up a mountain freeway in a fierce storm that dismal winter morning when her SUV suddenly flipped over. She had been airlifted to the trauma center we were now trying to reach, some twenty miles away.

I was heartsick. For the past year, Jenny had been on a mad dash from her problems. With her marriage falling apart, her natural spunk had given way to outright belligerence. Every family gathering recently had become a confrontation. She had refused to even speak to me for the past two months. Now, I was praying that her recklessness and anger hadn't finally resulted in disaster. *Please, Lord,* I prayed, *don't let her die with this wall between us. Please.*

The neurosurgeon at the trauma center was grim. There were serious head injuries, and Jen was in "very bad shape." We couldn't see her, but we could wait in a private room or the chapel. They would get us when we could see her, or if anything changed. We chose the chapel.

We found Steve, Jen's husband, in the chapel. He lifted his head from his hands when we came in. Carl held him as he cried. "We had a terrible fight last night, and I said some awful things," he sobbed.

Well, I thought, *this is where the rubber meets the road when it comes to my faith, isn't it?* I thought of the verse "All things work together for good to those who love God." *All things?* I wondered. *Even arguments and tragic car accidents?* I prayed for perspective. Fretting would not change the outcome. My daughter's life was in God's hands. Whether she lived or died, she was still with Him.

It was shocking to see Jen lying there in that hospital bed. She lay in a coma. Her swollen, shaved head was hooked to tubes, wires, and pressure monitors. Machines blipped and bleeped, nurses moved in and out. If she did survive, brain damage was certain. To what degree, they could not tell us. Still, she looked so peaceful that I could not help but feel that God was doing His healing work as she rested.

I was pulled from my thoughts by a voice behind me. "How's my girl?" I turned to see a young hospital technician. "My name is Phillip. I was at the accident scene with this little lady, and I wanted to see how she was doing."

Apparently Phillip had been late for work that day as he was headed down the mountain when he saw a sudden, massive billow of water and a tiny dot catapult from it. Realizing it was a car accident, he had stopped to help. When he reached the scene, a highway patrol officer was already there, covering Jen's curled, lifeless body with a yellow slicker, ready to pronounce her dead. Phillip, an orthopedic technician and trained as a navy field medic, flipped the slicker back and went to work on her. In a few minutes, she gasped a breath.

By then, a rescue helicopter was overhead but couldn't land because of the gusting wind and driving rain. It was imperative Jen get to a hospital as soon as possible, as she desperately needed help breathing. As discussion of lowering a respirator from the helicopter began, another car pulled up. It was an off-duty EMT who had seen the commotion and came to help. He had a respirator with him! Working together quickly, they got her going on the machine. The storm had finally begun to abate just enough for the helicopter to land and take off safely with Jen aboard.

As I listened to Phillip's account of these events, I understood what it means to feel the peace that passes all understanding. I could envision Christ reaching out to cushion Jen against what should have been a deadly fall, directing the EMT with the equipment she needed to the scene, and finally clearing the raging skies for the time the helicopter needed to pick her up. According to the doctor's charts, Jennifer's condition was not a hopeful one. It didn't matter. I realized that God works from His own heavenly charts, and I was at peace. It was very clear that He had a plan for my daughter, and this was not her time to leave us.

I shared Phillip's story and my feelings with Jen's husband when he came in to sit with her. He hugged me and said, "Whatever happens, I know God's hand is in it. Even if she's disabled, I'm committed to this marriage forever." All we could do was pray and wait.

Five days later, Jen twitched a foot and began to emerge from the coma. The doctors shook their heads in amazement. Not only was she not paralyzed, but she would recover. "A miracle," in their own words. Ten days later, she was transferred to a rehabilitation hospital.

After only two weeks, the doctor said he had never seen such progress. Jen's fighting spirit played in her favor now. She struggled to walk and to formulate sentences. Even chewing her food had to be relearned. But she fought to gain ground. Just three months after the accident which should have taken her life, we helped her walk shakily into her own house, back to Steve and their two little boys. "I'm so grateful that God is a god of second chances," she said with tears in her eyes.

It's been two years since we brought her back home. Her bruised brain continues to heal. She's still feisty, but there is a softness in her that I've never seen before. I look at Jennifer differently now. From an eternal perspective, I guess. Her strength and determination are gifts from God. Her life is a gift from God. She is a precious stone in the Master's hand that He is crafting for His glory. There are miracles. She is one of them.

All any of us need do is believe—and have hope and faith. He'll do the rest.

THE LONG ROAD HOME

by Rose Plihcik, Sun City, Arizona

Had anyone suggested to me that I would be able to drive on the busy highways of any large city, I would have responded with one word, "never." For twenty-five years, a phobia of highway driving held me firmly in its grip.

My fears began when my husband, Ed, and I traveled home to Connecticut on a balmy day in spring after a visit to his mother and stepfather. The traffic was heavy and had started to back up, when the car in front of us suddenly came to a complete stop. Ed slammed on the brakes. I was thrown forward, narrowly missing hitting my head on the dashboard. Neither of us was hurt, but I was so shaken by the incident that I could not bear to watch the traffic as we continued on our way. I shut my eyes and prayed that we would arrive home safely. My fears grew out of proportion to the incident, resulting in terror of being on any type of highway, interstate, or freeway.

I was a stay-at-home mom, and since we could not afford a second car, I rarely drove except on weekends. Even then, I drove only on familiar back roads and only to run errands no farther away than the next town. The thought of driving anywhere but those back roads was paralyzing.

When we traveled to destinations best reached by highways, Ed would try to take secondary roads whenever he could. Since that wasn't always possible, I developed techniques like reading a book or knitting until we reached our destination. I could not endure watching the cars and trucks careening past us. The apprehension and tension of knowing there had to be a return trip home served to take away any enjoyment I felt about where we were going. I became anxious about going anywhere and reached the conclusion that it was better to just stay home. I felt like a prisoner, captive against my will.

During this time, I had lost faith in God. I knew something was missing from my life, for there was a void that begged to be filled. I tried going back to church a couple of times, but I no longer felt comfortable in the church of my childhood. I felt lost in spirit and, in spite of a loving family, very much alone.

One day, while I was shopping for a book at a local discount store, I noticed a version of the Bible called The Living Bible. I picked it up and browsed through the pages. This version of the Bible was so much easier to read with its up-to-date language that I bought it and began to read it. I felt consoled by the words I read, and gradually I found myself praying again. I prayed to God to help me overcome my phobia. Nothing dramatic happened, but I began to feel less afraid. I knew God heard my prayers. I wanted a quicker response but realized that God does not answer prayers within our time frame or exactly as we wish. I started attending church again.

The following year, Ed had complications from diabetes. As a result of total blockage of blood flow to his legs, he developed gangrene in his left foot, which required extensive surgery to save his leg from amputation. This was soon followed by the need for bypass surgery on his right leg to prevent the same problem from occurring.

Ed's surgery seemed to go well. He had a follow-up appointment with the doctor in two weeks' time. I went with him, of course, although he insisted that he could drive. He was just going to have the stitches removed and then come home, but blood work revealed a massive infection. He was immediately hospitalized and scheduled for surgery the next day.

I was so worried and upset about this turn of events that at first it didn't occur to me that I would have to drive the car home. Alone. So it was that at rush hour on a Friday in January, I got behind the wheel of the car and exited the parking garage. The sky was thick with snow clouds. I struggled to find my way out of the city and onto the interstate, knowing I would have to merge with other traffic at some point, and cross three lanes to be in the proper lane. All I could do was say over and over, "Please, God, help me get home." Tears ran down my cheeks, but with my hands clenched on the steering wheel I couldn't wipe them away.

I reached the point where the highways converged. Interstate 84 loomed ahead, but I was in the wrong lane! I looked in the rearview mirror and saw nothing but headlights behind me. It was hard to judge how far away they were. My heart was beating wildly as I attempted to find an opening. Suddenly, a space appeared, and I slipped into it. It was a close call, the horns of the cars behind me were blaring, but at least I was in the proper lane. I repeated again and again, "Dear God, help me get through this, please."

At last my exit appeared. I was sobbing with relief, but I still had a twenty-mile drive to get home. Thankfully, the back road was quiet without much traffic.

Saturday and Sunday my son drove to the hospital, but he would not be able to come to the hospital during the week. I would have no one to count on but the Lord.

Monday and every day after that, I drove to the hospital to be with Ed. Each day I felt more confident than the day before. As the days Ed was hospitalized turned into weeks, I learned to put myself fully into God's hands before I set out for the hospital. With God's help, I could now drive the interstate to Hartford with a degree of comfort I thought I would never be able to achieve.

A lot has happened since that time. Ed's feet continued to worsen until he was in a wheelchair. Our son moved to Arizona, and two years later, finding I no longer wanted to deal with snow and ice, we moved there, too. With my son-in-law and daughter's help, I was able to drive cross-country from Connecticut to Arizona. There were many trips to a hospital in Phoenix from our home in Sun City West, but, with God on my side, I knew I would overcome any driving difficulty that came my way.

My husband went home to the Lord almost two years ago. I know now that God had prepared me little by little for the rough road I would face. I am never alone with God by my side. Whenever I set out on the road, I pray for God's guidance and help in getting me safely to my destination.

SALVATION THROUGH DEATH

by Carlin Hertz, Fort Washington, Maryland

January 27, 1994, was no ordinary day for Alabama State University. It was a day the whole Hornet football team would never forget. This day would forever be etched in the minds of sixty-six young men. It would change many lives for good.

The day was cloudy and a bit chilly. It had rained all day, but the rain let up just in time for the football team's daily conditioning session on the track. The players hated running in the cold on a slippery track.

"Zo, I do not feel like running today," I said to my roommate as we both laced up our running shoes and headed outside. I threw on a thick black sweatshirt to keep warm. We listlessly trotted over to Hornet Stadium. Within minutes, a gang of tired and complaining football players all walked in unison toward the track. Puddles splashed on our legs, dampening our clothes. We ignored it. Our minds were focused on the eight laps we would have to run.

The conditioning coach greeted us with a sinister smile. "Good afternoon, ladies. Welcome to my house." He laughed as he rubbed his thick beard and blew his whistle to get our attention.

I was stretching my hamstrings, trying to loosen up, when Darnell walked over and asked me to help him stretch. I really didn't know him that well, but he was a teammate. Besides, I'd heard nothing but good things about him. He extended his long, muscular arm to help me off the ground. He smiled, and then he sat down on the wet grass.

Darnell was no ordinary football player. He was a slender six feet six inches, 265 pounds of solid muscle. He had the biggest feet I had ever seen. His size would intimidate most men. But Darnell was different. Despite his massive frame, he was gentle, and the nicest guy I had ever met. I didn't know much about God then, but I heard that Darnell was a Christian. He never messed around with girls. He always went to church. If you had a problem, you could go to him, and he would help you through it. Darnell was a good influence on us all.

"You ready to knock these laps out, Carlin?" he asked as I stretched his hamstrings for him.

"I guess," I replied.

"Well, just keep up with me, and I'll get you through," he said as he jumped up and smacked my hand. The coach blew his whistle, and we all started running on the track.

We had to run eight laps, and then we had to do some sprints. I didn't know how I was going to get through it, but I stayed close to Darnell, like he told me to do. His presence kept my mind off the laps.

We were coming on the last lap, and I was a few feet behind Darnell. His long strides covered so much ground that I knew my baby strides would never catch him. I was determined to catch him, though, so that I could brag about it later at dinner.

Darnell was running at a good pace, not looking tired, when all of a sudden, he just collapsed. He crashed to the ground. I thought he was just tired and had fallen out, but he didn't get up. We all stopped and ran over to where he lay.

The student trainer ran over and frantically tried to help him, but she didn't really know what to do. By now, we could see Darnell was fighting for his life. His fists were balled-up tight, and he struggled to breathe. Finally, he just stopped. The trainer kept trying to talk to him, "Darnell, stay with me." In the distance, we could hear the blaring sounds of an ambulance siren.

By the time the ambulance got there, though, I think it was already too late. He just lay there as the paramedics tried to revive him. They placed him in the ambulance. We were told to go back to our rooms and wait for further instructions. We left the track in tears, hugging each other and praying, something many of us had never done. We were stunned.

A couple of us decided to go to the dining hall together instead of to the solitude of our rooms. As we sat down, a teammate ran over to us. "Everybody needs to go to the meeting room now!" From the look on his face, I knew that Darnell was gone.

"Hey, Kenny," I asked, "is Darnell all right?"

Kenny just looked at me and broke down.

Without thinking, I threw the glass in my hand, sending glass flying everywhere. "No! He can't be gone!" They had to hold me, because I couldn't control myself. People who didn't know what was going on looked at me like I was insane.

They told us Darnell had died of a massive heart attack. Apparently he had high blood pressure, but he wasn't taking his medication. I didn't want to accept his death. He was just twenty-two years old. I had just talked to him. Yeah, I had been to funerals, but to witness somebody alive one minute and dead the next was spooky. I had talked to him only minutes before.

During this time, a stranger from Cleveland arrived on campus. He was a missionary and had come to Montgomery to set up Bible studies on the campus. Jeff befriended a lot of the football players at a time when we really needed him and what he had to say. Learning that we had just lost a teammate, he set up weekly Bible studies in the football dorm. Every Wednesday night, the room where the Bible study was held would be packed with football players searching for answers. Many of my teammates had been very close to Darnell, and we couldn't figure out why he would die like that.

Through God and the Bible, Jeff soothed a lot of our pain and suffering. He told us the truth, and he told us about salvation through Jesus Christ. A lot of football players were saved during those Bible studies. Jeff and I became good friends. He told me that when he left Cleveland he didn't know what to expect. He said that God told him to take nothing with him, get on a bus, and head to Montgomery. He came right at the time we needed to hear God's Word the most. It was no accident he was here.

The good thing about Darnell's death was that he went to heaven. He was saved. The rest of us weren't, though. Any one of us could have died on the track that day. Where would we have ended up? Suppose Darnell had not died? Would a lot of those players have given their life to Christ? I doubt it.

Like Christ, Darnell died so that many of us might live. His death was the wake-up call it took to bring our entire team to Christ. I think Darnell is pleased.

Published in Parentlife *magazine in April 2000*

A MOM WHO USES A WHEELCHAIR

by Ronda Sturgill, Shalimar, Florida

A horseback riding accident at the age of eighteen left me a paraplegic, completely unable to walk. I was told a number of things by the nurses and doctors concerning my prognosis and recovery. As far as having children was concerned, I was told that I would be able to conceive and carry a baby, but that the delivery would probably be by cesarean section. However, my main concern at the time was that no one would ever want to marry me. After all, I was confined to a wheelchair.

I had no idea of what my life would be like as a paraplegic, but I did know that God was a loving God. Romans 8:28 says that "in all things God works for the good of those who love him, who have been called according to his purpose." Additionally, I claimed Proverbs 3:5–6 (KJV) as my life verse. "Trust in the LORD with all thine heart; and lean not unto thine own understanding. In all thy ways acknowledge him, and he shall direct thy paths." With that verse as my foundation, I struggled to adjust to my new life and create a new identity for myself.

After going back to college, between my junior and senior year, I worked as a counselor at an Easter Seal camp in the beautiful Blue Ridge Mountains of Virginia. Tim was the assistant director of the camp. One of Tim's best friends was also a paraplegic, so having a relationship with a disabled person was nothing new to him. He was able to look beyond my wheelchair and accept me for who I really was. I was so impressed by Tim's walk with the Lord and his knowledge of the Bible as he applied Christian principles to his everyday life that I immediately fell in love with him. Happily, it was a mutual feeling, and a few years later we were married.

We always knew that one day we would want to start a family, but I worried about the responsibilities of raising a child with my physical limitations. How would I ever be able to pick up my baby from a crib? How would I carry the baby around or give it baths? What would I do if he or she wandered out into a busy street?

Well, I soon got pregnant, and the worries temporarily took a backseat to the excitement. I loved feeling the baby kick and punch from inside. Eighteen hours of labor preceded the birth of our eight-pound twelve-ounce son. I will never forget the thrill and the rush of love I felt when I saw him for the first time. However, with his emergence from the protection of the womb, my worries about caring for him began in earnest.

I had to start caring for Toby right away in the hospital. I was very frightened at first and prayed desperately that God would help me take care of him. As I was getting him dressed and ready to bring home, he was lying on my lap with his feet toward my belly and his head on my knees. I turned my wheelchair to move across the room when, much to my horror, he went one way and I went another. I quickly reached out and grabbed him before he fell on the floor. *Dear Lord,* I thought. *What have I done? I almost dropped him, and I have not even left the hospital yet!*

I was very nervous going home. My mother carried him into the house for me and put him in his cradle for a nap. As he slept, I just stared at him and wondered how I was going to be able to reach him when he awoke. When I finally did lean over to get him, I fell right into his cradle!

I burst into tears as I realized that I could not even pick up my own baby. "I knew it," I cried to my mother. "This was all a big mistake. I cannot care for my own child. I should never have done this."

My mother looked me square in the eyes and said, "Oh yes, you can take care of this baby. This baby is not a mistake. He is a gift from God. And you will learn how to care for him the same way you have learned to do everything else in your life."

And so I did. I learned how to pick up Toby out of his crib, how to pick him up from the floor, how to carry him around, and how to get him in and out of the car. I gave him baths in the kitchen sink. As he grew big enough to sit in my lap, my friends were amazed at how still he sat. They could not imagine their eighteen-month-old baby ever sitting that still for any length of time. It was as if Toby knew he would fall if he wriggled and squirmed around. God, in His infinite wisdom, had given me a baby that I could handle.

I only dropped Toby once. I was carrying him around on my lap while we were out shopping when the front wheels of my chair caught on a raised part of a curb cut. When my wheels caught, my chair tipped forward, and Toby did a somersault right out of my lap onto the hard cement. I lost my balance, too, falling forward. I caught myself with my arms, but lacked the ability to get myself back into my chair. People who saw this came running over to us and very kindly picked both of us up and put us back together again!

Even before Toby started school, I dreaded the day that his friends would realize that his mom was different from their moms. I just knew that Toby would be made fun of because of me. Much to my delight, I was wrong. Toby invited me to come to his school and have lunch with him quite often. As his friends inquired about my disability, he answered their questions openly and honestly. He has never been ridiculed because his mom uses a wheelchair.

Toby is now eighteen years old. He fills our life with joy and makes our family complete. What if Tim and I had decided not to "take the risk" and have a child? We would have robbed ourselves of numerous "faith opportunities" that God has had to show us His love. God continues to equip me with the skills I need to take care of my son. As my mother said, having Toby was no mistake at all, but truly a miracle from God, for which I will always be thankful.

You know, the only limitations any of us have are those we place on ourselves, because it really is true, with God ALL things are possible!

THE NIGHT BEFORE. . .
AN AFRICAN CHRISTMAS STORY

by Peter Adotey Addo, Greensboro, North Carolina

Before this year, Christmas in my village had always been one of the most joyous of religious festivals for me. This Christmas Eve, things were different and I felt Christmas would never come. It was a profoundly desperate time. I was very sad because my family life had been severely disrupted, and I was sure that Christmas would never be the same. There was none of the usual joy and anticipation I always felt during the Christmas season. I was eight years old, but in the past few months I had matured a great deal.

Last April, the so-called Army of Liberation attacked our village and took all the young boys and girls away. Families were separated, and some were murdered. The soldiers burned everything in our village. During our forced march, we lost all sense of time and place.

Miraculously, some of us were able to get away from the soldiers during one rainy night. After several weeks in the tropical forest, we made our way back to our burned-out village. Most of us were sick, exhausted, and depressed. Most of the members of our families were nowhere to be found.

We had no idea what day it was until my sick grandmother noticed the reddish and yellow flower we call "Fire on the Mountain" blooming in the middle of the marketplace where the tree had stood and bloomed for generations at Christmastime. For some miraculous reason, it had survived the fire that had engulfed the marketplace. Grandmother told us it was almost Christmas because the flower was blooming. As far as she could remember, this only occurred at Christmastime.

Grandmother instructed us to celebrate Christmas. Those were the last words she spoke before she died that night. How could we celebrate the birth of the Prince of Peace, when since April we had not known any peace, only war and suffering? How could we celebrate life when death was all around us and had now claimed our beloved grandmother?

As I continued to think about our present suffering, several cars approached our village. At first, we thought they were cars full of men with machine guns, so we hid in the forest. To our surprise, they were just ordinary travelers, whose detour had led them straight to our village. All of them were on their way to their villages to celebrate Christmas with family and friends. They were shocked and horrified at the suffering and the devastation all around us. They confirmed that tonight was really Christmas Eve. Now, circumstances had brought them to our village at this time on this night before Christmas.

They shared the little food they had with us. They even helped us to build a fire in the center of the marketplace to keep us warm.

In the midst of all this, my ill and pregnant sister went into labor. She had been in a state of shock and speechless since we all escaped from the soldiers. Just like the Virgin Mary, she gave birth to a beautiful baby boy. This called for a celebration. War or no war, Africans have to dance, and we celebrated until the rooster crowed at 6:00 A.M. We sang Christmas songs, with everyone singing in his or her own language. For the first time, all the pain and agony of the past few months escaped us.

A miracle occurred that blessed evening. Christmas really did come to our village that night. It came with the birth of my nephew in the midst of our suffering. When morning finally came my sister was asked, "What are you going to name the baby?" For the first time since our village was burned and all the young girls and boys were taken away, she spoke. She said, "His name is Gye Nyame, which means 'Except God, I fear none.'"

Christmas came to our village that night with the birth of a baby. For us, this birth turned our village around. It personified for us the universal story of suffering turned into hope—the hope we find in the baby Jesus.

I knew we were not alone anymore, that God indeed had a purpose for us, and He would see us through what was to come. I realized there was hope, and I learned that Christmas comes in spite of all circumstances. It is always within us.

CHAPTER THREE

Love One Another

Dear children, let us not love with words or tongue
but with actions and in truth.
1 John 3:18

THE HUG FUND

by Cheryl Norwood, Canton, Georgia

You would think that getting married somewhat later in life than most couples, Mike and I would have been more established financially. However, neither of us brought much to the marriage cashwise. We had decent jobs but not much in savings. Mike was your typical bachelor before our marriage; i.e., new car, expensive furniture and stereo equipment, but no money in the bank. I had been supporting an antique habit and a shoe addiction. But we were comfortable and enjoyed being able to contribute money to several worthy causes on top of our tithe to our local church. God had truly blessed us, and we enjoyed sharing those blessings with others.

Then the bottom fell out. Four months into our marriage, an uninsured driver hit me. Then Mike's company closed its doors. My insurance was limited and did not cover home nursing care for me. Even with the help of our wonderful family and friends, Mike had to stay home with me and missed out on several job opportunities. Finally we were both able to go back to work, but our meager savings were depleted, and debts had added up.

We knew we would be back on our feet eventually, and we were very grateful for the physical healing that God had given me. God had really watched out for us, blessing us not only with my physical healing but a deepening of our love for each other, as well as an awareness of all the wonderful people around us.

What could we give back? It was a struggle just to pay our tithe each week. There was no money for anything extra. We stretched those pennies so far that Lincoln screamed! Every time a need came up, we would empty our pockets, but we felt it was so little, and the needs were so great. We wanted so badly to share God's goodness to us with others.

One day I received a check for just over $10, a rebate on an insurance overpayment. I cashed it and brought the money home. I put it in an antique tea tin on the shelf in the living room. Mike and I decided to start a fund and let God tell us how to spend it.

We prayed about this little fund, asking Him to show us how our tiny sum of money could make a difference for Him.

The next week, a friend at work was very depressed. She was recently divorced and feeling overwhelmed by loneliness. She didn't share much with us, but one day as I was going down the hall I overheard her say, "I feel invisible, like no one would even notice if I just suddenly disappeared." I went home to Mike, and we prayed about it and then decided we would put the $10 in a card to her. Since she knew my handwriting, Mike addressed the card. We bought a little encouragement card and wrote in a short note and signed it, "God loves you and so do we. You make a difference!"

Not much of a gift, but when I saw my friend at work a few days later, she was just bubbling. She had never shared anything personal with us at work, but around the coffeepot that morning, she told everyone about the card and gift. She said she treated herself and the kids to pizza with the $10 (this was ten years ago!), and they had a little party for no reason. She said to us, "I felt like God reached down and gave me a big hug!"

Thus began God's Hug Fund.

We would put in leftover change and money saved by using coupons. Occasionally one of us would have a little overtime in our check, and we would pitch that in the tin. Sometimes it would be Mike who would notice someone that needed "a hug from God." Sometimes God showed me a person in need of a hug. We kept it anonymous. We didn't always send a card, and we didn't always leave the cash; sometimes we bought something and left it. Sometimes it was groceries for a family having hard times. Sometimes it was something silly to get a laugh from a grouch!

Through it all, we learned that you don't need to have a lot to give a lot. We also learned the sweet blessing of giving in secret. When you give in secret, God gets the credit He deserves. Without your pride and their pride getting in the way, God has room to work!

While we are very grateful to be able to contribute financially to God's work in a bigger way now, we still look for little ways to give out those hugs. The neatest blessing to come out of all this is that we are also more aware of all the little hugs God sends our way. Last week alone I received a smile from a child, a thank-you note, a great afternoon shopping with a friend, a free lunch dropped off by someone who knew I was working through lunch at my desk, and help from a neighbor carrying in the groceries.

Someone's tea tin must be empty! Because I think God emptied it out just for me!

NICHOLAS

by Susan Fahncke, Kaysville, Utah

My son Nicholas has always had a soft heart. It's the thing I love best about him. At thirteen, he is now struggling with the "macho" role society expects of him. I am proud that he has remained a compassionate and kind person, even though the teenage years have struck. One such moment of pride was when he decided to give Christmas to a family in our neighborhood.

Chad and Derek are two boys who attend Nick's junior high. Junior high is painful enough for anyone, but for Chad and Derek, it was a daily nightmare. Living alone with their mother, they were the smallest boys in junior high. They wore the same worn, outdated clothes to school every day and were picked on constantly. Their mother is a loving, hardworking woman, but as most single moms know, there is rarely enough left over for clothes.

My son has always been sensitive to the pain of others. What most teenage kids wouldn't have even noticed, Nick immediately understood as embarrassment and pain lived out daily. They quickly became the subject of Nick's prayers and worries. He appointed himself secret protector to Chad and Derek.

Every year at Christmastime, we select a family for whom we are "Secret Santa." Last Christmas, we had a family meeting and a vote for who would be the best candidate. The majority of our family voted for a disabled friend of ours, who also happened to be a single mom with two teenagers. Except Nick. He resolutely stuck to his decision to help the Williams boys. Not wanting to squelch my son's desire to make a difference in the life of someone else, I hesitated. I knew how important this family was to him. My husband and I conferred. We would be Secret Santa for both families.

Nicholas's eyes lit up. His thirteen-year-old grin made my heart soar. How many mothers were blessed with a teenage angel? Seeing the kindness in my child's soul brought tears to my eyes. I knew what a rarity he was.

It is our tradition to provide the makings of a Christmas dinner, as well as carefully selected gifts for our "Secret Santa" family each year. Without a doubt, Nick knew that we needed to buy the boys clothes. And they couldn't be just any clothes. They had to be "cool," they had to be "in" clothes. Nick was determined to give Chad and Derek clothes that would stop the taunting and make them feel good about what they wore to school every day.

To many of us, this is a trivial, worldly thing, but when you are a young teenager, it is everything. Whether he realized it or not, Nick wanted to give them self-esteem, a chance to fit in. Quite a gift for a thirteen year old.

As we spent endless hours looking for just the right outfits for both boys, I concentrated on their mother. Having once been a single mom, I remembered the days of my own single motherhood. Every little bit of "extra" went to my children's needs. It had probably been a long time since she had done anything nice for herself.

Abandoning the kids to the boys' clothing department, I took a quick detour to the bath aisle. Smiling to myself, I selected a luxurious bath basket, filled to the brim with bubbles, soaps, lotions, and all kinds of "take me away" things that only a mom can truly appreciate. I found myself getting into the spirit of Nicholas's gift. I looked at clothes, makeup, jewelry, books. I finally selected a book of uplifting stories for mothers and a box of truffles. Delighted with myself, I couldn't wait to show everyone else what I had done. The spirit of Christmas filled my heart and overflowed into a joyous, childlike feeling of giddiness.

Returning to my children, I found they had finally settled on several articles of clothing that my son thought were "in." Judging the boys' sizes was difficult, but we did our best. Nick suddenly remembered the boys wore only old, worn coats to school. Utah winters make good gloves a must. We chose the thickest, warmest, "coolest" gloves in the store, and I didn't even look at the price tag! We were all grinning with the sheer joy of giving.

We next added a good family video, two great books, and then put the Christmas dinner together. A fat turkey, all the trimmings, dessert, and candy for the boys went into the cart. We couldn't wait to deliver our packages and picture the looks on Derek's and Chad's faces. I secretly hoped their mother had as much fun opening her gifts as I had shopping for her.

Our cart overflowing, we headed for the checkout line. At first worried about spending too much, I was now filled with a great sense of peace. I knew my husband wouldn't mind and, as blessed as we were, we ought to share those blessings with others. Standing in line, the thought kept coming back to me that money would be a much appreciated gift. Maybe there was something this family really needed that I didn't know about. Next to the counter, there were store gift cards on a rack. I carefully looked at the amounts and said a quick prayer for guidance. I reached for the fifty-dollar gift card, but my hand picked up the one hundred-dollar card. Praying again, I knew this was right and laid it on top of my purchases. I made a quick call to my husband to make sure this was not too much, and he surprised me with his assurance to go ahead.

I looked at Nicholas as his eyes fell on the gift card and laughed as he wheeled around in shock. "Is that for them?" he asked me. I nodded, and my eyes filled with tears as he threw his arms around me and thanked me as if the gift were for him. What an amazing kid I have.

That night, we wrapped the presents and delivered the huge box to the family's doorstep. Nick rang the bell, and we all ran giggling down the street. The feeling of joy stayed with us long past that night. And it returned the day school resumed. Nick ran all the way home from school to tell me Derek and Chad wore their new clothes to school. They fit and boy, did they look cool!

The planning and executing of our "Secret Santa" was the greatest gift our family got that Christmas, and I saw a side to my son that would make any mother weep. Teenage angels are hard to find these days, and I am so blessed that God placed one under our roof.

CROSSING THE BRIDGE OF FRIENDSHIP

by Elizabeth Turner, Ontario, Canada

Maybe it was his crippled stature that first drew me to the old man across the road. My years as an ICU nurse had developed my high level of interest in anyone with an obvious debilitation. The level of his impairment was extreme. The arthritis, so apparent, had bowed his limbs to a grotesque degree. On the very few occasions that I saw him out of his motorized wheelchair, he was a piteous site. Shrunken to perhaps four feet, it is difficult to aptly describe the severity of his body's betrayal. His age was difficult to decipher, but his eldest son, a strapping six-footer, appeared to be approaching his thirties.

Their arrival in our neighborhood caused many tongues to wag. It wasn't so much the fact that they were East Indian by nationality. Our typically Canadian street represented the best of our nation's "tossed salad." It was, perhaps, the number of inhabitants in the home that we thought odd. There seemed to be at least three adult couples residing in the home. Making things even more intriguing was that fact that the three women residents were each in various stages of pregnancy.

As I customarily do with all new arrivals on our street, I delivered a home-baked pie and welcome card shortly after they moved in. With a distinct language barrier, we depended on body language to express ourselves. After my initial introduction, very few words were spoken between my new neighbors and myself. Waves and smiles were the best we could achieve.

Through their first winter, I seldom saw the old man outside, but he maintained a strident vigil at the lovely picture window at the front of the home.

By the spring, three new inhabitants had made an appearance. With interest, or nosiness, depending on your outlook, I watched the arrangement of the household. Leaving early each morning were the three young men and two of the wives. By eight each morning, as I took my own children to school, the old man would be perched in their driveway, one child strapped to his back and another occupying each of his arms. I always waved.

The two little girls and the tiny boy were gorgeous babies. All had sooty lashes that accentuated their beauty. The old man would smile and nod his head as I admired his charges. By 9:30, the remaining wife would come and take one child at a time, presumably for feeding and diapering. Throughout the rest of the day, it appeared the babies were on a rotating schedule. While one was inside, the old man would have one on his back and one in his lap. At the end of the day, the other adults would arrive home, and the old man would be released from his duties. Remarkably, this was the time when, from his wheelchair, he would toil in the garden. In short order, my appreciation of the old man grew.

Over the course of the next few years, I watched from the sidelines. The children grew rapidly, each delighting in the old man's attentions. The highlight of the day appeared to be "The Race." Placing one child on his lap, he would put his chair in high gear and rush to the corner. The remaining two would count off the amount of time that it took, and in a language I didn't understand, urge the old man to go even faster on their turn. It was a sight to behold. Unable to turn away, I have occasionally felt like a voyeur, vicariously feeling a bit of their joy.

While leaving the house one day, I was met with a curious spectacle. Standing in their driveway were the three sons, their wives, and the children. They all had an unmistakable air of sadness about them. As I watched, the entire group moved toward me from across the street. Bowing, the eldest of the sons handed me an envelope. My heart was pounding as I saw the tear-swollen faces of the three women. It didn't take long for the realization of their loss to set in. No more would I delight in the antics of the children and their grandfather.

My grief was genuine, and I shook each of the sons' hands in turn, unable to stop my own tears. The "home wife," as I had come to call her, came forward, and for the first time looked me directly in the eye. Not a word was spoken, but when I felt her arms around my shoulders, our hearts spoke words that neither of us could find. I prayed silently for God to comfort them all in this time of sorrow.

After delivering the kids to school, I realized that I had driven with the unopened envelope clutched in my hand. Opening it, I was surprised to see the very card that I had presented to them four years earlier. I started crying, thinking of the dear present that the old man had left for me. Boldly scrawled across the front of the card, he had left me the one word that he knew I would understand. . .FRIEND.

SOMEONE ELSE'S CHILD

by Janice Thompson, Spring, Texas

She wasn't born our daughter, though it might have taken more than a quick glance to establish that fact. She had the same shiny chestnut hair, the same rosy complexion, and a sense of humor to rival that of each of our other three daughters. But she was born someone else's child.

We first met Betha when she was thirteen. She was a neighborhood kid, new to the youth group at church, and my kids had taken a liking to her. She wasn't exactly the kind of kid that a parent would be drawn to immediately. In fact, she was plenty rough around the edges.

I often asked my daughters about Betha. Who was she? What were her parents like? Where, exactly, did she live? The fact that she kept showing up at our door, day after day, was a clear indication to me that all was not well at home. I hadn't met her parents and really knew very little about this child who seemed determined to become one of mine. Who was this little waif, and why did she have such a desire to be with us? Why had she taken to calling me "Mom" and treating my own girls more like sisters than friends?

I got all the answers to my questions late one night. She had just returned home after spending a full day with us when our telephone rang. I answered to a tearful Betha, her voice laced with panic.

"Mom, my dad is. . .sick. Can you come and drive him to the hospital?" Of course I would drive her father to the hospital! I found my way to their house and watched as her dad, frail and thin, got into my car. He looked gravely ill. Betha climbed in the backseat, face pale.

As we made our way to the hospital, I learned, much to my shock, that he was not suffering from the stomach flu, as Betha had suggested, but from alcohol poisoning. He was beyond being "just drunk," and in was clear he had struggled with alcoholism for years.

I didn't know if it was the alcohol speaking or the fear of impending death, but this man, a complete stranger, began to speak to me as a friend, pouring out his heart to me. He told me of Betha's mother, who had left him when Betha was five years old, never to be seen or heard from again. He spoke of a faith in God that he clung to with trembling hand, despite his situation. He bragged about Betha, his precious little girl, who had walked hand in hand with him down this rocky road.

I peered into the rearview mirror at Betha's tear-stained face and suddenly understood everything. Her eyes sought mine in the mirror. They met with silent understanding. She needed me. She needed us.

This was not the first time Betha's father had been rushed to the hospital in critical condition that summer, nor would it be the last. His battle with the bottle would continue for quite some time beyond our initial meeting. Days turned into weeks, and weeks into months. All the while, Betha stayed with us. We prayed, as a family, that God would protect her father, heal him, and help him but also recognized the decision to quit drinking had to be his.

It was a cool October evening when Betha's father came to us, asking the question we had known would eventually come. Could we keep Betha for a year so that he could enter a treatment facility? We happily agreed. He signed a power of attorney that same night, and Betha came to live with us. . .legally.

Sadly, her father checked himself out of that facility after only four months, hitting the bottle once again. He wandered from state to state looking for work, looking for peace. In a moment of desperation, he arrived at a Christian facility accustomed to dealing with men in his situation, and he checked himself in. He remains in their care to this day.

And Betha? Ah. . .she is a happy, well-adjusted fifteen year old, whose most current concern is whether or not she will get to drive soon. She has had to struggle through the difficulties that being the child of an alcoholic brings but is conquering them all in Jesus' name! She has committed her life to Christ and lives daily to please Him. She's completely "family" now, arguing and bickering appropriately just like our other girls. She has a laugh that could turn any frown upside down.

All in all, she is pure delight.

Betha writes her daddy often, and he sends childhood photos, a signal that he is thinking of her and loves her. And when I overhear people talking about Betha, hear them discussing her "situation," I am reminded of how far we've all come together.

"She's someone else's child," I sometimes hear them whisper. I correct them quickly.

"No," I respond, looking them squarely in the eye. "She's our daughter, and God planned it that way."

ROSES AND SILVER MAPLES

by D. L. Young, Cleveland, Tennessee

We all lived on the same street in the same neighborhood. Each house was identical. Each had a five-foot silver maple planted in the small patch of lawn between the sidewalk and the street. The country flourished, progressing at an astounding rate. It was the sixties.

I lived in the eighth house on the right, from the city end of the street, with my mother, Joann, my father, Woody, and my big brother, Lee. Our twelve hundred-square-foot rancher never had a thing out of place. In my house, you could literally eat off the kitchen floor without worry of eating dirt. My mom was the best housekeeper in town.

Each day, my dad came home around 6:00 from his job at the car dealership and kissed my mother hello. He was in charge of eight "bump and paint" men. I was proud because, in my seven-year-old eyes, my dad was THE BOSS.

"How was your day, Squirt?" he'd ask me, swinging me high in the air.

"Great, Daddy," I'd reply. "Guess what happened today."

It never made a difference what happened, he always listened. We sat on the front stoop, and he wouldn't say a thing until I'd finished my rambling. Occasionally, I would have to pause for him to wave to a neighbor, or a kid passing by on a bike, who'd yell, "Hiya, Woody."

Two doors down from us, on the left, lived Greg and Cathy and their four kids, all under eight years old. As a kid myself, I wondered about them because I seldom saw any of the children. If they were in the front yard playing and I waved, they immediately ran into the backyard, out of sight.

"Cathy sure has her hands full with those four kids," I heard my dad tell my mom.

"Somebody needs to do something about that husband of hers," my mom replied. I wondered what kind of something she meant. Late one autumn afternoon I found out.

I was skating up and down the driveway in the new skates I had received for a good report card. The sound of Greg's rattly old Chevy pickup caught my attention. He pulled into their driveway and left the engine running. Soon he reappeared from the house, arms loaded with boxes. Cathy ran after him.

"Greg, please don't leave. I'll do better."

"You're worthless, Woman," he yelled. "You can't do one thing right, and you're the worst mother in the world." Cathy was crying. She tugged at Greg's shirt as he passed her.

"Please?" She held on. I stood silent under the silver maple, not believing what I saw. Then he slugged her, and she fell to the ground.

I fumbled across the narrow sidewalk into the safety of the grass and ran to get my dad.

"Daddy, Daddy, come quick. Greg just hit Cathy. They're fighting."

By the time my dad got to the front door, Greg was gone, clunking down the street in his beat-up Chevy, never to be seen again.

"Stay here, Squirt."

Cathy hugged her silver maple, tears flowing. My dad pried her away from the tree, and Cathy wrapped her arms around his neck and sobbed.

"It will be okay." He patted her back, holding her until she pulled away from him.

My parents' faces were solemn at the dinner table that night. My brother and I ate our food in silence. We knew they were contemplating solutions. We could tell because my mother's hand rested on top of my father's arm, and a warm, loving look waited for his answer.

Daddy stabbed his fork into the air. "I've been meaning to hire a secretary. The paperwork is getting too much for me to handle." My mother smiled.

"Rita Dumont, on the next street over, said she wanted to find a job close to home," Mom added. "Maybe I'll talk to her about baby-sitting. We can pay her for a couple of months. Cathy will never have to know. Right?" Mother lifted her eyebrows to Lee and me. "Right?" she said again.

"Um, right." We smiled at her.

The next day I skated again. Practice makes perfect, and I was determined to master the art of staying erect. A white panel van pulled into Cathy's driveway, and a man got out carrying a big, long package. After he left, Cathy walked toward our house.

"Smell," she said to me, opening the box. Inside were a dozen white roses, perfectly bloomed and swimmingly fragrant. I had never seen (or smelled) anything so beautiful. Cathy must have felt the same, she smiled so big. I wondered if the corners of her mouth would reach her ears. Then she showed me the card; it said:

> *Keep your chin up!*
> *Woody and Joann*

My heart burst with love and pride for my dad and mom.

Today, I am forty-seven years old. My parents are in their eighties, living in that same brick rancher. The silver maples have grown to wondrous heights, and Woody still makes every effort to help whomever he can.

The image of Cathy receiving those roses lives in my mind like it was yesterday. And the scent of roses makes me smile with a delicious secret I will always hold dear to my heart.

REUNION

by Gerry Di Gesu, West Chatham, Massachusetts

When one of my adopted sons, Chris, met his biological mother for the first time at the age of twenty-two, it was one of the most joyful days of my life. For reasons I don't fully understand, the idea of adoption still carries a mystique and often a negative connotation for many people. That's why I want to share my joy.

When I mentioned to close friends that my son was being sought by his birth mother, I was surprised to find that the majority assumed I would feel threatened and fearful. Actually, I was delighted.

I cannot imagine being either the mother of a child given up for adoption who never knows what happens to her child, or being the adoptee who goes through life not knowing his background and who he really is.

My husband and I had told Chris and his older brother, Kevin, that we would help them find their natural parents, but they had to realize it could be either wonderful or a traumatic, upsetting experience, depending on the person they found.

I realized Chris's meeting could go either way, but the fact that this woman had waited until he was twenty-two to inquire about him so she wouldn't disrupt his family gave me good feelings about her. Chris's easy acceptance of her invitation and his attitude convinced me he was sound and ready to cope with whatever he might find.

After initial separate interviews with the social worker at the agency which had made the placement, Chris and his birth mother met at the agency office. I was a wreck the whole day, watching the clock, trying to imagine the emotions in that room.

Just as he returned home, I arrived home from work with a million questions for him, but I didn't want to crowd him because I knew he was a swirl of conflicting emotions. He had to rush out to work but asked if she could come to our home and meet the family later that evening. Of course we said yes; I was dying to meet her.

Later, I opened my front door to greet a bright and smiling woman whose sparkling eyes reflected the joy of her day. We hugged and cried and then sat down with the rest of my family to get acquainted. Tentatively, we felt our way around each other, not wanting to pry but wanting to know everything. What I remember most was the constant sound of laughter in our living room that night.

Calmly and without self-pity, she shared her story, relating the callous and harsh treatment she received from her family, social agency, and hospital staff, none ready to offer compassion. She explained how desperately she had wanted to keep her baby and only at the last minute, when she realized there was no hope of caring for him, had she signed the adoption papers.

She had been terrified of contacting the agency for help in finding Chris, expecting the same harsh treatment, only to be delightfully surprised to find warmth and empathy instead. She battled the constant fear that neither my son nor his family would want to meet or accept her. How I admired her courage as she risked rejection each step of the way on her search for her child.

At last we finally said good night. I felt happy knowing I had a new friend and that Chris knew who he was and how much he was wanted. Time will tell how this relationship will develop, but I know that the look on my son's face and the joy in this woman's eyes as they said good-bye and she hugged him reinforced my belief that we can't be afraid—we have to risk and reach out in love. Christ did no less for us.

First appeared in The Standard *1995*

THE MISSING CASSEROLE

by Vivian M. Preston, Barberton, Ohio

Our maple tree near the back door grew so large the branches hung menacingly over the roof of the house. Reluctantly we cut it down and for a long time mourned the loss of the tree every time we passed the remaining stump. Presently it became a catchall for packages, garden tools, and other odds and ends.

Near noon one sunny day, I backed the car out of the driveway and went to a covered-dish luncheon. When I arrived, I looked in vain for my casserole.

"I must have left it on the stump," I called to my table companion while I raced out the door. I chuckled at her puzzled look as I drove home.

The stump was empty. I quickly checked the kitchen counter,

oven, and refrigerator. No casserole.

As I backed out of the driveway for the second time, my new neighbor's little boy smiled and waved across the street. My daughter had commented on how friendly the youngster seemed.

I returned the greeting and felt guilty. I hadn't been over to welcome them to the neighborhood as was my custom. I usually took along something I had baked. During our initial conversation, I would ask if they went to church. If they did not, I invited them to a worship service with us. However, like Martha in the Bible, I had been too busy with household chores. "I'll bake some bran muffins and go over tomorrow," I vowed.

Upon my return to the luncheon, I explained to my friend that I couldn't find the casserole I had prepared. "Are you sure you made one?" she teased and put a big spoonful of baked beans on my plate. I laughed, accepted her good-natured kidding, and enjoyed the rest of the afternoon. As usual, there was more than enough food to go around, and my dish wasn't really missed.

When I came home, I glanced at the stump. There was my casserole dish! I lifted it to carry it indoors and found it curiously light. Taking it to the kitchen counter, I lifted the lid. It was clean and empty except for a folded piece of paper.

My surprised eyes read:

> *Dear Neighbor,*
> *Sending the casserole over with your daughter was so*
> *neighborly of you. It was truly an answer to prayer. The*
> *gas company has not regulated my oven yet, and my*
> *parents came today to see how we were settled in.*
> > *Gratefully,*
> > *Ellen*

My daughter entered the kitchen as I finished reading the note.

"You did mean the casserole for our new neighbors, didn't you?" She gestured toward the empty dish.

"Not really," I laughed and handed her the piece of paper in my hand. "It was for the Mothers' Club luncheon."

As she scanned the words, I closed my eyes and prayed, "I'm sorry, Lord, for my procrastination, but thank You for sending the casserole where it was most needed today."

DADDY HANDS

by Susan Fahncke, Kaysville, Utah

I awoke in the night to find my husband, Marty, gently rocking our baby, Noah. I stood unnoticed in the doorway, watching this amazing man with whom I was so blessed to share my life. He lovingly stroked Noah's fat little cheeks in an effort to comfort him. I watched as my husband moved Noah's cheek up against his own chest, so that Noah could feel the vibrations of his voice.

Noah is deaf. Learning to comfort him has been a whole new experience for us. We relied on our voices, audio toys, and music for our other children, but with Noah, we need to use touch, sight, the "feel" of our voices, and, most importantly, sign language to communicate with him and comfort him.

My husband made the sign for "I love you" with his hand, and I saw a tear roll down his cheek as he placed Noah's weak hand on top of his own. For a week and a half, Noah's fever had been very high and dangerous in spite of everything the doctor had tried. When I touched my husband's shoulder, we looked at each other and shared the fear that Noah wasn't getting any better. I offered to take over for him, but he shook his head. Many men would have gladly handed over the parenting duties for some much needed sleep, but Marty stubbornly and resolutely stayed with his child.

When morning came, we called the doctor, already knowing he would probably put Noah in the hospital. Our hearts were filled with dread as we waited in a small room different from the usual examining room. The doctor told us Noah needed to be admitted to a hospital. Now.

If the drive to the hospital was surreal, the night in the hospital was torturous. It was filled with horrible tests that resulted in Noah's screams echoing through the halls. Marty reassured me that he felt in his heart Noah would be okay. He never wavered. He comforted me, Noah, and everyone who called to check on Noah. Marty was a rock.

When the first batch of tests was completed, a nurse informed us that a spinal tap might be necessary. Meningitis was suspected. Marty and I prayed together. With our hands intertwined and tears streaming down his face, my husband lifted his voice to the Lord. As he humbly asked for the Lord to heal our son, my heart was filled with comfort. Marty's prayer was speedily answered. A short time later, the resident doctor came in to tell us that test results showed Noah had Influenza A. No spinal tap would be needed, and he felt that Noah would recover soon and be back to his old, zesty self.

A few days after Noah was released from the hospital, I was cooking dinner when I peeked into the living room. I chuckled at the picture I saw. There was my husband, sitting in his "daddy chair," with Noah in his lap. They were reading a book. Marty would take Noah's teeny hands and help him form the signs for the words. They caught me watching them. My husband and I simultaneously signed "I love you" to each other, then to Noah. And then Noah put his little arm up, trying to shape his chubby hand in his own effort to sign "I love you" to his daddy. I watched with tears as my husband carefully helped Noah form his tiny fingers into the sign with his own gentle hands.

Daddy hands.

Published in Stories for a Faithful Heart

THE TATTOOED STRANGER

by Susan Fahncke, Kaysville, Utah

He was kind of scary, with tattoos running up and down both arms and even on his neck, sitting there on the grass with his cardboard sign and his dog (actually his dog was adorable). His sign proclaimed him to be "stuck and hungry" and to please help.

I'm a sucker for anyone needing help. My husband both hates and loves this quality in me. I pulled the van over and, in my rearview mirror, contemplated this man, tattoos and all. He was youngish, maybe forty. He wore one of those bandannas tied over his head, biker/pirate style. Anyone could see he was dirty and had a scraggly beard. But if you looked closer, you could see that he had neatly tucked in the black T-shirt, and his things were in a small, tidy bundle. Nobody was stopping for him.

It was so hot out. I could see in the man's very blue eyes how dejected, tired, and worn-out he felt. Sweat was trickling down his face. As I sat with the air-conditioning blowing, a Scripture suddenly popped into my head. "Inasmuch as ye have done it unto one of the least of these my brethren, ye have done it unto me" (Matthew 25:40 KJV).

I reached down into my purse and extracted a ten-dollar bill. My twelve-year-old son, Nick, knew right away what I was doing. "Can I take it to him, Mom?"

"Be careful, Honey," I warned and handed him the money. I watched in the mirror as he rushed over to the man and, with a shy smile, handed it to him. I saw the man, startled, stand and take the money, putting it into his back pocket. "Good," I thought to myself, "now he will at least have a hot meal tonight." I felt satisfied, proud of myself. I had made a sacrifice, and now I could go on with my errands.

When Nick got back into the car, he looked at me with sad, pleading eyes. "Mom, his dog looks so hot, and the man is really nice." I knew I had to do more.

"Go back and tell him to stay there, and we'll be back in fifteen minutes," I told Nick. He bounded out of the car and ran to tell the tattooed stranger.

We then ran to the nearest store and bought our gifts carefully. "It can't be too heavy," I explained to the children. "He has to be able to carry it around with him." We finally settled on our purchases. A bag of "Ol' Roy" dog food, a flavored chew-toy shaped like a bone, a water dish, bacon-flavored snacks (for the dog), two bottles of water (one for the dog, one for Mr. Tattoos), and some people snacks for the man.

We rushed back to the spot where we had left him, and there he was, still waiting. And still nobody else was stopping for him. With hands shaking, I grabbed our bags and climbed out of the van, all four of my children following me, each carrying gifts. As we walked up to him, I had a fleeting moment of fear, hoping he wasn't a serial killer.

I looked into his eyes and saw something that startled me and made me ashamed of my judgment. I saw tears. He was fighting like a little boy to hold back his tears. How long had it been since someone showed this man kindness? I told him I hoped it wasn't too heavy for him to carry and showed him what we had brought.

He stood there, like a child at Christmas, and I felt like my small contributions were so inadequate. When I took out the water dish, he accepted it from my hands as if it were solid gold and told me he had had no way to give his dog water. He gingerly set it down, filled it with the bottled water we brought, and stood up to look directly into my eyes. His were so blue, so intense, and my own filled with tears as he said, "Ma'am, I don't know what to say." He then put both hands on his bandanna-clad head and just started to cry. This man, this "scary" man, was so gentle, so sweet, so humble.

I smiled through my tears and said, "Don't say anything." Then I noticed the tattoo on his neck. It said "Mama tried." Mama tried.

As we all piled into the van and drove away, he was on his knees, arms around his dog, kissing his nose and smiling. I waved cheerfully and then fully broke down in tears.

I have so much, a home, a loving husband, and four beautiful children. I have a bed. I wondered where he would sleep that night. My worries seemed so trivial and petty now. My stepdaughter, Brandie, turned to me and said in the sweetest little-girl voice, "I feel so good."

Although it seemed as if we had helped him, the man with the tattoos gave us a gift I will never forget. He taught me that no matter what the outside looks like, inside each of us is a human being deserving of kindness, of compassion, of acceptance. He reminded me that each of us has a holy Father, no matter where the circumstances of life have brought us. And most importantly, he taught me that as a mother, I must never, never, stop trying. He opened my heart.

Tonight and every night I will pray for the gentle man with the tattoos and his dog. I hope that God will send more people like him into my life to remind me of what's really important.

TUSLOG DET 66

by Jacque E. Day, Chicago, Illinois

It was at TUSLOG Detachment, "Det" 66, where in 1964 at age nineteen, my father spent his first Christmas away from home. Det 66 housed the Signal Corps, which was in charge of long-range communications. My father, Private First Class Charles Day, worked as a cableman, laying cable from Turkey all the way to Ethiopia.

TUSLOG (The U.S. Logistics Operational Group), they were told, was the first line of defense against a Soviet attack, and instant communication over very long distances was essential to thwarting invasion efforts. And it was there, in the barracks of Det 66, that a little Turkish man of Islamic faith who shined shoes for a living, gave one hundred lonely American boys a surprise Christmas gift that brought each of them to tears.

They didn't know him by name, but they came to count on him. Each day he greeted the American soldiers as they came off duty. He sat cross-legged in the entryway of the barracks with his shoeshine kit, good-natured and relaxed. The American soldiers welcomed the small, inexpensive comfort afforded them by the little man who shined their regulation shoes each day—two pairs per man, per day. He was perhaps forty-five years old, the same age as their fathers, and definitely too old to shine shoes, at least by American standards, but he worked deftly, making his way through two hundred pairs of shoes each night with the speed and skill of a true craftsman. Hours after he started, the little man would finish the last shoe, pack his kit, and head off for the bus stop. For his labors, each paid the little man the U.S. equivalent of twenty-five cents a week.

They liked him. His quiet, polite demeanor relaxed them, and his work made their lives easier. Each night as he made his way through the bunks, the soldiers made attempts to strike up conversation. He knew about as much English as they did Turkish, which wasn't much on either account, so they communicated mostly through hand gestures. But sometimes, some understanding would seep through.

He lived in the capital city of Ankara. He had a wife and five children. He was Islamic. Two of his sons were about the same age as the soldiers, who were anywhere from seventeen to twenty-three. He rode the bus. It was a long ride that sometimes took three hours. Apparently the income he generated at the barracks must have been worth spending six hours a day riding a bus over a bumpy road.

On December 23, 1964, PFC Charles Day made his typical off-duty hike to the mess hall. For Christmas week, the Army decided to treat the boys with generosity, which meant more white meat in the creamed turkey, bigger desserts, apple cider, and a few lights strewn around the mess hall. Still, it was less of a comfort and more a reminder of what they were missing at home. They ate the better than usual meal in solemn silence, all thinking the same thing. Most of them barely out of high school, all still closer to being boys than men, there they sat, two days away from Christmas, eight thousand miles away from home, wearing regulation work gear and eating from metal trays. The feeling wasn't just sadness or emptiness or loneliness. It was a combination of all those things. They quietly finished their meals and headed for the barracks.

At the barracks, they found their little Turkish shoeshine man, seated cross-legged as always in the entryway. Next to him sat a decorated tree so small that it stood no higher than he sat. Under the tree were one hundred small wrapped gifts, one for each soldier. Not one man was forgotten.

This poor, uneducated little man who shined shoes for a living had reached into their hearts and relieved the feelings that silenced them in the mess hall. How did he understand? How did he know? Perhaps as a father, he saw his own sons in each of them. This little man who traveled six hours a day to earn a fraction of their wages, who seemed to have nothing to give, had somehow managed to give them everything. And so these soldiers of TUSLOG Det 66 wept openly as a poor Islamic shoeshine man, whose name they didn't know, handed each of them a gift.

In a few weeks my father was transferred and never returned to TUSLOG Det 66. But he never forgot the man who, perhaps without knowing it, gave a handful of lonely boys the most memorable Christmas of their lives. My father's five-foot, eight-inch frame towered over the tiny man. But to this day, close to forty years later, he swears that the little Turkish shoeshine man was a very big man indeed.

Published in Celebrate Life, *November/December, 1998*

CHILDREN ARE A GIFT

by Maryella Vause, Blanco, Texas

In mid-December, a Texas Blue Norther swept into the hill country west of Austin. Temperatures dropped twenty degrees in twenty minutes. As my husband and I drove over the frozen, rutted back roads across cattle guards to a small farmhouse an icy rain began to fall. *Swell,* I thought, *just what we need now.* My hands and my heart were cold. I was mad at God and mad at my husband.

We were on our way to attend a birth—a birth that seemed far less than a blessing to me. Doesn't God's Word say that children are a blessing, a heritage, a gift? How could He allow this to happen? *Why would you send a child into a situation like this?* I ranted in my heart. *It's awful. It's unfair. People who would bring a child into an environment like this surely don't deserve a baby.*

The first time we were asked to attend a home birth, I thought my husband would "just say no" and that would be the end of it. I was shocked when instead he said, "We'll pray about it." We had never even considered delivering babies at home. With our training and experience, we knew the risks and possible complications, not to mention the possible legal tangles and the outright scorn and opposition of our peers. Our local fifteen-bed hospital had closed, though, leaving many of our patients with either untrained, granny-midwives, or expensive obstetrical care at distant hospitals.

That first home delivery was a child for one of our regular patients. It was a beautiful birth, a deeply meaningful, blessed experience for each of us. It was a joy to be a part of the welcome of a baby into the arms of a loving family. However, it also established us as the doctor and nurse who would deliver babies at home. Exactly what I dreaded and feared. On the other hand, I admired my husband's faith and courage, his willingness to help when no one else would. Maybe his experience as a medical commander in Vietnam during the Tet Offensive had given him the courage required to think of others and not of the risks to himself.

When he had answered the phone this particular night, I knew he was tired. As the only physician in our part of the county, he was putting in sixty to eighty hours a week. I thought he would say, "Call EMS and have them take her into the city." My heart sank as I heard him saying, "We'll be right over."

"Don't go," I pleaded. "You said that we would do these home births only at the Lord's direction. Surely He's not directing this. Did you even pray about it?"

"Yes, I prayed about it," he answered with some irritation in his voice. "That poor old woman is trying to deliver the girl by herself. God wants me to go. You don't have to come if you don't want to."

Right. How could I not go with him?

And now, here we were, on this miserable night, in this filthy weather, in some godforsaken corner of the county looking for a farmhouse. And I was still mad.

The girl lay in the drafty back bedroom of the dilapidated old farmhouse. Hardly more than a child herself, she writhed in pain with each contraction. The macho boyfriend swaggered around in the front room while I helped her get into a better position and began coaching her to relax and focus on her breathing rather than her pain.

The twenty-something boyfriend was one the local boys who had dropped out of high school to take up truck driving as a cover for drug running. He had brought this pathetic, seventeen-year-old girl back from California with him on one of his "runs." Instead of marrying her, when she was well along in her pregnancy, he dumped her at his middle-aged mother's little shack of a house here in rural Texas. It was his mother who had called us begging for help. Wearing a cowboy hat and boots, and grinning from under a two-day stubble of beard, he extended his hand to my husband. "Hey, Doc. Glad you could make it. MY BOY's about to be born."

Oh no, I inwardly groaned, *one of those. Could this possibly get worse?* Just then the girl screamed, and he went three shades of pale. So much for his bravado.

"I'm going into town now to tell my buddies. This is. . .great." As he reached for his faded blue jacket, my husband put his hand on the young man's shoulder and said firmly, "You can't leave now. You've got to help us get the baby here."

With a look of fear on his face he said, "No way, Doc. I can't do that. I'm going down to the cafe, and you can just call me when the baby gets here. No offense meant, but having babies is women's work. I'll set off some firecrackers when my son gets born." He pulled away and started to back toward the door. My husband caught his arm, stopping him.

"You don't understand, Son. We need you to help. We don't have a hospital here. Without those nice delivery tables, YOU'VE got to be the one to hold up her shoulders and be our birthing bed. You're strong. You can do it."

As I set up the bed and the room to receive the child, my husband showed the inexperienced, truck-driving cowboy how to support the mother's head and shoulders during the birth. It just wasn't right in my mind. How could God send a child into this mess? The poverty, an out-of-wedlock birth, the risks to the mother, the risks to us, and it all seemed so unfair to the baby.

We coached and encouraged the mother as she became focused and intent on delivering her child. We worked together, sweated, and prayed. Within two hours, the little baby girl slipped into my husband's strong, gentle hands. When he placed the wet little one on her mother's breast, I looked over at the young father. He was tired from the effort of holding up his girlfriend's shoulders. I was surprised to see tears running down his cheeks, unheeded and unchecked. He was gently stroking her hair with one hand as the fingertips of his other hand caressed the newborn baby's head. As he continued to stare, enthralled, at his daughter, he whispered, "Ain't it a miracle, Doc?"

I looked at the three of them, mother, father, and child. Suddenly I saw—a family! Maybe not a "perfect" one, but, I thought, what right had I to judge? After settling mother and child and leaving instructions, we packed up to leave. Holding his new baby girl, the young man thanked us repeatedly. As we left, he said, "Hey, I still gotta go out and shoot off some firecrackers. My buddies gotta hear that MY GIRL is born!"

It was a quiet ride home. We were too tired to talk. I kept wondering what the future would hold for those three. To my way of thinking, it was such a shabby, rough start. I just prayed it would get better for them.

Well, he did run out and shoot off firecrackers. More importantly though, he quit drug running and went into legitimate trucking. He took his young girlfriend, who had been raised Catholic, down to the local Catholic church to visit the priest. St. Ferdinand's Catholic Church beside the Blanco River never saw a sweeter couple take their vows. They stepped into a new chapter of their lives. Heavenly light shone through the stained glass windows of the chancel as the ancient, yet timely, words were exchanged.

As husband and wife, they set up housekeeping in their own little home. They have had two more children. He has become one of the more stable, upstanding members of the community. He waves and grins as his truck meets our car along the highway these days. She smiles and chats with me when we meet in the grocery, often telling me how well the children are doing in school. Sometimes she shows me the latest pictures of them, or I notice one of the children's names on the honor roll in the local newspaper.

When I see this family in the town today, I remember that cold, stormy night so long ago and ponder that "His ways are not our ways." It still amazes me that God would entrust the care of a baby to us. He even placed His only Son as a helpless infant into the hands of a teenage girl. I still blanch when I remember my judgmental and narrow-minded stance that night so long ago. I would never have sent a child into such circumstances.

God in His wisdom and mercy did!

"Behold, children are a gift of the Lord."

ANGEL OF KINDNESS

by Linda Knight, Woodslee, Ontario, Canada

It was only a hug, a seemingly insignificant hug, and yet its gentle power helped to make a miracle happen.

She was new to our church. All I did was counsel her for a few brief moments after an altar call. She had been living in Canada for three years now, having escaped an abusive relationship in South Africa. I remember commenting on the beauty of her accent as we spoke that day. She told me of her escape from her homeland. At the airport, friends and neighbors had rallied around her, shielding her and her children from her outraged husband and the local police as they tried to stop her from boarding the plane to freedom.

I gave her a Bible and my phone number. I told her if she ever needed to talk to give me a call. That was when I hugged her. And then we parted company.

Three weeks later, the call came. At the first sound of my voice, she hung up. But she said something nudged her to try again. Thank heaven she did. She was beside herself with worry and grief. Her seventeen-year-old, special needs son couldn't handle the cultural differences between his homeland and his adopted country, or the taunts and the ridicule of classmates. Her own life since coming to Canada had been equally challenging. Thoughts of suicide began to occupy her mind, increasing daily. She was frightened of what she might do.

Then she remembered our encounter. She told me how much that hug had meant to her. The warmth of that touch had felt to her like Jesus assuring her that everything would be all right in time. It had planted a hope in her that she'd never experienced before. We talked for a long, long time that night. It was the beginning of a lovely friendship.

One day she phoned to say she had a gift she wanted to give me. There was a catch to the gift, though. I had to promise to give it away. My curiosity was piqued, and I waited anxiously for her to arrive.

She gave me a beautiful china angel. Its arms were outstretched, and it held a tiny dove in its right hand. It was, she told me, The Angel of Kindness, given in appreciation of random acts of kindness. It had been given to her some time ago by a person she had once helped. She said my hug and phone number had, quite literally, saved her life, and now The Angel of Kindness was mine for the moment. When I experienced a random act of kindness in my life, it would be time for the angel to take flight again.

No one is sure where the angel originated, but we know where it's going—from one act of kindness to another. We never know when the Lord will use us. Sometimes, we don't even see the way He uses us, especially through random acts of kindness. Yet these simple acts can be the glue that will hold a life together. And that act could be something as simple as a hug.

First appeared in: Touch *magazine c.1995 December under the name Debra Young.*

OUR ANGEL

by D. L. Young, Ooltewah, Tennessee

"There!" Mom said, as I topped the tree with our traditional angel. "Now our Christmas season is officially under way. It wouldn't be Christmas without our guardian angel to watch over us."

Her tattered wings don't stand up anymore. There's a hole in her stomach that we've covered with aluminum foil. It came from a Christmas bulb that was too hot. But our angel has always been at the top of our Christmas tree, filling our family with the spirit of Christmas, and completing the holiday for us.

My grandpa bought our angel for my mom's first Christmas in 1953. He said it would be my mom's guardian angel for the rest of her life. When my parents got married, the angel was the one thing she insisted on taking for her own tree.

"Isn't the tree beautiful?" I said to my two older sisters. "Our very own Christmas tree. It's the most beautiful sight in the world."

This tree was very special to us. It had been three years since we had our own Christmas tree. The previous year, a neighbor let us borrow a tiny tree. It was a very nice tree. My sisters, Sally and Valerie, and I strung popcorn and made paper ornaments for it. We had fun working together to make it feel like Christmas. Our angel sat on top of the tiny tree, guiding us along.

"Make sure the lights are evenly spaced," Mom told Sally, sixteen, who had been in charge of the lights for the last three years. "We don't want too many in one place."

The year before last, we had a tree made from the limb of an apple tree. We lived in the country then and had a lot of apple trees. Valerie came up with that idea. Sally wrapped the lights, and we put on our angel. It was pretty, especially in the dark. The lights looked as if they were just hanging in the air.

"Valerie, do you have the ornaments you made?" Mom asked as we continued decorating our tree. "They are so beautiful."

Valerie, fourteen, is my creative sister. She makes the prettiest ornaments from old light bulbs, glitter, and crepe paper.

The Christmas tree I remember most, though, was three years ago. I was eight, and we were living in Michigan. My dad left us right after Thanksgiving. Mom said he needed to be alone, but he still loved us very much. Mom was sad and cried a lot. She told us there wouldn't be a Christmas tree that year. Dad was always the one who went out to cut a fresh tree.

The day before Christmas Eve, our furnace broke down. Winters in Michigan are very cold, so we all snuggled around the fireplace to keep warm. We sang songs, popped corn, and roasted hot dogs. Things were bad, but we didn't notice. We had each other, and our angel was sitting on top of the bookcase.

All Christmas Eve we played in the snow, making snowmen and having snowball fights. Mom worked hard to have a traditional Christmas Eve dinner. She roasted a chicken instead of a turkey, but we didn't care. In her spare time, she piled enough wood on the fire to keep us warm.

On Christmas Eve, we went to church. I was one of the Cratchett kids in our version of *A Christmas Carol*. Afterwards, we watched "Rudolph, the Rednosed Reindeer" on television and drank hot chocolate with marshmallows floating in it.

"We had fun today," I said. "But it just doesn't feel like Christmas without a tree."

"I know, Annie," Mom said sadly. "Next year we'll have a tree. Things were tough this year. Sometimes you have to face the bad times to understand the good times."

We all snuggled that night, knowing we had each other, and we had our guardian angel for a touch of Christmas.

When we got up the next morning we were in for the surprise of our lives, for what should we find in our living room but the most glorious Christmas tree imaginable. Sally had stayed up all night making it. She had cut up paper bags and glued them together in the shape of a tree. She taped it to a wall and decorated it with paper ornaments. She strung the lights around the outside edge and on the top—taped to the wall—was OUR ANGEL!

"Plug in the lights, Annie," Sally said to me. I rushed to do it. This was the most beautiful tree I had ever seen. A tree made with love and decorated with the real spirit of Christmas.

Three Christmases have come and gone. It has been my job, ever since, to light the tree. Every time I put the plug into the wall, a light seems to go on in my heart, too. I look at our angel, remember, and thank the Lord for showing all of us the true meaning of Christmas—giving from your heart—giving from love. Just like God did when He sent His only Son to be born in that stable.

HANDCRAFTED, WITH LOVE

by Lanita Bradley Boyd, Fort Thomas, Kentucky

"This smoke is more than I can bear!" Mom whispered in exasperation. "Having my blood taken twice a day and chemotherapy is bad enough without choking to death on her cigarette smoke!" I, too, disliked the smoke but hesitated to complain. I knew Mom never wanted to be a bother to the nurses, with whom she was a favorite. Most of them had been recipients of her handmade crafts as well as her pleasant spirit.

Mom, usually cheerful and optimistic, soon admitted her distress to her nurse and was quickly moved to another room. Moving her myriad of cards, flowers, and craft projects was quite a task. It was worth it to her, though, to get away from the smoke.

Then she glimpsed her new roommate. She turned to me, eyes wide. "She's colored!" she whispered, and I winced. It always amazed me that my mother, this lovely Christian woman, could be so racially intolerant.

The next night, fortunately, the whispered remarks were favorable. "She's ninety-four," Mom informed me. "Had surgery. I don't know what for. Her granddaughter has been here all day, and now that's her son and her great-granddaughter. They're real nice and quiet and seem real concerned about her. I think she's a religious woman, too."

So far, so good, I thought. I had never heard Mom speak so kindly of a black person, but then she'd never really known any African-Americans personally. I showed my interest and concern. Inwardly, I rejoiced. Knowing that Mom's cancer was terminal, and she wouldn't be with us much longer, I had felt confident that she was at peace with the Lord except in being so racially prejudiced. Perhaps this would work out well.

It did. Mrs. Lyles was gentle and gracious. It was obvious Mom had a great respect for her.

"Why, I could talk to her just like anybody else," Mom said in amazement.

Then one day Dad came home, head drooping. "Dorothy's roommate left today, and the new one arrived right before I left. I'm afraid Dorothy is going to have a hard time adjusting. It's the worst it could be—she's black, and she smokes!"

Lord, why can't You give her roommates that won't upset her? How little I knew of His great plan! God's plan became encapsulated in one word: Charlotte.

I couldn't visit Mom that night and hesitantly entered the room the following evening. She was smiling broadly, and the curtains separating the beds were open—always a good sign. I noticed that Charlotte was not much older than me. "I want you to meet Charlotte," Mom bubbled. She couldn't quit talking about all they had in common.

They'd found their lumps at about the same time, each had had the same breast removed, and each was fighting the relentless cancer with every ounce of will possible. Differences in skin color, age, cultural background, children, and religion were irrelevant.

Charlotte's personality was the perfect complement to Mom's. Whereas Mom could be talkative and assertive only if she knew someone well, Charlotte had no such reservations. Her beautiful smile and loving attitude welcomed everyone as an instant friend. Her dark skin and hair were in sharp contrast to Mom's pale face and smooth white hair, but in spirit they were the same.

Charlotte felt she had no creative skills and fell in love with every item Mom made. She seemed to sense Mom's needs for reassurance as well as physical assistance and always said and did just the right thing. At that time, Charlotte could move more easily about the room, so she was quick to get Mom a drink or pick up something that had fallen from the bed. Every time I arrived, they seemed to be laughing about something, though I knew they also had serious moments. As far as Mom and Charlotte were concerned, there was no longer white and black. They were sisters in the deepest sense, sharing the same pain, with the same faith, fears, and hope that some miracle would be performed by the chemotherapy.

After a few days of observing this glowing—and to us, incredible—relationship, I just had to bring up the unmentionable.

"Mom," I asked, "does Charlotte smoke?"

"Oh, sometimes," she replied in an offhand way, "but she stands by the window and blows the smoke outside."

And she did! This was no one-sided relationship. Charlotte loved and respected Mom and would have done anything to please her. I knew it was hard for her to smoke so much less than usual, but she limited her cigarettes as much as possible, taking just a few puffs and then extinguishing her cigarette quickly.

After that chemotherapy was over, they were on similar return cycles for a while. Even though no longer roommates, they would visit each other's room when their hospital stays coincided. In between, Mom, living in an adjacent state, would write Charlotte letters, and Charlotte would make long telephone calls to Mom. They sympathized and joked about their hair loss and other distressing side effects, making it all more bearable for each other.

One day, as Mom was waiting to see if her blood count was high enough to be admitted for chemotherapy, she kept peering around the room and down the hall, hoping to catch a glimpse of Charlotte, who also had an appointment that day. In her hands she clutched the newest doll she had exhaustingly made to give her. It was the only one of that kind she had been able to finish, and she wanted to be able to give it to Charlotte in person.

At the very moment the nurse called Mom's name, Charlotte was wheeled out the door and into the elevator.

"Just a minute!" Mom said to the nurse. Dad leaped to hold the elevator door until Mom could slowly make her way over to speak to Charlotte. Mom laid the doll in Charlotte's emaciated lap and leaned over to hug the fragile body.

"I love you, Charlotte," she said softly.

"I love you, too, Dorothy," Charlotte answered, squeezing as tightly as she was able. They smiled at each other as the elevator door closed.

Mom found out that her blood count was now too low for further chemotherapy. She began calling Charlotte daily. By the time Mom returned for her next checkup, Charlotte had been admitted to the hospital. Officially, Charlotte was not allowed any company, but Mom used her familiarity with the nurses and her considerable powers of persuasion to gain entry anyway.

As Mom held her friend's hand, she knew that this was indeed for the last time and was grateful that Charlotte seemed to recognize her.

Charlotte's husband called the next day to say that Charlotte had died that night after Mom had left. Mom, though tearful, took it calmly.

"We both knew we didn't have long. She was so young, I just didn't think that she'd be the first to go," Mom said. "But then of course I could see that she was always just a little further along than I was."

It was only a few weeks before Mom was gone, too. Even in our grief, we could accept it more easily knowing that, through God's grace, Mom had overcome her bigotry. He had given her the opportunity to learn that love and friendship are not based on outward appearances but on the condition of the heart.

CHAPTER FOUR

Angels Among Us

*Keep on loving each other as brothers.
Do not forget to entertain strangers,
for by so doing some people have
entertained angels without knowing it.*

Hebrews 13:1–2

THE GARDEN

by Alex and Dawn Edwards, Aurora, Illinois

Carl was a quiet man. He didn't talk much. He would always greet you with a big smile and a firm handshake, but even after living in our neighborhood for over fifty years, no one could really say that they knew him very well. All we really knew about him was that he had worked for the gas company and that he had won an award when he retired for never having taken a sick day in all his fifty-one years with the company.

Before his retirement, he took the bus to work each morning. As his retirement approached and he grew older, the lone sight of him walking down the street often worried us. He had a slight limp from a bullet wound received in World War II. The bullet itself was still lodged very near his spine. Watching him, we worried that although he had survived World War II, he might not make it through our changing uptown neighborhood with its ever increasing random violence, gangs, and drug activity. How could we have known that an angel limped in our midst?

Carl was in his early seventies when he began what was to be a fifteen years plus job of caring for the gardens behind the minister's residence. He was then retired, and his wife had died a few years earlier. When he saw the flyer at our local church asking for volunteers, he responded in his characteristically unassuming manner. Without fanfare, he just signed up to do the weeding, watering, and seeding of flowers and vegetables that were planted each spring.

He was well into his eighty-seventh year when the very thing we had always feared finally happened. He was just finishing his watering for the day when three gang members approached him. Ignoring their attempt to intimidate him, he simply asked, "Would you like a drink from the hose?"

The tallest and toughest-looking of the three said, "Yeah, sure," with a malevolent little smile. As Carl offered the hose to him, the other two grabbed Carl's arm, throwing him down. As the hose snaked crazily over the ground, dousing everything in its path, Carl's assailants stole his retirement watch and his wallet and then fled.

Carl tried to get himself up, but he had been thrown down on his bad leg. He lay there trying to gather himself as the minister came running to help him. Although the minister had witnessed the attack from his window, he couldn't get there fast enough to stop it. "Carl, are you okay? Are you hurt?" the minister kept asking as he helped Carl to his feet.

Carl just passed a hand over his brow and sighed, shaking his head. "Just some punk kids. I hope they'll wise up someday." His wet clothes clung to his slight frame as he bent to pick up the hose. He adjusted the nozzle again and started to water.

Confused and a little concerned, the minister asked, "Carl, what are you doing?"

"I've got to finish my watering. It's been very dry lately," came the calm reply. Satisfying himself that Carl really was all right, the minister could only marvel. Carl was a man from a different time and place.

A few weeks later, the three returned. Just as before, their threat was unchallenged. Carl again offered them a drink from his hose. This time they didn't rob him. They wrenched the hose from his hand and drenched him head to foot in the icy water as he tried unsuccessfully to fend them off. When they had finished their humiliation of him, they sauntered off down the street, throwing catcalls and curses, falling over one another laughing at the hilarity of what they had just done. Carl just watched them. Then he turned toward the warmth-giving sun, picked up his hose, and went on with his watering.

The summer was quickly fading into fall. Thankfully, things had been quiet and uneventful. Carl was doing some tilling and getting the rose beds ready for their winter mulch protection when he was startled by the sudden approach of someone behind him. He stumbled and fell into some evergreen branches. As he struggled to regain his footing, he turned to see the tall leader of his summer tormentors reaching down for him. He braced himself for the expected attack. "Don't worry, old man. I'm not gonna hurt you this time." The young man spoke softly, still offering the tattooed and scarred hand to Carl. As he helped Carl get up, the man pulled a crumpled bag from his pocket and handed it to Carl.

"What's this?" Carl asked.

"It's your stuff," the man explained. "It's your stuff back. Even the money in your wallet."

"I don't understand," Carl said. "Why would you help me now?"

The man shifted his feet, seeming embarrassed and ill at ease. "I learned something from you," he said. "I ran with that gang and hurt people like you. We picked you because you were old, and we knew we could do it. But every time we came and did something to you, instead of yelling and fighting back, you tried to give us a drink. You didn't hate us for hating you. You kept showing love against our hate." He stopped for a moment. "I couldn't sleep after we stole your stuff, so here it is back." He paused for another awkward moment, not knowing what more there was to say. "That bag's my way of saying thanks for straightening me out, I guess." And with that, he walked off down the street.

Carl looked down at the sack in his hands and gingerly opened it. He took out his retirement watch and put it back on his wrist. Opening his wallet, he checked for his wedding photo. He gazed for a moment at the young bride that still smiled back at him from all those years ago and then put the photo back in its place. He pocketed his billfold once again and went back to mulching his roses.

He didn't make it to the following spring to see those roses bloom again. He died one cold day after Christmas that winter. Many people attended his funeral, in spite of the weather. In particular, the minister noticed a tall young man that he didn't know sitting quietly in a distant corner of the church. The minister spoke of Carl's garden as a lesson in life. In a voice made thick with unshed tears, he said, "Do your best and make your garden as beautiful as you can. We will never forget Carl and his garden."

That spring, as the ice thawed in the yard, another flyer went up. It read: "Person needed to care for Carl's garden." The flyer went unnoticed by the busy parishioners until one day when a knock was heard at the minister's office door. Opening the door, the minister saw a pair of scarred and tattooed hands holding the flyer. "I believe this is my job, if you'll have me," the young man said. The minister recognized him as the same young man who had returned the stolen watch and wallet to Carl. He knew that Carl's kindness had turned this man's life around. As the minister handed him the keys to the garden shed, he said, "Yes, go take care of Carl's garden and honor him."

The man went to work and, over the next several years, he tended the flowers and vegetables just as Carl had done. In that time, he went to college, got married, and became a prominent businessman in the community. But he never forgot his promise to Carl's memory and kept the garden as beautiful as he thought Carl would have kept it.

One day he approached the new minister and told him that he couldn't care for the garden any longer. He explained with a shy and happy smile, "My wife just had our baby last night, and she's coming home Saturday."

"Well, congratulations!" said the minister as he was handed the garden shed keys. "That's wonderful! What's the baby's name?"

It was Carl.

THE IVORY QUILL

by Darlyn Bush, Abbeville, Louisiana

Some adventures in life stay in your memory always. That day in the spring of 1923, in New Orleans, Louisiana, was one such day.

I was twenty-one and depressed beyond measure. With the clip-clop of horse-drawn carriages along the cobblestone streets following me down the sidewalk to Jackson Square, it felt as if everyone had a purpose for being, except me.

I sat on a park bench quietly praying that God would send me a sign, something that would give me a glimmer of hope to my invading disenchantment with life. Tears surfaced as I glanced up at the towering steeple of Saint Louis Cathedral. *Lord, please help me to understand my path to happiness,* I silently prayed.

As the last of my plea took flight with the spring breeze, a beautiful white dove perched on a bush in front of me. And just as suddenly as it had come, it flew across the square. My tear-filled eyes followed its course toward another park bench where it landed at the feet of an old gentleman sitting all alone. He had been feeding the pigeons the last of his sandwich. The last of his crumbs were thrown to the newcomer. . . the dove.

His clothes were rumpled and tattered, and his eyes revealed much loneliness. Something moved me to go and join this old soul. As I walked across the park, I stopped to buy two cups of coffee and some French beignets for the two of us. His joy at having someone to talk to and the merriment portrayed on his face after sipping his coffee and nibbling his sweets were more than enough thanks for me.

Before long, he was talking at length and with great pride about the memories of his past, mostly as a Civil War soldier. He told of how his younger brother had fought for the other side and been killed by a Southern soldier from his own troop. He told of the cannons' thunderous roar as they lit the skies of twilight. Stories of how the soldiers, most of whom were wounded, marched wearily across fields of dead bodies. Food and water were in short supply, and dysentery plagued the exhausted soldiers.

His pride, of course, was understandable. . .he was a proud veteran. But his obvious love and joy over mentioning these matters baffled me greatly. Maybe this was the only time that he ever remembered himself being needed or having a purpose in his life. It was soon obvious there was no one left who cared anything about him. He lived in a long-ago past, virtually oblivious to his current state.

Yet he never complained of his present plight. He was without socks to protect his feet from the ground that rubbed his flesh raw where the holes in his shoes were. He had no home, just a cardboard box to sleep in. Neither did he complain of his tattered clothes and lack of food, no, not this soldier of war. He was merely grateful for every day that he was able to make his way to the park to sit and feed his feathered friends.

How ashamed I became. Compared to his present circumstances, my life was bountiful. I had food in my pantry, a comfortable bed to sleep in, and good clean clothes on my back. I had friends who loved and cared about me. I now understood that I had my whole life ahead of me and realized that the things we might want are not always the things we really need.

This courageous old soul had instilled in me faith, insight, and enough determination to see life through—no matter what the odds might be. I, in turn, felt the glory of being responsible for the twinkle in his eyes and the contented smile on his lips.

I bowed my head in prayer, thanking God for bringing this gentle soul to my rescue. I made a decision at that moment to invite the old soldier home for dinner. As I raised my head to talk to him, I found he had gone. The dove had also disappeared. I looked in every direction but could not find them.

Suddenly, something on the bench where he sat captured my eye. I reached down and lifted a white feather that was left in his place. *How peculiar,* I thought, as I studied the ivory quill. The dove never perched upon the bench, and yet its plume lay next to me.

I returned to Jackson Square for months on end trying to find that gentle soldier. I finally gave up the search when a white dove finally landed at my feet. I knew in my heart that I would never see the old man again.

I have kept that treasured feather throughout the years between the pages of my Bible. In my darkest hours, I have removed that ivory quill and recalled the finding of it. It never fails to always bring me hope and joy.

Today is December 13, 1987. It is my seventy-fifth birthday. My oldest great-granddaughter, Amanda, is coming to visit me. She, too, is filled with despair. It is time to pass on the ivory quill and the old soldier's story with it.

So my precious Amanda and I will sit this afternoon, enjoying a cup of tea, and I will tell her of the tale that so long ago filled my life with hope and joy. I know in my heart that afterward, Amanda will always love and remember this old, gentle soul—just as I have remembered him so well. And it will bring her hope and joy throughout her life until she, too, passes it on.

SHE'S PROBABLY SINGING IT RIGHT NOW

by Pastor John Roberts, Sterling, Colorado

Her name was Rebecca. My wife's niece. "Bekah" is what we called her. She probably had the cancer since before she was born, the doctors said. The kind Bekah had usually starts during the early days of development, not long after conception. Something goes wrong as the cells begin to divide, some genetic malfunction occurs, and the cancer begins to spread, slowly, silently.

There are several kinds of this rare childhood cancer, called rhabdomyosarcoma, most of which are easy to detect and remove. Bekah's was the worst kind, however. Growing deep inside her abdomen, the tumors produced no symptoms until they had invaded her spine and several internal organs.

By the time the cancer was detected, she had grown up and become a cheerful and lovely newlywed, with a bright future in music ministry ahead of her. She had traveled to Russia with a choir, helped lead dozens to the Lord in her church's youth ministry, and blessed literally thousands with her incredible musical gifts.

And then came the awful news: On the Fourth of July, her new husband, Dallas, and her family got the word that she had just a few weeks to live.

After the initial shock, Bekah saw this turn of events exactly as she had seen every other circumstance in her life—an opportunity to tell others about God's goodness and love.

She shared the gospel with her nurses and told her coworkers about God's love. She continued to sing for the Lord every chance she got. She phoned kids that she and Dallas had been working with and invited them to her house to pray for them and love them.

Four weeks ago, she had what proved to be her last opportunity to sing in church. She invited her doctors to come hear her. One of them did. As she shared and sang, she told once again of God's love and goodness and encouraged everyone there to trust God like she did.

Last Saturday was her grampa's birthday. Weak and sick as she was, she invited him over, because she wanted to pray a blessing for Grampa Jim on his birthday. So she did.

Finally, on Monday, just a day before she died, she told her family not to cry, because she was going to be fine, just fine.

Well, now she is fine, just fine.

A thousand unanswered questions rise up for believers in times like this. Most of them begin with the word "why" and end with the silence of heaven.

I think I know what Bekah would say in answer to our questions.

I think she would say, "Just keep loving God. Keep doing what He says. Let God be God. You do what He calls you to do. He'll take care of the rest."

Come to think of it, she probably wouldn't say that.

She'd sing it.

In fact, she probably is singing it right now.

GRANDMA

by Linda Knight, Woodslee, Ontario, Canada

I was a shy, sixteen-year-old teenager when I met my boyfriend's beloved grandmother, and she first stole my heart. Grandma was only four and a half feet tall but had a heart as big as a cathedral. In no time at all, I was totally enraptured by its wonderful power.

She was a devout woman, faithfully at mass every Sunday morning. Although she never traveled more than three hundred miles in all her ninety-seven years, she had fascinating stories to tell of her long and wonderful life. Stories of faith, survival, and remarkable courage were written in every line upon her face. Her faith in Jesus was evident in every twinkle of her sparkling brown eyes.

One story I really enjoyed was how, at the age of nineteen, she had given birth to premature twins. One baby weighed a pound, and the other a pound and a half. There were no hospitals close by, and doctors could take hours or even days to get to someone who needed help. Grandma knew something must be done right away to save her two girls. Wrapping them in blankets, she put them near their old wood burning stove and set jars of water around them so the steam would help them breathe. Days later when the doctor finally arrived, he said he couldn't have done a finer job himself. One of those baby girls lived to be eighty-seven years old.

But the thing which always astonished me was the way you were always made to feel welcome and loved when you visited her. Whether invited or not, she would always be waiting with open arms to give you a smile and a great big hug. There would always be a pie baking as if she knew you were coming. The house would always be full of people, half that she didn't even know. At mealtimes, even though she was on a limited income, you could not have found a finer feast. Just like Jesus, Grandma's life was filled with the real thing; a love you could taste, touch, feel, and experience firsthand.

One day I asked her, "Grandma, how do you do it? You always seem to have more than enough food for everyone who walks through your door. You always have a smile, a hug, a word of encouragement, and a pie baking in the oven!"

Grandma turned toward me with her arms wide open and said simply, "I just love everybody!"

I feel so blessed to have witnessed the grace of God at work in her life. Grandma was the first "angel on earth" I had ever met. Now, as a grandmother myself, my prayer is that I'll somehow learn to walk in her footsteps.

CHAPTER FIVE

God's Plan

In his heart a man plans his course,
but the LORD determines his steps.
Proverbs 16:9

*Published in "Stories for the Family's Heart,"
1998, and* Lutheran Woman Today, *1996*

TWICE BLESSED

by Kathryn Lay, Arlington, Texas

We knew the call would come eventually, but we weren't sure when.

"Her name is Michelle," our caseworker said. On that day, November 2, 1991, we learned of the imminent adoption of our nine-month-old daughter.

It was time to celebrate. As promised, we called our closest friends and treated them to a special celebration dinner.

While we laughed and talked at the restaurant, telling them of what we knew about our soon-to-arrive and much prayed for daughter, I became aware that the older couple in the booth behind us laughed as we did and nodded knowingly as we voiced our excitement and nervousness.

We weren't quiet. After ten years of infertility; of prayers too numerous to count; and eight months of parenting classes, paperwork, and home studies—we were full of joy at the good news. It bubbled over as we talked and planned in the restaurant.

"What if we're not good parents?" I asked.

"What if the adoption doesn't go through, and we lose her after we've fallen in love?" Richard asked.

"I'll bet she's sweet and adorable and full of smiles," I said.

"I'll bet she'll be a daddy's girl," Richard said.

The louder we got, the more I noticed how quiet the neighboring diners had become. But I was too excited to worry, too scared to stop talking.

When the couple behind us left their booth, they paused at our table.

"Congratulations," the woman said, patting my shoulder.

"Thank you," I said, grateful they weren't angry at our loudness. "We know we've been kind of loud, but, we're a little excited," I explained.

She leaned closer and quietly said, "I have several children of my own. I also have a granddaughter that was adopted by a couple not long ago. I have never seen her. Hearing your excitement, I feel in my heart that, somewhere, she is loved and well taken care of by a family like you." Patting my shoulder once more, she whispered, "I'll pray for you and your baby."

At a time when we were blessed and overflowing with joy, God put us in a place where we could be a blessing and comfort to another. I pray for that grandmother, that God will continue to give her peace and comfort for the granddaughter she wonders about. I know my husband and I, along with our little Michelle, were in her prayers that night.

I also pray for the grandmother of our daughter, that she will know how much this little girl means to us. That she, too, will find peace in knowing God's perfect plan.

Previously published in Mature Living, *April 1992 and* Alive! *July 1995*

DAVE'S APPLE TREE

by Martha Larche Lusk, Dallas, Texas

I sighed as I looked at it. Dave's apple tree was stubbornly and sadly unproductive. Not a bud in sight. It hadn't borne fruit for the entire five years of its life in our yard. Each spring my husband and I inspected the tree daily for buds, thinking this would be the year, and visualizing the ripened fruit. But it had remained barren. If vegetation were capable of speech, this tree would have been a mute. It hadn't broken its silence with so much as a blossom in all the time since we had planted it.

This past spring, we finally decided we had waited long enough for the tree to "establish" itself, and we sought some professional help. In early March, we spoke to the nursery we had purchased it from and got some authoritative answers to our questions. All of which confirmed our suspicions. Yes, this particular species was self-pollinating. Yes, it definitely should have bloomed and produced fruit by now. In their opinion, our tree did indeed appear to be barren. To sum it all up, they suggested that, if we wanted apples, we should buy another apple tree.

When we got home, Dave issued an ultimatum. Either the tree

blossomed this year, or he would cut it down and replace it. We wanted apples, but wasn't that sort of drastic? It was still a beautiful tree to me. Why couldn't we just keep it as an ordinary tree? "No," Dave said. It wouldn't be in keeping with nature's balance. A fruit tree should bear fruit. If this one didn't, then we had no space for a sterile fruit tree. That view of things upset me, but it was Dave's tree.

A couple of weeks went by, and spring was abundantly evident in our garden. The peach tree had put out its usual mass of buds which soon opened into a blanket of snowy elegance. The pear tree followed suit shortly thereafter, as did the two apricot trees. The buttery-colored daffodils were everywhere. Shrubs burst into flower to add their share of interest to the landscape. I was still rooting (forgive the pun) for the apple tree. I checked it every day. I gave it pep talks. I reminded it of the peril it was in. But it remained the only thing growing in our yard untouched by spring's promise.

I had resigned myself to the tree's fate just as it got its reprieve—a reprieve obtained for the worst possible reason. Dave died suddenly.

The first few days after his death passed in a haze of grief and shock. I often retreated to the garden. It was where Dave loved to be, and I could feel his presence there. I also felt God's strength and love as I observed nature's life force all around me in the unfolding of spring. Everywhere except the apple tree. Its branches remained devoid of promise.

As I sat there one evening staring at this tree, I knew beyond a shadow of a doubt that Dave had been right. There was no longer any hope for bloom and fruit. I would honor Dave's wishes and have the tree cut down and replaced. Still alive and thriving, that tree seemed a mockery of Dave's memory. Dave was gone. The tree had to go, too. Once again, though, the apple tree was spared.

The Saturday after Dave died, I suddenly understood why the garden had offered me peace and serenity during the last few painful days. As it says in Ecclesiastes 3:1 (KJV), "There is. . .a time to every purpose under the heaven." Nature, the right hand of God, pointed out to me the power and beauty of the divine plan, whether it be for man or tree.

Overnight, Dave's apple tree had burst into full bloom.

I REMEMBER

by Pat Toornman Bales, Brighton, Colorado

"Quick, John, run inside the house and get a bunch of bath towels," James commanded. "Call Frankie NOW—and tell him to hurry! Joseph, hold the hind legs as tightly as you can. Mom, I've talked to Frankie. He's raised sheep for years. He told me what to do, and he promised to help. I've read books, and I know I can do it. Quit worrying." James tried to reassure me, but somehow those words, coming from a twelve-year-old boy, were anything but reassuring.

A ewe had ruptured during pregnancy. Torn muscles in her side prevented her lamb from entering the birth canal. Knowing she couldn't have a normal delivery, I had wanted to get rid of her, but my oldest son, James, insisted that he could handle her and her pregnancy. He insisted he would keep an eye on her and do what was necessary when the time arose. The time was now, and we were preparing to operate.

I was not ready for this. I felt totally overwhelmed. Struggling to keep the farm after my husband left, working, and trying to raise the boys myself had all taken their toll. I thought I was independent and could handle anything. I believed my faith was strong. Now, circumstances tested all that confidence.

My boys had to grow up fast when their dad stepped out of their lives as well as mine. It took over three months to get into court for the temporary orders. We lived hand-to-mouth. Everything we had taken for granted was gone. Our world had been turned upside down. We owned the farm and animals, but I didn't have a full-time job. Counting pennies to buy a gallon of milk became the norm. Even though my boys were helpful, they were still young. The daily problems rested solely on my shoulders, and there were lots of them. Emotionally, we were all drained.

I remembered the first time I felt I was all alone. The second year of my marriage, my next door neighbor found me crying. I was pregnant with James and very unhappy with the state of my marriage. As I sobbed about my marriage, she held me and dried my tears. Then she prayed with me. Sharon explained to me that the God I vaguely knew as a child was there for me every moment of every day. I started attending church, reading my Bible, and building my relationship with Him daily. God used that time to change me. Whenever I became frightened, I could remember God loves me, and I was not alone. I would pray, and it quieted my fears.

But, there were still times like this, when I felt overwhelmed. I forgot the promise that He would always be with me. I had been depending on myself and barely surviving. I needed to depend on Him. When I prayed, peace flooded over me. I could get that same peace now, if only I asked Him. Closing my eyes, I would try it.

My body rigid with tension, I prayed silently.

God, You're in control. You know I can't do this alone. I keep trying, but I just can't do it by myself anymore. . . . Please help me. . . . Please show me Your love. I need You. The prayer calmed my quaking body.

Eight-year-old John came running back with a stack of towels. "Frankie's on his way. He said James knows how to get her ready and that the timing is REAL IMPORTANT."

"James, what does he mean by that?" I asked, worry creeping into my voice.

"Mom, just grab her front legs and hold them apart and steady." James's voice came as a whisper but braced with control. My grip held steady.

"John, help Joseph hold her back legs 'cause she'll start kicking."

With methodical precision, James cut the ewe's belly. Joseph and John held tightly to her back legs. Opening my eyes, looking at my three young sons' faces, I saw something I hadn't noticed before. John and Joseph were looking at James with complete faith. They followed orders and held fast to the kicking legs. James looked up at me with a determination in his eyes that went well beyond his twelve years. Right then, I knew we were going to make it. Peace flooded over me.

"I feel a lamb! I think I got it! John, hold both legs! Joseph, grab a towel!"

James pulled out a wet, wiggly lamb still attached to its mother and handed it to Joseph. We all felt the peace as James cut the cord. Joseph, only six years old, started rubbing the lamb dry.

"Hey, James, how's it going?" boomed Frankie as he strode into the barn.

"Look, it's alive! We have a baby!" James squealed, sounding more like a boy of twelve than the confident, determined young man I just watched deliver a lamb.

"Remember, there are usually more than one. Twins are the norm," Frankie said.

"Here, you take over." James started to move to the side of the ewe.

"No way, young man. You started it, you can finish it. I'll take John's place, and he can take care of the next lamb."

During the next ten minutes, James found not just twins, but triplets! All three were given to John and Joseph who dried them off and carried them into the house.

Those lambs are grown and gone. Joseph and John are now teenagers. James just finished his junior year at the Air Force Academy and is applying to medical schools. He wants to be a doctor. It is a dream he has had since he was twelve. When I asked him what made him choose a career in medicine, he answered, "Mom, do you remember the day our ewe ruptured, and I had to deliver triplets? That day I knew what I wanted to do with my life. I felt God there with me."

I looked at him, and I did remember. I remember that day and my boys' expressions as clearly as if it were yesterday. I also remember all the other days that have come and gone and how thankful I am for them. Most of all, I remember I am not alone. I always have a friend, someone Who loves me and helps carry my everyday worries and concerns—just as He did the day James delivered triplet lambs.

MICHELLE

by Tracy Bohannon, Riverview, Florida

Michelle came to us at the age of two as our first foster child. As I looked at her for the first time, I prayed, "God, please let this work out." She had shoulder-length, wispy brown hair, and enormous blue eyes that were the saddest I have ever seen. I hoped we were up to the challenge of parenting a foster child. Before taking this step, we had attended a class for prospective foster parents, which was supposed to teach us everything we would need to know. What they couldn't teach us was the incredible love and affection we would experience.

Every day Michelle grew, and every day we loved her more and more. Gradually, as the days passed, Michelle's eyes went from sorrowful to the sparkling, mischievous eyes of any other toddler. She brought so much joy to our family. We all adored her, especially our four-year-old son. Michelle opened our eyes to simple joys that we had always taken for granted.

I learned how fortunate our own son was to be born to parents who loved and cherished him as the miracle of God's love that all children are. Michelle showed us that just a walk in the park was much more than a simple pleasure—it was a way to connect, to be one with God's creations. Holding Michelle's hand in one of mine, and my son's in the other, I marveled at the simple but powerful act of love and protectiveness in just holding one small hand in mine.

Then one night, after the children were in bed, we received a telephone call. A relative had been found who was willing to take Michelle. Although we knew that a child could leave at any time, we were completely unprepared. I silently climbed the stairs as Michelle slept and quietly packed her things. The next day, her social worker arrived promptly at ten. I carried Michelle out and, after a long hug and a kiss, followed by many tears, I placed her in the car and watched her leave.

To have had the privilege of loving her was a miracle granted to us from God. We learned so much from this very special little girl. She paved the way for all the children who would follow her. We were able to love and cherish each child that came to us, no matter what the circumstance. Most importantly, we learned how to let go, no matter how painful it might be. With God's help we tried to love them as Jesus loved us—unconditionally and with a steadfast love that can only be given by God.

Although we don't see Michelle anymore, the love she gave and the changes she brought to our family continue to be seen and felt. She will always be a part of our hearts and souls, always reminding us of the blessings that are ours every day.

THE RULES OF LIFE

by Linda Parker, Windermere, Florida

Andrea played by the rules. She always played by the rules. Andrea's world was a neat, tidy package.

At seventeen, she had carefully evaluated the scholarships she had been offered for four years of paid college education to prepare her to teach music. She sought advice from her high school guidance counselor, discussed her options with the church music director, and made her final decision by considering her parents' preferences as well as the cost of commuting. After mailing in the commitment letter, there was nothing left to do but stand back and bask in the praise for making such mature, sensible choices.

Her life followed an orderly progression. Four years of college, National Music Honor Society, and, three weeks before graduation, she received an offer to teach in Hardinsburg Elementary School.

At Hardinsburg Elementary School, she was quickly recognized as a first-rate teacher. Every summer she returned to the university, each time taking on a new area of specialized study.

Andrea learned methods of music therapy in order to use music to unlock doors of silence and isolation in emotionally disturbed children. She took course work in physical therapy so she could help children with physical challenges to participate in Hardinsburg's beginner band. Her final summer in graduate school was spent mastering sign language so that she could bring deaf and hearing-impaired children into the music classroom for the first time. Miss Andrea was not far from sainthood in the eyes of her students, their parents, or the Hardinsburg Elementary School administration.

When a young attorney opened a new practice in town, no one

was surprised that he, too, would take notice of Andrea. Nor were folks surprised when, a few months later, Mike and Andrea proceeded with a proper plan—marriage; wait two, well-planned years; then start a family.

Andrea, true to form, managed her pregnancy with textbook precision. Milk became her drink of choice, jogging was replaced with yoga and stretching, and she played classical music for her unborn child.

Early one rainy morning, just before Thanksgiving, Mike and Andrea became the parents of a tiny baby girl with delicate features. Ann Marie had beautiful brown curls, large blue eyes framed by dark lashes, and ten elegant piano-player's fingers. She also had permanent brain damage—cause unknown. How could this have happened?

While Mike worked overtime, Andrea alternately wept, worried, and shook her fist at God in her frustration. "How could He do this to me?" she ranted. *I paid my dues in advance,* she thought resentfully, *with my service to handicapped children.*

Christmas was soon only days away. Andrea and Ann Marie rarely left the house. Unable to postpone it any longer, there were some unavoidable holiday preparations to be completed, even for the small-scale celebration Michael and Andrea had planned.

Ann Marie wore a warm pink bunting as Andrea loaded her into the stroller for their first shopping trip. Every store display they passed was alive with moving figures, musical sounds, and twinkling lights, all designed to draw the delight of children. The elaborate decorations seemed to be designed for the sole purpose of reminding Andrea of God's unfair decision to deprive her of a healthy baby and to burden her life with the care of a handicapped child.

After pushing the stroller through the crowd of shoppers, Andrea took a few minutes in the ladies' room to stop her tears. As she wept in the privacy of a toilet stall, she heard a woman speaking to a child. It was a happy conversation, filled with the anticipation Christmas brings to a child's chatter. Andrea felt another sharp pang of jealousy for what this other mother and daughter obviously shared.

Pulling herself together, Andrea parked the stroller near the counter so she could wash her hands before she and Ann Marie returned to the crowded mall. The woman and her daughter continued to talk enthusiastically about their upcoming holiday plans as they washed their hands. Andrea's heart pricked with true envy as she watched them, but she stopped short when she saw the child's face for the first time.

The little girl in front of her was probably not more than eleven or twelve. She had long dark hair, almost as curly as Ann Marie's, and she wore a red cap turned at an impish angle. She also had the unmistakable features that identify Down syndrome.

Andrea realized she was staring openly at the pair. She struggled for something to say, a way to explain her rudeness. Finally, she stammered, "I'm sorry to stare. You two just sound so happy." It was an awkward moment.

The mother could have reacted indignantly, but sometimes empathy prevails. In the instant that she peeked into the stroller, the woman remembered being Andrea, being a new mother engulfed in hurt and misdirected rage.

"You have a beautiful baby," she said.

Andrea nodded, but she could not think what to say.

"You know, God only picks special mothers to have special children," the stranger added, and with a "Merry Christmas!" she and her daughter went on their way.

Special mothers? Special children? Suddenly, it did not matter that Andrea's world was no longer the same neat, tidy package. It was the surprise and wonder of a gift from God, and it took a stranger in the ladies' room to point that out to her. This was the blessed task for which God had prepared her. How could she have been so blind?

Andrea scooped Ann Marie into her arms and held her tightly. "You," she said to the sleepy, blinking bundle, "are my greatest blessing. God entrusted you to me." And looking heavenward she said, "Thank You, God, for opening my eyes. Thank You for sending Your Son, thank You for sending my daughter," and laughing she added, "and thank You for sending us into the ladies' room!"

This would be the best Christmas ever.

SOMETIMES THERE ARE NO U-TURNS

by Shanna Hoskison, Pecan Gap, Texas

Early in 1982, we weren't exactly planning a child. Ideally, we had wanted to wait five years before starting a family. Two years into our marriage, those plans changed. Our daughter was conceived.

At twenty years of age, I didn't think too much about it. I guess I was too young to be worried, scared, or expectant in any way. Being pregnant and having babies was what everyone was doing. We were no different. The pregnancy was uneventful, although I did have to have a cesarean section.

Our baby was perfect in every way, with a wonderful disposition. Except for some typical thirteen-year-old rebelliousness, she grew to be a wonderful child. She was a good student, loved by peers and teachers alike, and always made us proud. Throughout her growing up, however, I wanted a sibling for her. Coming from a family of five children, I couldn't imagine not having a brother or a sister. I wanted this for my daughter. She deserved the closeness of a sibling. It just didn't seem to be God's plan. As she turned eight, nine, ten, I resolved myself to raising an only child.

A couple of years ago, when she turned sixteen, I began to prepare myself for the "empty nest" thing. I had no idea how God was going to help me through this "syndrome." Then, early in the spring of 1999, I began to feel what I had only felt one other time in my life, some seventeen years before. How could this be? I ignored the symptoms for some time, thinking my mind must be playing tricks on me. My body had to be going through some phase.

Surely I wasn't pregnant.

Oh, but I was.

I wasn't sure how was I going to explain this to my firstborn, but this was a path that had no U-turns. I remember crying for two days and nights, my husband holding me and consoling me. When I called my mother to ask her for words of wisdom she said, "God doesn't make mistakes." When I told my seventeen year old that I was expecting, she simply looked to heaven and said, "Well, it's got to be God, after all these years. You may be carrying a prophet, great leader, or who knows, but I know this baby has a very special calling on its life."

We now have a young daughter of only a few months. Our daughters are seventeen years apart in age. Was this our plan? No. This was definitely God's plan for our lives. It surely wasn't ours.

As I watch her in her walker, running across the kitchen floor in pursuit of the stream of light from the window, I laugh. My oldest says I think everything the baby does is funny. I explain, no, it's just when I think about my feelings when I found out about her that I have to laugh. I have to laugh at the tears I shed, and the hesitancy and fear I felt when I first found out I was pregnant. Accompanying my laughter is a deep and abiding thankfulness for God's wisdom and His plan for my life.

I am so glad that He is driving this car called "Life" and not me. I never would have taken this road myself. And I would have missed so much.

GOD'S PLAN—NOT MINE

by Joel Holtz, Minneapolis, Minnesota

I had it all figured out. I was finally moving back to live in one of my favorite places, central Oregon. My job was ending, my condo had a buyer, I had gotten rid of all my furniture, and I was set to leave in a couple of weeks. It had been over ten years since I had last lived there, and I could hardly wait to get back. The Deschutes river, the mountains and forests, and the aqua blue lakes were all in my mind constantly. What would I do first? Maybe some white-water rafting, or a hike in the forest. Maybe a drive along the Cascade Lakes Highway. I was following my own path, charting my own course, never expecting the Lord might have other plans.

After leaving church one Sunday morning and approaching my car, I noticed someone had left a note on my windshield. Just weeks before, I had put a notice in the church bulletin, asking for help with refreshments. Since I was leaving, I thought I should try and find a replacement for pouring water and coffee, which I had done for the last couple of years. I figured the note was about that request.

As I started to read the note, however, it became evident the person who wrote it was not responding to the notice for help with refreshments, but rather inquiring whether or not I was married. My immediate thought was, "Someone in church who knows my car is playing a practical joke." But why would she leave a name and a phone number if that was the case? So, when I got home I decided to call and get to the bottom of it. I got an answering machine, left my name and number, and having gotten rid of my bed a few days earlier, promptly took an afternoon nap on my carpeted living-room floor.

Later that night, shortly after supper, the phone rang. It was the person who had left the note.

"This must be Joel. Hi, I'm Rita," she said.

After finding out how she had known my car, and when she had started attending the same church, I felt I had to be totally honest with her.

"I would love to get together with you sometime, but I am moving to Oregon in a couple of weeks."

"Oh sure, I finally get the nerve to meet someone new, and now you are leaving," she responded with a laughing lilt in her voice.

"Well, I would be happy to take you out to dinner before I go," I offered, not knowing why I had even suggested it.

"I would like that," she said. "My birthday is next week, how about then?"

"Sure, that would be great," I said, again wondering what I was doing.

"Don't you want to know what I look like?" she asked.

"That would make me rather shallow, wouldn't it?" I responded. We were off to a flying start.

We both had a busy week coming up, so we decided to meet the following Friday for dinner. She gave me directions to her home, and I found myself looking forward to the day. I found her house easily. I was pleasantly surprised to see it was in one of my favorite areas, about fifteen minutes from my home. I calmly rang the doorbell, waiting for her to answer. When she did, standing before me was one of the most beautiful women I had ever seen.

"I know you," I said, relieved that in fact she was someone I had seen in church before.

After a few minutes of conversation, we left for the restaurant. We had a great time at dinner, and when I drove her home, she invited me inside to continue our conversation. We talked until 2:00 in the morning, at which time I realized I probably would not be moving back to Oregon. As I left to go home, I asked if I could see her again.

"Of course," she answered, smiling.

As so often happens, God had a plan that did not coincide with mine. Thankfully, I followed His lead, and not my own.

We have been married now for almost three years. I never made it back to Oregon, and you know what? It doesn't bother me a bit.

TIME OF MY LIFE

by Stephanie Welcher Buckley, Edmond, Oklahoma

"Teach a life-skills class in an inner-city school?" I asked during staff meeting. "Why in the world would I do that?" As a single woman in my thirties, I had a comfortable workload and didn't want to add another job responsibility. Besides, what did I know about teaching? I had no interest in public education. I didn't even have children!

"As employees in the community health department, our mission is to make the city a healthier place to live," my boss explained.

How this goal would be accomplished by teaching a roomful of high school kids was beyond my comprehension. My duties as a community development specialist in an Oklahoma City hospital were mundane compared to the competitive career I'd had in journalism and broadcasting eleven years earlier. However, my job was simple, and the salary was excellent. I had traded challenges for security.

"The last thing I want to do is baby-sit twice a week," I complained to a coworker at lunch.

"Then make it easy on yourself," she suggested. "Have guest speakers come in and talk about topics like careers, managing money, nutrition. . . . We work with those kinds of people right here at the hospital."

That afternoon, I planned the curriculum and made a prospective speakers list. Rather than class assignments or homework, I would base the student's grade on attendance, writing thank-you notes to classroom guests, and keeping a journal of the points they heard from each speaker. *The less work for me the better,* I thought.

When the day arrived for me to go to the classroom, I was nervous. Standing at the front of the class, I saw a sea of multicultural faces. They seemed so fragile, not at all like the images I had seen watching MTV. One boy's dyed red hair was tipped green; another sported large tattoos on his neck, ankle, shoulders, and forearms; and two pregnant girls sat together on the second row, their stomachs bulging behind the desk. *A class full of misfits,* I thought. But from somewhere inside myself I heard a voice say, "You've gotten as far off track as they are."

As the semester wore on, I began to see the students as children in need of encouragement and acceptance. "You did an excellent job on this thank-you note, Maria," I praised the Hispanic girl with gang signs on her hands. "A whole page! Way to go!"

She smiled, pleased by the compliment. "I liked the way Ms. Daigle talked to us," Maria said. "Someday I want to be a counselor and help people like she does."

The speakers were making a difference for some students, but I never imagined that I, too, would be changed by one of these lectures. Back at the office, my boss stopped at my doorway one day. "I booked a friend of mine for your class. He is one of our doctors and likes to encourage young people."

"There is a change in your syllabus," I said at our next week's session as a tall, handsome black man walked into the classroom. I introduced Dr. Johnny Grigg. He had grown up in poverty, but he used his physical ability as a football star to win a scholarship to college. Instead of playing professional sports, he focused on education and became a neonatal intensive care pediatrician. The students were mesmerized by the soft-spoken man in green surgical scrubs.

"Think of your life as the face of a clock. Most people live to be about eighty years old, so that would be the twelve o'clock position. You are almost twenty years old and that puts you at three o'clock, so a quarter of your life is gone." This analogy seemed to hit home as the class listened thoughtfully to our speaker.

"None of you are here today by accident," he said scanning the room making eye contact with each student. Then he said something that reached to my core, just as it seemed to touch the class. "God has a purpose for your life." He paused to let this sink in and then continued. "One of my favorite Bible promises is found in Jeremiah 29:11, 'For I know the plans I have for you,' declares the LORD, 'plans to prosper you and not to harm you, plans to give you hope and a future.' "

I hadn't anticipated our guest would discuss spirituality, but it was soon evident this aspect was the very foundation of his life. . .and the kids were listening intently.

"God has a blueprint for us all. He wants us to discover our destiny through a relationship with Him," he confided. Dr. Grigg went on to explain the importance of making every day count. His presentation was filled with encouragement, support, and love. His eyes glowed with excitement as he said, "Choose wisely how you spend the time you have left." We all sat and listened, spellbound, until the buzzing of his beeper broke our somber trance. Dr. Grigg had to get back to the hospital, but he had left us all enough to think about for a lifetime.

On the way home, I realized the hands on my clock approached six! For all practical purposes, my life was half over. The dreams of a journalism and broadcasting career put aside, I had focused on a safe, uncomplicated, mediocre life.

That evening, I prayed God would lead me to a career that glorified Him and fulfilled me. In my journal the next morning, I wrote about the regret of giving up on the gift God had given me—the ability and desire to write.

Although not a morning person, I began waking up at 5:00 A.M. to write before going to work. Almost daily, I remembered the clock analogy and prayed about how to serve God through writing. Soon, a concept for a book emerged. I felt energized by my passion. What a contrast from the lethargy and apathy I felt doing my job at the hospital.

Several months later, I told a coworker about my writing routine and the lack of time I had to write. "They are going to have to fire me before I have enough time to finish that book," I joked. Twenty minutes later, my boss called me into her office. A reduction-in-force caused me to lose my job! Just as Dr. Grigg had said, I suddenly realized God had a plan for me. The hospital's severance package allowed me to launch a career as a Christian communicator. I had time and money to follow God's plan.

Never again would I comb the want ads and accept an easy or meaningless way to make a living. No longer would I hide my talent and desire to write. Dr. Grigg's words reminded me that following God's direction would fulfill my destiny. The hands on the clock of my life warned that there was no more time to waste. Instead of regretting years wasted following my path instead of God's, I focus on Dr. Grigg's advice to "choose wisely how I spend the time I have left."

Today, I am having the time of my life following God's plan and serving in a career that glorifies Him. Never again will I chart my own course.

MABEL'S MIRACLE

by Charles S. McKinstry, Roanoke, Virginia

Mabel was sixty-seven years of age and had been a "goer" and a "doer" all her life. As a leader in her church, she never missed any opportunity to serve. She was an indefatigable lady, dedicated to praising God by leading an exemplary life.

In December of 1998, Mabel suffered her first heart attack while caring for children whose mothers were at work. She was rushed to the nearest hospital emergency room gasping from chest pains.

After a needle in the heart and an EKG, she was hooked up to a beeping monitor, a respirator, and a feeding tube.

Five days later, she had recovered sufficiently to function without the tubes and needles and was allowed to sit up in the easy chair in her hospital room. Two days of slow walks around the halls produced no further signs of a heart malfunction, so Mabel was sent home to rest and fully regain her strength. Unfortunately, "rest" was not a word found in Mabel's vocabulary. She jumped right in, doing whatever needed to be done. The following week, she collapsed again in the church kitchen. Clutching her chest with both hands, she petitioned God, "Take me home now, Father, if I can no longer serve You."

This time, she lapsed into unconsciousness as the medics worked on her lifeless body during the siren-screaming ride to the hospital. They were in touch with the emergency room personnel by radio, so everything was ready when they wheeled her through the swinging doors. A highly qualified heart specialist had been alerted, and he worked on her faltering heart for two hours before declaring her condition critical, but stable. They had no sooner made this pronouncement than the alarms went off and the monitor showed a straight line, indicating that Mabel's heart had stopped, despite their belief that she was stable.

The respirator, IV, and other lifesaving paraphernalia were put into action again as Mabel observed all the activity from a vantage point overhead. She could hear a voice telling her that she must return to tackle the job that God had lined up for her. When they administered the electric shock paddles to her chest, she watched as her body jerked on the gurney. Finally, the monitor showed a heartbeat again.

Mabel survived and was ultimately transferred to CCU for a week and then to a private room. Three weeks after she had been returned from the dead, Mabel was strong enough for a series of extensive tests that would determine the amount of damage to her heart and associated arteries.

The results were not encouraging. She had four blocked arteries which seriously limited the amount of blood that flowed through her heart. She was in desperate need of quadruple bypass surgery immediately. However, as is so often the case, the operating room and the surgeons were fully scheduled until February the twentieth, six long weeks away. The doctors convinced Mabel that she had to go home and rest to build up her strength so she could hope to survive the long and dangerous bypass operation.

Mabel rested for the first two days at home. She really was too weak to do much else. Her daughter came and took care of her. The third day, though, she bounced out of bed at the first light of morning, said a prayer, got dressed, drank some coffee, and headed for the front door.

"Mama, you get back to bed," her daughter admonished her.

"No, Dear, the Lord needs me, and I'm going to do His work." From then on, she kept busy until the day of her bypass operation.

She walked into the hospital looking like the picture of health, rather than a woman close to death from a blood-starved heart. The doctors couldn't believe she looked and sounded so vibrant, but they had no idea that Mabel knew God wanted her for a job He needed done.

In surgery, when they opened her chest, moved aside the ribs and examined her heart and arteries, they were amazed. The four blocked arteries were pale and unhealthy, as they had suspected, but Mabel's heart was pumping blood like a sixteen year old's.

"That's impossible," the doctor said, shaking his head. "Her heart should be struggling to pump, not acting like a teenager's." Then the surgeon saw something that had not appeared on the latest MRI. A new artery, beautifully pink, and pulsing with life, was now feeding blood to Mabel's heart. It had apparently developed since her first MRI and accounted for her remarkable preoperative performance, when she should have been unable to do anything more than remain in bed.

After Mabel was returned to her room and fully conscious, the doctor visited her. "I've been opening chests and examining hearts and arteries for twenty years," the surgeon told her. "This is the first home-made bypass I've ever seen. It's truly a miracle. I had serious doubts that you would be alive for this operation; now I can see why you are."

Mabel smiled broadly as she said, "I hope those three man-made bypasses are as good as the one He gave me, 'cause I'm going to need all the energy I can get. My daughter just lost her husband, and she has to go back to work. I'm going to be a full-time nanny to my two-year-old twin grandsons, and that takes a lot of get-up-and-go!" Then, she exclaimed with glee, "Doctor, God has work He wants me to do before He takes me home."

A HARD WINTER'S PRAYER

by Lynn Terrell, Wichita, Kansas

It was a hard winter—not just because it was especially cold, but because it was especially lean. The recession had permeated the country, and it was starting to affect entire communities.

We had suddenly been laid off from the aerospace industry, and there were no pantries of canned goods to see us through. Even the temporary construction jobs had dried up; so, until spring, there was no work at all. To complicate matters, our rental house was being sold, so we would have to move. And our baby needed medicine—expensive medicine. With no insurance, that was our major concern that cold Wednesday afternoon.

"If worse comes to worse, maybe we could manage an apartment building," I remarked, turning to the classifieds. "At least it would pay the rent, the utilities, and the phone. I'm sure Mr. Hill would extend our credit at his store through the winter," I encouraged my husband.

"But we can't buy the baby's medicine from the grocer," he observed.

Also, with thousands of people out of work, and with no apartment experience, we weren't even confident in our ability to land one of only three manager's positions listed in the paper.

I asked the Lord for guidance as I reached for the phone, then jumped in surprise at its sudden ring. The caller was a distant relative—very distant—someone new to the family, whom we had only met twice. I barely knew her name.

"I hate to bother you," she apologized, "but we have a friend who has an apartment building, and his manager has to be in Florida in a week for a new job. He is desperate for a replacement, and I offered to ask around. Do you happen to know of anyone who might be interested?"

My heart raced, as I finished my interrupted prayer with a silent, but rousing *Thank You, Lord!* But, aloud, I managed to maintain my composure. "Where is it?"

It was just a few miles from us. I had even lived there for a year when I was a teenager.

When we met with the owner that evening, he explained that he had another business across town, and he wanted us to move that weekend when he could help. The timing was perfect!

"That is fine," my husband said, "but, we need to take care of something very important. Could you also hire me for some extra work, so I could make some cash?"

"Sure. And if you need anything from my store, I can just deliver it on my way home. In fact, I'll just run a tab for you, and you can work it off by painting."

"Oh, thank you for the job, Mr. Hanson," we exclaimed in excitement. "But we have already arranged for groceries."

"Well, good; I don't own a grocery store," he laughed, while chewing on his cigar stub. "And just call me Doc. I'm a pharmacist."

Even as God was arranging the job for the former manager, He had met our future needs.

Amen! I silently prayed—formally ending one more prayer that had been answered—even before we bowed our heads.

ALICE

by Charlene Cook, Murfreesboro, Tennessee

Sometimes God steers us into a course of action which may not always seem what we wanted or what we had in mind. But if we listen to Him, our lives will be greatly rewarded. Such is the story of how I came to know Alice.

After becoming disenchanted with Denver's smog and traffic, my husband and I decided to move. We discussed many different places, but, one night, Nebraska seemed to pop into my head from out of nowhere. "Nebraska!" my husband said. "Why Nebraska?" I didn't have an answer for him, but I knew in my heart that was where we were to go.

The very next Sunday in the Denver newspaper, we found a job offer in Omaha, Nebraska, that was perfect for my husband. Within a month, we were moving to Omaha.

Since we were not in the market to buy a house, our plan was to rent an apartment. However, God had other plans. We were out sightseeing one day and chanced upon a realtor's sign on a small, wood-frame house in a farm village named Yutan. Once inside, I knew this house was exactly what I wanted. Within two months, we were moving in.

After a while, I noticed an older woman taking walks around our neighborhood each day. She reminded me a lot of my own grandmother, so one day I decided to go walking with her. I was warmly welcomed, and it wasn't long before we became good friends.

Her name was Alice. She was a sweet and generous woman. It didn't take long before I was visiting her at least a couple of times each week. During these visits, I would help with little tasks she needed done. I really didn't mind. Her husband was not in good health, and I knew what little I did made her job easier. My grandparents had died years ago, and with my husband changing jobs and our moving around so much, I hadn't felt like I had any real family for years. Alice's love made me feel a part of her family.

Her love also helped return me to God's family.

Before long, Alice had me going to church with her each Sunday. Although I prayed and read my Bible, with our frequent moving it had been a long time since I really belonged to any church. I was so thankful to be "home" again.

The next step in my "Alice-led-journey" occurred when I raised my hand and volunteered to teach seven and eight year olds on Wednesday nights in a Christian education program. My first Wednesday, I was faced with a roomful of rowdy kids. Before the class was over, I was having as much fun as they were. I had found my niche.

As time passed, Alice needed more and more help. As soon as I came home from work, my phone would ring; Alice would be watching for me to come home so she could ask me to help her with something. She called me "her little angel." I never minded helping her, but I knew she was upset that she had to call upon me so often.

Herb, Alice's husband, needed more and more help getting around. If he fell, she needed help getting him up and, before long, she needed help getting him into and out of bed each day. It was getting to be too much for Alice to handle. Her own health began to fail.

After discussing the situation with our pastor, we contacted Alice's daughter and shared our concerns with her. Not long after, Herb was placed in a nursing home. It wasn't more than a few weeks later that Alice had a stroke and she, too, needed to be placed into a nursing home. Things changed quickly after that, but I felt secure in knowing that God had a plan and that He was in control.

A few months later, I found myself tearfully helping the church ladies prepare a luncheon for Alice's funeral. It was a bittersweet time. I will not forget her, the way she made me feel at home again. That was wonderful. She taught me that I must be active in the church to be a happy Christian. It's ironic that shortly after Alice's funeral my husband's company moved out of state, and we went along with them. Who can say the hand of the Lord was not at work in this journey?

Looking back at the way things happened, I know in my heart it was the hand of God that brought me to Yutan to help Alice in her time of need and to help me find my way back into the church. This was where I needed to be. Others may think it just a coincidence, but Ephesians 2:10 tells me differently, "For we are God's workmanship, created in Christ Jesus to do good works, which God prepared in advance for us to do."

All we need to do is listen and obey.

CHAPTER SIX

Life Lessons

I will instruct you and teach you in the way you should go;
I will counsel you and watch over you.
Psalm 32:8

Whether you turn to the right or to the left,
your ears will hear a voice behind you, saying,
"This is the way; walk in it."
Isaiah 30:21

THE PERMISSION SLIP

by Lynn Roaten Terrell, Wichita, Kansas

He'd always been our rebel. Ready to take the road less traveled. "Would you please have a talk with your son?" our pastor's wife begged. When his teacher wanted to know what he would like to make in art class, he replied, "Let's make one of those 'obscene gestures' grown-ups talk about, so I'll know what one looks like."

His second-grade teacher had approached us in desperation. "Please ask Ken not to turn in his homework in "code" quite so often. Even with the key he gives me, it just takes too long to grade his papers."

That same year, democracy was nearly toppled when the sixth-grade gifted students elected him their class president. The school apologized, "We spent a month studying about the sanctity of free elections. Now we have to explain that their class election is not valid. You see, Ken can't serve as president of the sixth grade. He's only in the second grade!"

As he got older, the issues became more complex. We were more frequently challenged by moral or ethical dilemmas. Such talks always ended with "Let's see what the Bible says about that." It became something of a game. A sort of biblical "Name That Tune."

"I can show you in two chapters that dinosaurs roamed the earth with man." Or, "I can tell you in ten verses where the Bible says we can use animal fur for clothing." I would counter with, "That's nothing! In only one verse, I can disprove Einstein's Third Law of Thermodynamics!" I don't even know what a thermodynamic is, but I created an interesting hypothesis with Scripture to back it up! It remains one of our favorite theories for discussion.

So when Ken, now eighteen, strolled in that afternoon, plopped down to pull off his running shoes, and asked, "What are you doing, Mom?" I immediately recognized the opening lines of our after school talks.

I lowered my favorite part of the newspaper, the crossword, and he casually tossed a crinkled piece of paper toward me. I recognized it immediately. It was the "permission slip." I hated them! I had signed hundreds for summer camps, field trips, flu shots, an ear piercing or two. There were also those for twenty-one operations, and dozens more when they mistakenly thought our son had leukemia. Oh, how I had waited for the day it would all end! Six months before, on Ken's eighteenth birthday, I had joyfully sung "Happy Birthday to You," followed by a rousing ad lib of "And I'll never have to sign another permission slip as long as I live."

"What's that for?" I inquired. "Why are you bringing me a permission slip? You're over eighteen."

"It's a release form for my trip to the Navajo Reservation at Four Corners, remember? They asked for your signature because I am still on your insurance. Four Corners is a long way away from a major medical facility."

Four Corners? Medical facility? There was a pregnant pause. What was wrong with this picture? . . . FOUR CORNERS?! Suddenly, I dropped my crossword puzzle and flipped back to the front page of the newspaper. For days, the headlines had flashed the same frantic message: Navajo Youth Claimed by Mystery Illness. That afternoon's paper echoed the alarm: Another Teen Struck Down at Four Corners.

I shoved the newspaper under his nose. "What's the matter with them, anyway? They still expect you to go to Four Corners? Don't they read the papers? People are dropping dead out there." I shrieked. "You're not going!"

"I'm going, whether anyone else goes, or not," he responded, in a well-modulated tone.

"Why?" I demanded.

"Because I promised them I would. Remember? When I went to teach last year, I told them I would go back and help remodel their church." Picking up the pen and shoving it assertively toward me, he added, "You know, I don't need your consent, but I would like it."

When he was growing up and the issues were simpler, I always seemed to have so many clever answers. Where were they now, when I really needed them? The discussion was rapidly heating up, and the more hostile I became, the more determined he was.

"Remember?" I was searching. "Remember last year, you postponed shoulder surgery to do mission work with the Indians, and I signed the release anyway? Against my better judgment, I might add. This time, people are dying. Young people, your own age. You'd be crazy to expose yourself to that disease. Why, they don't even know whether this thing is carried by air, water, animals, human beings. . . . No!" I said, tossing the permission slip toward him. "Go if you must, but don't expect my endorsement."

"Mom?" he inquired carefully, deliberately, pacing the question for maximum effect. "Did Jesus go to the lepers, or did He wait for them to come to Him?"

Where did he come up with this stuff, anyway? I wondered. Now he was actually throwing Scripture in my face!

"Well. . .Jesus wasn't my son," I shot back.

And then that handsome young man broke into the dimpled "gotcha" kind of grin he's so famous for and calmly replied, "But Mary let Him go!"

So, as I signed that last permission slip, I realized that I was not only "letting him go," but I was also "letting go of him." And I can prove that was the right thing to do in only part of a verse: "Go ye, therefore, into all the world. . ."

THE BROWN PAPER BAG

by Heather Collins-Hamilton, Collierville, Tennessee

Having recently left an abusive marriage and gotten a divorce, I was told by my daughter's pediatrician that I should consider seeking counseling to help Hope through her emotional problems. Instead, I moved us across the state and enlisted the help of my parents. Hope relaxed in their presence and reveled in the attention of her grandparents.

Later that summer, my father died. Actually, he committed suicide. I couldn't find the words to explain my father's suicide in toddler terms because I didn't understand it myself. My grief spilled over to Hope, and she became very angry at the sudden change in her mom and the recent changes in her life. She felt betrayed at losing her dad and then losing Granddaddy.

As a new divorcée, my bitterness toward my ex-husband was palpable. Added to that were my mixed feelings of love and anger toward my father for his suicide. Unfortunately, my anger and cynicism expanded to include all beings of the opposite sex. Hope, whose antennae-like perception picked up my feelings, became a confirmed cynic in her own right—fearful of all men.

"Promotion Sunday" at our church is the day when children are promoted to the next grade level and meet their new Sunday school teacher for the upcoming year. A short, slender man with sandy brown hair and wide, hazel eyes greeted us. He introduced himself as Grant, the teacher for the three-year-old classroom. My heart sank as I watched Hope hug the wall on the opposite side of the room. She refused to join the curious children huddled around Grant, who held a large brown paper bag in his hands as he asked them if they wanted to see what was inside. He proceeded with his object lesson without approaching Hope or insisting she participate.

At one point, I noticed Grant found a moment to make eye contact with Hope and extend a kind smile as he continued the Bible lesson. At the end of the Sunday school lesson, Hope still stood with her back against the wall; her hands groping the plaster behind her as she edged her way out of the room, suspiciously eyeing Grant. Again, Grant offered a warm smile.

The next Sunday, Hope reluctantly returned to the door of her Sunday school class. She was the last child to arrive. With much coaxing from Grant's wife, Maureen, she agreed to go inside. Grant's brown paper bag held a puzzle piece which he allowed Hope to place into the puzzle. Hope's addition to the puzzle completed a picture of an old, one-room church with white wooden siding, a green roof, and a tall steeple. The church sat atop a hill in the countryside. Grant used the puzzle to illustrate to the children that just as every piece of the puzzle was important to the whole puzzle picture, so was each child important to the household of faith. As brothers and sisters in Christ, they were each an important "piece" of the household of faith. It was a wonderful analogy.

After admiring the puzzle, I described where I would be sitting in the sanctuary should Maureen need to find me. I walked to worship service and sat down in the back pew on the far right nearest the door. I prayed that Hope would be spared from anxiousness, and I prayed for the couple teaching the three-year-old Sunday school class.

At the end of worship service, I walked down the hall toward the Sunday school wing of the building with the other parents who were retrieving their children. Grant knelt to tell Hope good-bye. To my surprise, Hope wrapped her arms around Grant's neck, planted a kiss on his cheek, and skipped into the hallway toward me.

As we walked hand in hand to the car, Hope said, "You know, Mom, Mr. Grant's got kids. He's a real daddy, and we are all part of God's family." I brushed away a tear of thankfulness.

For many Sundays thereafter, Hope eagerly attended Grant's Sunday school class. She absorbed Scriptures and simple Christian concepts from Grant's "Brown Bag Bible Stories." One Sunday, each child was given a paper bag of his own that contained a donut and a donut hole. Grant explained that the donut hole symbolized that they were children of God, whose love was like a never ending circle—just like the one that was formed by the donut ring. The donut hole fit perfectly inside the donut, completing the relationship between them and God. The children savored every word of Grant's lesson!

I found myself looking forward to the lessons that emerged from Grant's brown bag. One week, Grant demonstrated the detriments of anger with a skein of yarn and a pair of scissors. Grant instructed the children to extend their hands. He bound their hands together with the yarn and said, "Anger can control your life. Pray about it. Then let it go." Using the scissors to trim away the yarn, he freed their hands from entanglement and explained the healing power of prayer.

What a U-turn in our lives this man brought about! I was learning right along with Hope, and she was becoming a happy, well-adjusted young lady. God was surely watching over Hope and me as He allowed us to be in the right place at the right time to meet Grant. As it says in Romans 8:28 (RSV), we know that "In everything God works for good with those who love him, who are called according to his purpose."

Several years later, I bumped into Grant and Maureen while

Christmas shopping at the mall. For the first time, I shared with them what had occurred in our lives during the time Hope was in his Sunday school class. I expressed my heartfelt appreciation for the positive impact his class had upon my young daughter and upon myself. A tear streaked Grant's face. I was shocked when he thanked me for the opportunity to make a difference in my child's life!

I discovered that Maureen had been present to support Grant's effort in teaching the Sunday school class because Grant had never taught preschoolers before in his life! A victim of corporate downsizing, Grant had been unemployed for the previous sixteen months and was struggling with low self-esteem and depression. He had volunteered to teach the three-year-old Sunday school class as a way to combat his despair and to contribute to our church in the only way that he felt he could, considering his limited financial resources. God certainly works in mysterious ways. Not only was Hope turned into a happy child, Grant's experiences with her and her classmates prompted him to change career paths. Grant entered the teaching profession.

Written by an unknown author are words which ring true, "The greatest gift a child can receive is a good teacher early in life." Hope received Grant, and together we received God, the greatest teacher of them all.

Previously published in the Portales News-Tribune, *May 7, 2000*

FOOTPRINTS ON MY HEART

by Joan Clayton, Portales, New Mexico

Jimmy was big for his age. He towered above my other second-grade students and outweighed them by at least twenty pounds. Being so robust and strong made him the number one choice for soccer at recess, but the game always ended up with complaints and skinned knees. "Jimmy knocked me down! Jimmy made me bump my head. Jimmy tore my shirt. Jimmy kicked the ball in my face."

I tried several methods. Making Jimmy the referee was not a good choice. That trick put Jimmy in the thick of the game. I changed "free play" into directed activities only to hear: "When are we going to get to play soccer?" I banned soccer playing for awhile, only to hear the same complaints about Jimmy's roughness on the playground.

Jimmy was a sweet child. He loved to play, and he really didn't mean to hurt another child. It just kind of happened because of his size and awkwardness. I couldn't take Jimmy's recesses away. I didn't want to be on him about his roughness all the time either. I prayed for guidance. I needed wisdom in providing the best I could for each child.

One day Jimmy groaned to me, "Nobody likes me. Nobody plays with me. I don't have any friends." Jimmy had tears in his eyes, and I could feel his hurt. Rejection is so painful, especially from peers. I began to talk to Jimmy. I was praying inside of me for the right words.

"Jimmy, you are a very special boy," I said. "You are big and strong, and that's good. But you see, the other children are much smaller, and they are not big and strong like you. I know you don't mean to run into them or accidentally bump someone." Suddenly, God's inspiration came to me loud and clear. "Jimmy, since you are so strong, why don't I make you the 'class bodyguard'? You can watch over the children. You can be my assistant. When you see someone playing too rough or getting into trouble, you can gently remind them of our playground rules. Then you can show them how to play safely. Jimmy, you can show them how someone can be big and strong, yet soft and gentle, too!"

Jimmy loved the idea. He could hardly wait for the next recess. Neither could I! I was overcome with gratitude for an answered prayer as I watched Jimmy mingle among the children. He walked around with a big smile on his face, protecting, helping, and defending. If he accidentally stepped on a toe or brushed against someone, he immediately said, "I'm sorry. Are you okay?"

I thrilled to the children's reaction. They became extremely receptive and were visibly touched that Jimmy was cheering them on. As the end of school approached, the children began to hope they would be in Jimmy's room in third grade. On the last day of school, I announced the teachers the children would have for third grade. There were many "hoorays" for those who were going to be in Jimmy's new room and many disappointments for those who were not. This reaction was far removed from how things had been at the beginning of the school year. Jimmy told me good-bye, hugged me real tight, and ran to the bus. I ran to my classroom and cried.

I cried tears of thankfulness for my ability to teach these precious children, tears of gratefulness for what God had done in Jimmy's life this past year, and tears of hopefulness that He would continue to work not only in Jimmy's life, but in the lives of each child God put in my care. And I prayed that He would continue to "inspire" me to touch their tiny souls in ways only He can.

After the third grade, Jimmy changed schools, and I lost track of him. Three years later I received a phone call from him. It was in the middle of summer vacation. I was surprised but glad to hear from him; he would be entering the seventh grade and sounded so mature from the little boy I once knew. "Hi, Mrs. Clayton! This is Jimmy. Remember me? I just wanted to call and tell you good-bye. We're moving to Kentucky. I'll never forget you, Mrs. Clayton. You should see me now. I'm even bigger and stronger! Thank you for teaching me that I can be big and strong, yet soft and gentle, too."

That lesson on the playground had stayed with him over the years, and although I was deeply touched that he wanted me to know it, I was more touched by how my prayers were answered, how God so often changed these little lives in ways only He could. I was merely His messenger.

From first grade to graduation to adult life, I keep receiving blessings from my former students. As I write this, I distinctly remember another incident that happened many years ago.

We were playing "Follow the Leader." I was the "leader." The playground was sandy. Everywhere I stepped the children stepped. In my mind's eye, I can still see their tiny footprints on mine. After thirty-one years of teaching, I understand how I may have touched their lives, but will they ever know how they changed mine? Will they ever know they also left their tiny footprints on my heart? God bless them all.

A YOUNG MAN CALLED CLINTON

by Dorothy Rieke, Julian, Nebraska

Even after children "leave the nest," they often require their parents' support and physical involvement. Recently our daughter, who had resided in Omaha for ten years, decided to move. Of course, we immediately offered help. After we cleaned out the stock trailer and pickup, we left early one fall morning for the large city about sixty miles away. About an hour later, we pulled into the parking lot of our daughter's apartment complex.

As we entered our daughter's studio apartment, we were amazed that she had accumulated so much. Boxes were stacked to the ceiling on two sides of the room! I wondered if we would ever finish moving her in one day. Not being as young as I once was, I dreaded the trips up and down three steep flights of stairs. However, when Cindy explained, "A young man from my church will soon be here to help," I breathed a sigh of relief. Feeling thankful for another helper, I started carrying boxes down the stairs to load in the pickup and trailer. Huffing and puffing, up and down the stairs I went.

Suddenly my attention was drawn to another person helping. His tall, thin figure spryly ran up the stairs to the apartment and rushed back down carrying boxes. As he loaded the trailer, I realized that he knew exactly how to pack the trailer to get the most out of the space.

This young man, different from those neatly dressed young people who attended our small town church, was tall with long black curly hair partially covered with a man's kerchief tied pirate style. Dark eyes peered out of a bearded face. He was dressed in clean but faded jeans and shirt. To be quite honest, if I had met this fellow in an alley at night, I would have taken off at a brisk pace—a very brisk pace.

My daughter, bringing another load downstairs, took time to introduce her friend, Clinton, a member of her church. It seemed that some members in her church's "Twenties Class" regularly volunteered to assist the old and young alike who needed help. We greeted Clinton, telling him we were glad to have his help.

As the morning progressed, we discovered that no load was too heavy for Clinton. Soon my husband was asking his advice about moving certain items and was talking nonstop with him as they carried some of the heavier furniture downstairs. I don't know exactly at what point we both accepted Clinton, but before we reached our daughter's new home, we were both thinking that he was a fine young man.

After the boxes were carried into the new house, Cindy opened her purse prepared to pay Clinton for three hours of very hard labor. Clinton spoke up quickly, "As long as God provides for my needs, I will not charge for helping people." In the next minutes, we begged him to accept payment, but he would not. I even told him I would like to help God a bit to supply his needs, but he was adamant. Looking at his clean but worn jeans, we understood that he was not particularly interested in material possessions.

Later, after staying to help my husband make some minor repairs to the house, he joined us for lunch. As we sat around a makeshift table preparing to eat, he said grace for the food. During the meal, he confided that his parents recently became members of his church. He also told us that he and his parents met each week for a Bible study.

Clinton's own story was another surprise. After graduation from high school, he lived in a pretty "loose house" with other young people. He was aware of the presence of sin but put it from his mind until he accepted Jesus Christ as his Savior, at which point he turned his life around and had not looked back since.

In a world often distorted by those doing for themselves and never thinking of others, we discovered a young man, not raised in a Christian home, who had fully embraced religion and its principles—shunning the shimmering hypnotic gleam of material possessions. He was really applying biblical knowledge to his daily activities. More than that, his actions that day touched every worker—influencing their lives.

After this experience, my husband and I learned better how not to judge. Sadly, in the past, first impressions and appearance had, at times, governed our behavior toward others. No more would we fail to see the whole person. Clinton, without realizing it, helped us make a U-turn of actually walking the talk of biblical principles. He provided a lesson in Christian living that most of us wish we could duplicate had we the courage and the opportunity.

"Judge not, that ye be not judged. For with what judgment ye judge, ye shall be judged: and with what measure ye mete, it shall be measured to you again."—Matthew 7:1–2 (KJV)

"Let us not therefore judge one another any more: but judge this rather, that no man put a stumblingblock or an occasion to fall in his brother's way."—Romans 14:13 (KJV)

NO ONE IS EVER TRULY BROKEN

by Gil Stadley, Paynesville, Minnesota

Several years ago, my wife and I were visiting her family in Okinawa, Japan. A friend of ours, a fellow Christian, asked us to visit Miss Uema, a former coworker of mine. Miss Uema had recently retired and was making plans to do some long-awaited traveling when she suddenly became very ill. Japanese doctors, not being able to find out what ailed her, sent her to the U.S.A. where it was discovered she had Lou Gehrig's disease. I had not seen her in over twenty years, yet somehow my wife and I felt compelled to pay her a visit.

We were at a loss how to approach this woman during our visit. Miss Uema was a woman who did not know God and was now diagnosed with a terminal illness. How would we share the gospel with her and tell her of God's love? Nevertheless, we visited her, shared memories, sang gospel songs, and read Scriptures. Before leaving, we gave her a Japanese edition of Philip Yancey's book *Where Is God When It Hurts?* We prayed God would touch her heart, and we continued praying for her after we returned to the United States.

Several months later, we received a call from our friends in Okinawa. The Lord had created a miracle U-turn in Miss Uema's life! After seeing the love of Christ through the many Christians who visited her faithfully and witnessed to her, Miss Uema had accepted Christ as her Savior. She wanted the love that had been shared with her for herself and within the month was baptized. Praise the Lord for His mighty power!

Two years later, we had the great privilege of visiting with her again. Her illness had progressed considerably, and this time she was in a Christian hospital, unable to move any part of her body except to blink. A single tear greeted us. Yet, she had the most beautiful smile you could imagine!

We spent a few hours with her and came to learn how she had come to this Christian facility. It seems that patients in the room she had previously shared, in another hospital entirely, wanted to know more about this loving God after seeing the constant flow of Christians coming to visit her. A neighboring Christian doctor was so moved at discovering this that he was inspired to build a wing onto his hospital. There, patients like Miss Uema could live out their days in a medical facility that would love them and allow them to have daily Christian fellowship. Other patients wanted to go with her, having witnessed God's love in action. In no time, the new wing was filled with patients praising the Lord.

Here was a woman who could no longer move, who could not serve God outwardly, but who could simply smile and love God in silent prayer. She reminded us that God loves everyone, no matter what shape we are in, and He will never forsake us. There will come a day when Miss Uema will have a perfect body, with no more pain and suffering. Until that time, she is a living testimony to the power of the Lord Jesus Christ and how He loves us as we are and will always remain faithful!

Even though we have always walked with God, this life story of Miss Uema created a U-turn in our lives. My wife and I have learned how important it is to see people through God's eyes and that nothing, no matter how small, done in the name of the Lord is without value. All of us are "broken" in some way, but that is when God steps in and touches our hearts and souls and helps heal us. He can always be depended upon to help us turn around and chart a new direction for our life. For as it says in Ephesians 3:20: "With God's power working in us, God can do much more than anything we can ask or imagine" (author's paraphrase).

CROWNS WORTH SEEKING

by Marilyn Phillips, Bedford, Texas

I am the coach of a varsity cheerleaders team. My squad has outstanding skills and more often than not wins first place at cheerleader competitions. Until recently. . .when much to our amazement and to the astonishment of the crowd, my girls were not awarded the coveted title and the huge trophy that went with it. The varsity cheerleaders had never experienced such a disappointment. We held hands and prayed together.

While we prayed, I thought back to a time when winning the trophy and prestige that went with it meant everything to me.

I had been a consistent winner of high school beauty contests for many years. Each contest I won brought another huge trophy, rhinestone crown, and moment of glory. I kept the trophies in prominent positions in my apartment so they could easily be seen. They made me feel like I was a beautiful and special person.

That was until a devastating fire destroyed them all. How I had mourned their loss and questioned God as to how He could take away these things that had been so dear to me. In despair, I began searching the Bible for answers. . .and found many.

I questioned what type of crown is considered worthy in the eyes of God and read in Proverbs 14:24 (RSV) "the crown of the wise is their wisdom." Next I wondered how one might gain wisdom and read in Proverbs 4:8–9 (NLT) "If you prize wisdom, she will exalt you. Embrace her and she will honor you. She will present you with a beautiful crown." In 1 Peter 5:4 (KJV) I was promised that one day I would "receive a crown of glory that fadeth not away." And the best was found in 2 Timothy 4:8 (NLT) "And now the prize awaits me—the crown of righteousness that the Lord, the righteous Judge, will give me on that great day of his return." And not just to me, but also to all those whose lives show they are eagerly looking forward to His coming back again.

I soon realized that along with my trophies, I had many other material crowns and treasures in my life like my job and my car. Although these things are important, when they become the focal point of your life, they block any meaningful relationship with God. God had used a fire to change my attitude toward worldly recognition and material objects.

I thought about all this as we prayed in defeat. Then, I openly talked to my girls.

The day my squad of varsity cheerleaders failed to place first, I was able to share what God had revealed to me—that sometimes God has other plans, and His plans are always right.

News quickly reached us after the competition that proved this to be true.

We learned the winning team had traveled from a flood-stricken area to come to this competition. There was even one girl on the winning team who had lost her house and every worldly possession in the flood. We were humbled at how they had come through such adversity to win, and my team felt compassion for the winning girls.

All eyes were on my varsity cheerleaders as they graciously congratulated and hugged the winners. Tearfully, we prayed for the other team.

I shared with my girls that God was in control, and any team could have won the competition trophy that day. However, what we seek should not be worldly honors. The character of my cheerleader squad was strengthened, realizing that God knew we could handle defeat. Knowing God was in control helped us focus on His will for our team, instead of focusing on the fact that we were not awarded a trophy for an outstanding performance at the competition.

What I discovered twenty years ago through a fire in my apartment still remains true today; the trophies that are worth seeking are eternal, and we have the promise to receive the crown of life.

Could there be anything better?

THE STAND OF CEDAR

by Amy Jenkins, Wauwatosa, Wisconsin

Once I fought my way off public assistance, I didn't know how to enjoy life. At only twenty, I'd found myself in a deep, dark hole. I was determined to make up for the mistakes that led me to early marriage, divorce, single parenthood, and lack of job skills. I devised a plan to quickly get an education that would provide a career opportunity and a livable wage. For nine months, I accepted welfare while studying to become a licensed practical nurse. After that, I worked full time, bought a house, and continued in college until my daughter was in high school. By then I was an R.N. with bachelor's and master's degrees.

A decade later, I married a physician and was given a surprise blessing, a baby boy, who brought an unanticipated level of joy. We moved to a larger home on a gracious parkway facing a small stretch of woods and a river. I still hadn't learned how to slow down or to stop struggling. Years of double shifts, full-time college loads, mowing the lawn, helping with homework, planning children's parties, and trying to excel at everything had turned me into a machine. My cure for everything was hard work. My new interests in gardening and bird-watching seemed frivolous. I could not, however, squelch these new interests and was compelled to pursue them. So I made a garden.

With enticements of native prairie plants and a few bird feeders, our yard began to attract wondrous visitors. I pored through *Peterson's Guide* to identify the spirited bands of chickadees, the noble woodpeckers, and the crimson cardinals who made me sigh in awe every time they entered the yard. Every week, one or two more species came. I bored my family and friends with accounts of sighted species, how I attracted them, which would stay for the winter, and which were nesting. I still had one nagging wish. Every time I used the Peterson's Guide, I was drawn to a picture between the vireos and the thrushes. It was the cedar waxwing, a sleek, crested bird with red and yellow accents. The guide listed them as occasional visitors to feeders, but they were mainly insect eaters. There was no way to attract them. They would come if they wanted to. I wondered through my first year of birding if I would ever see one.

Like most everything in my life, "birding" was not a leisure activity. No, I gave it the maximum effort. I tracked the migratory patterns and bought appropriate seed. Investigations revealed all sunflower seed was not the same. Cardinals prefer the striped seed, not the black. Golden finches turned out to be finicky about their thistle and wouldn't eat it if it became damp. When attracting wrens, I mounted two houses about twenty feet apart, as one acts as a decoy home. A combination of baffles, special positioning of feeders, and cayenne pepper solution foiled the squirrels. I spent more time studying, filling and washing feeders, and fighting squirrels than enjoying the birds themselves. This was how most of my life was lived—too busy to enjoy.

One late summer day, I uncharacteristically decided to take a solitary walk to the river; I didn't even take the dogs. As it was near dusk, the attacking mosquitoes made me question the wisdom of my jaunt. The river drew me over, and I sat on a rock and looked in and thought of nothing. It was a welcome respite for my overoccupied mind. The water soaked up my errant thoughts and made me just "be." I kept sitting and looking, and then way down the river I saw them. A huge swarm of birds was sweeping down back and forth over the river. I waited for a good twenty minutes for them to make their way to my stretch of the river. Sitting quietly anywhere for two minutes, let alone twenty minutes, was unusual for my frenetic life. Yet I felt a peace in my soul that this quiet time was very much needed—that somehow, I needed to slow down.

It's a wonder bugs didn't fly into my gaping mouth as the birds got close enough for me to identify. There must have been two hundred sleek, crested birds with yellow-tipped tails and red-tipped wings. The cedar wax-wings I had longed to see stayed right in front of me eating mosquitoes. They were even more beautiful than their Peterson's picture.

As I smiled through my tears, I remembered a Bible verse: "The LORD, the LORD God, [is] merciful and gracious, longsuffering, and abounding in goodness and truth" (Exodus 34:6 NKJV). My gracious God gave me this beautiful display of abundance to teach me that everything does not have to be a struggle. God wants me to live abundantly. My long-suffering Lord, who had given me two awesome children, a wonderful husband, a beautiful home, and everything I had ever really wanted, was still trying to convince me that He can bless play and joy and rest just as He does hard work.

I walked out of the dark woods, covered with mosquito bites, with a tear-stained face and the ability to take a deep breath and a few minutes every day to watch the birds in the presence of God's grace. I have learned to "be still," to take time to enjoy, and be thankful for all the Lord has given me.

I have never seen another cedar waxwing.

LAUNDRY LINES AND BROKEN CLOTHESPINS

by Michele Howe, LaSalle, Michigan

There are two tasks in this life which make my hair stand on end when-ever I contemplate them: grocery shopping and hanging laundry. In the past several years, my husband has taken me off the grocery shopping hook ever since he offered to do most of our buying at a warehouse store near his school. Every now and then, I still am required to enter a grocery store and can almost feel the hackles rising when I get to the checkout counter. But it's not negotiable—eating, that is. I just simply cannot reconcile paying so many hard-earned dollars for something that vanishes within twenty-four to forty-eight hours. If the food lasted longer, stayed fresher, or perhaps even did a bit to earn its own keep, I might be willing to not begrudge our food budget on a regular basis. Be that as it may, none of the above scenarios is likely, so I'd best make my peace with the grocer.

But hanging laundry on the line is an entirely different matter. It has caused me great mental stress through the years. My husband qui-etly opens our electric bill, and I can almost (but not quite) hear him calculating how many students he tutored before and after school, how many boys he lectured on not using the headlock move during wrestling practice, and how many coupons he collected—to pay for my extravagance in using the clothes dryer. It is a mystery. For some un-known reason, our bill really is higher than anyone else around us. We have checked. Still, I get that "I'm really wasting my time, talents, and energy here" attitude whenever I trek outdoors with clothes, basket, and pins in hand.

I have it bad in the attitude department. As I go through the rou-tine of wiping off the clothesline which overnight is covered with cob-webs, checking the ground for any misdirected horse manure, and looking into the sky for any sign of rain, I find myself sighing, quite loudly and audibly. "Won't someone see my distress and rescue me?" I desperately plead. With no sign of relief in sight, I grab the first piece of clothing within reach, pick out a couple of clothespins, and start hanging. If it's a really good day, not one clothespin will crack under my tender grasp, the wind will be blowing. . .but not too hard, and I won't find a spider making its lodgings under the clothespin's wire spring right after I squish it on my clean white T-shirt.

Still, even on the best of days, rules, rules, and more rules run through my mind. I hear my husband reminding me that the heavy stuff goes on the ends of the lines, hang the shirts from the bottom, etc., etc., etc. . . , yeah, yeah, yeah. . . , my mind rebels, my emotions rebuke, and my mouth mutters, well, I won't go into that foible. Once the deed is done, I head back inside to begin other less painful chores on my "to-do" list. But in the back of my mind, I continue to hear that ominous chant from somewhere out back, "We're still here, we're almost dry, we're waiting for you. . . ." Why? Oh, why, can't I escape that haunting refrain even as my hands turn to other more deserving accomplishments?

Recognizing that being indoors and busy offers no retreat, I acquiesce and head back to the clothesline. With the hanging clothespin carrier in hand (a loving gift from a friend who feared for my sanity), I begin removing every last article of laundry all while thinking about how stiff the towels will feel on my wet skin after showering, how wrinkled the pants have become so they'll require ironing, how all the invisible pollen is sticking to my daughter's sheets so she will be wheezing later on. . .enough!

Enough is enough, I say. True. . .enough. But exactly what "enough" am I referring to? Enough complaining? Enough begrudging? Enough of the pity poor me? Yes, to all of the above. I see the hollow faces of children whose bellies are never full. . .and my children eat like kings. I see the empty eyes of the man whose wife has left him. . .and my husband lies beside me every night. I see a friend whose body is wracked with a disabling disease. . .and I am healthy. I see. . .or do I?

All around me are signs and evidences of creative genius, marvelous workmanship, and abundant opportunity. The question remains, do I see? Honestly, realistically, humbly, do I see what blessings I have in my life? I wonder. How often do I look at what others have, what others have done, what others appear to be, and compare my life with theirs, my wealth with theirs, my accomplishments with theirs? All too often I am guilty of this, and every time I foolishly make a comparison, my life seems a bit shallower and a great deal more unattractive. That well-known saying "circumstances aren't important. . .it's our attitude toward the circumstances which matters" is so undeniably true.

Taking pleasure in the simple, daily, repetitive tasks is the key to enjoying life in the here and now. Gaining satisfaction from the insignificant, grungy chores we're responsible for each day is a pivotal point both in attitude and maturity. Seeing life in its entirety through the many small, seemingly trifling acts of service, love, and faith is the truest act of worship to which we can aspire. Each of us has our own prickly areas of life which bring out the worst in us. But we can see past the outrageous grocery prices and the stiff laundry by recognizing the work of our hands means someone we love won't go without. The labor we disdain means another won't have to work so hard. The positive outlook we exhibit means others can get a glimpse of heaven's love. . . and when they do, they'll be able to truly "see," too.

So, today, if the sun is shining, my hands (and heart) will be eager to offer some ready service to those under my care. I'll happily hang every piece of laundry, wind or no, and spiders beware!

THE PERSPECTIVE OF A PANSY

by Laura Smith, Roswell, Georgia

In Atlanta, we have the luxury of planting pansies in the fall and viewing their curious faces all winter long. That is how my grandma described their blossoms—as "faces." You know what? She was right. If you look into a pansy's velvet petals you can see its eager expression peeking out at you. It was my grandmother's love for this flower which drew me to *Viola tricolor hortensis* when I was a little girl. My favorites were the white petals with purple centers, or "faces." They remain my favorite flower today.

Since pansies are annuals, last year's flowers had long since died and been pulled from the ground, never to be seen again. I hadn't taken the time to plant even one flat of pansy seedlings this fall. Actually, I hadn't found the time to do much of anything but work since September. My job had become especially demanding due to a project which required me to fly weekly to Washington, D.C. Between airports, delayed flights, cancellations, taxicabs, trains, and countless hotel rooms, I hadn't spent enough time with my husband, hadn't returned phone calls from my parents, hadn't sent birthday cards to my dearest friends, and certainly hadn't made time to focus on God and His plans for my life. Most importantly, I hadn't taken the necessary time to come to terms with the death of my beloved grandma.

Perhaps by skipping the whole pansy planting process this autumn, I was putting off facing the reality that Grandma, the only grandparent I had ever known, had died. My connection between her and the flowers was so strong. I told myself I was just "too busy" for gardening enough times that I convinced myself it was true.

As I drove home from the airport one chilly November evening, I was overwhelmed by an empty pang in my heart. It had begun as a slight ache that Thursday and had built up to a deep hollow throb after five straight days of deadlines, lists, conference calls, and meetings.

I hadn't allowed any time for myself to read, visit with friends and family, or even to pray. I had tried to ignore this vacuous feeling inside of me. I had just kept going and going, like a robot following programmed commands, forgetting about all of the things in life that gave it deeper meaning.

The pain was especially great this particular evening due to a canceled flight which delayed my getting home until long after my lonely husband was already in bed. After fighting eight lanes of stop-and-go traffic for over an hour, caused by what appeared to be a fatal accident, I arrived home frazzled. As I pulled into my driveway, my headlights shone into the empty flower beds. I glimpsed something white resting on the ground. I parked my car in the garage and walked around to the front yard to collect what I assumed was a piece of garbage and throw it away. But I did not find any trash. Instead I found a lone white pansy with a purple face flourishing in a barren bed of pine straw.

The determined flower had fought all odds to spring from a ripped up root, which is not bred for regrowth, and to return this year. It didn't seem possible, and maybe it wasn't. Yet, here was a perfect posy grinning at me and asking me from its remarkable face why I, too, couldn't break through the soil and let myself bloom. If loved ones who have passed away can speak to us from heaven, I knew this was Grandma's way of letting me know that although she had left this earth, she wasn't really gone. Just like the pansy, which had been pulled from the dirt yet was still blossoming, my grandmother's spirit would always flourish inside my heart and with God.

Grandma would never have put work first. Her family and friends were the priorities in her world. She didn't know the meaning of timetables or of deadlines. Although her life was simple, she was always happy and saw only the good in others and the beauty in the world around her.

Hers was an example God would be proud of, one that I should follow. Perhaps it was time to open up my heart and my eyes to the important things around me, to fill up the empty hole inside me with the nourishment which only God could give me. Work could wait. Life, as the pansy showed me (through God's miraculous powers), could not.

CHAPTER SEVEN

Grace

*All over the world this gospel is bearing fruit and growing,
just as it has been doing among you since the day you heard it
and understood God's grace in all its truth.*
Colossians 1:6

*For it is by grace you have been saved, through faith—
and this not from yourselves, it is the gift of God.*
Ephesians 2:8

LOOKING FOR GOD AT
CHARLES DEGAULLE AIRPORT

by Cheryl Norwood, Canton, Georgia

There we were, in Charles DeGaulle Airport, Paris, France, Sunday morning, 6:00 A.M., bone-tired from an eight-hour flight from our home in the Atlanta, Georgia, area. The seats on the plane had been very comfortable, the service was great, but we were one row away from the lavatories, a popular place on a long flight. We would just doze off and then hear the door open or close or have someone stumble into us. We never got more than a few minutes' uninterrupted sleep.

In the airport, we were as helpless as children. We knew only a few phrases in French. We almost turned this trip down due to that very fact but then decided we needed a break. We both worked full time outside of the home in high stress positions. In addition, our families had both been going through health crises and struggles. Maybe a free trip to France would help renew us!

Our enthusiasm for this wonderful gift began to drain with each passing moment as we waited in the airport terminal for our train. We had thought to exchange dollars for francs before we left, but at 6:00 A.M., nothing was open anyway. We were thirsty, but all the vending machines took only coins. We tried several times to get change from other airport inhabitants, but none understood our limited French or cared enough to be of any help. We found a bench to sit on, but it was hard, shiny, slick sheet metal. My gabardine slacks made it difficult to sit comfortably because I kept sliding off the bench onto the floor! I finally piled up our entire set of luggage in front of me as a barricade.

Miserable and concerned that this was a sign of what the rest of our week would be like, I began to pray. "Please, God, help it to get better. Please help Mike have a good time. Right now things don't look too good, and we are tired and hungry and anxious. Give us Your peace." When I opened my eyes, I noticed Mike had a big, goofy grin on his face. "What's so funny?" I asked.

He answered, "Listen to the PA system. Can you hear what they are playing?"

I strained to hear the music. Ray Charles was singing "Georgia on My Mind."

Slowly the same goofy grin slipped across my face. God had heard my feeble little prayer even before I prayed it, and this was His answer. Georgia was on Ray Charles's mind, and two Georgians were on God's mind. Suddenly we both felt better, and we both knew that the next week would be wonderful. It's great to be on God's mind!

SOMETIMES LIFE JUST ISN'T FAIR!

by Pastor John Roberts, Sterling, Colorado

We met Lisa—all three feet of her—when she was introduced to us by a young man named Phil. He had befriended Lisa, led her to the Lord, and brought her with him when he came to visit us.

She had a condition called osteogenesis imperfecta (O.I.). She could not walk or stand. By age sixteen, when we met her, she had reached her full stature and had already exceeded her life expectancy.

Most who saw her would whisper as they turned away, "Isn't that a shame?" Those who actually got to know her saw something else. It was in her eyes. They were. . .well, fascinating, to say the least. One of the effects of O.I. is that it turns the eyes blue—all blue—including the "whites." Yet, more amazing than the color of her all-blue eyes was the fact that there was no hint of bitterness in them, no anger about life's unfairness.

In fact, she didn't seem at all troubled by her condition. It didn't bother her to have Phil carry her around like a sack of potatoes, or tease her about being so tiny, or call her "Old Blue Eyes." She even told jokes about herself.

One Sunday, Phil brought her to our church to sing a solo. He carried her to the platform, seated her on a stool, and went to the piano to accompany her. Here are the words she sang:

"I may not be every mother's dream for her little girl.

"My face may not grace the mind of everyone in the world.

"But that's okay, as long as I can have one wish, I pray.
"When people look inside my life, I want to hear them say,
" 'She has her Father's eyes.' "
I wept then, as I weep now, remembering.

If ever there was someone who could have protested, "It's just not fair," it was Lisa. Yet, I never heard her complain. She knew that expecting life to be fair is undiluted foolishness in this broken world. She taught us that, instead of fairness or justice, we should fix our hope on the grace of God.

One day, at the end of all things, God will balance the scales of justice. Until then, all of life's unfairness is the crucible in which the followers of Jesus testify, not so much to the justice of God, but to His grace. For though we yearn for justice and fairness, what we really need is grace and mercy.

What do we seek from God? His justice? I hope not. Not if we understand what seeking His justice implies. If we were to get justice from God, and not His grace, we would be doomed.

Next time we are tempted to complain "it is just not fair!" remember blue-eyed Lisa, who knew that while life is not fair, God is full of grace.

Which, of course, is what we all really need anyway.

UNPLANNED BLESSING

by Cathy Herholdt, Bothell, Washington

"Pink indicates pregnancy. . . ." I read the instructions on the pregnancy test over and over, hoping to find a mistake. But as I stared at the bright pink results on my own test, I knew there was no mistake. I was pregnant. The moment suddenly became so clear. I fell to my knees and began to pray out loud, pleading with God to let this be a dream. "What am I going to do? Dear God, please help me." I was twenty-four years old, single, and had never felt so totally alone in my life. I must have sat there for an hour, letting reality soak in and feeling the sheer terror of it.

As I sat there on my bathroom floor, crying out to God, a sudden peace flooded my entire body. It seemed so strange, but at the moment of the greatest crisis in my life, I felt calm, like being in the eye of a hurricane. I knew then that there really was a God and that He was going to help me. I kept wavering between panic and peace, hearing Him say in my heart, "Everything is going to work out. Trust Me, I will be with you."

The rest of the day was a blur. I told Bret, my boyfriend of only three months. He, too, was scared but also felt that somehow everything would work out. We knew we should have been more careful. We knew what we did was wrong and irresponsible. Yet what was done, was done. I made an appointment to see my doctor, but I remember little else about that day.

That first appointment with my doctor confirmed my home pregnancy test results. The nurse asked me if I'd like to discuss my "options" or go upstairs and schedule my first OB visit. Abortion was one of those options, but, as if I was being led, I went upstairs and scheduled my first prenatal appointment. The receptionist startled me when she congratulated me as I turned to leave. I thanked her as another bit of reality sank in.

I spent the next few weeks slowly informing relatives and friends about my pregnancy. Mostly people were shocked but supportive. Some suggested we should "take care of the problem" without anyone ever knowing. Bret and I went through the motions of making the decision to keep the baby, even though we felt like this decision had already been made for us. I went to talk to a family planning counselor just to cover my bases. I told her I was done with college, had a good job, as well as a supportive boyfriend and family. The counselor mentioned adoption, but I had already begun to form a deep bond of love with this baby growing inside me.

In the months that followed, my pregnancy progressed, but so did my anxiety about becoming a parent. Once again, God showed me His love through the support offered by other people. Friends and family showered me with gifts, bags of used baby clothes and other necessities, as well as information and advice about parenting. It seemed that everything we needed was provided for us, often from unexpected sources.

Another miracle that took place over the course of my pregnancy was the undying love that grew between Bret and me. I began to see in him all the qualities of a wonderful father and partner. On the day before Easter, in my seventh month of pregnancy, Bret asked me to marry him. We sat in my car outside my little apartment after dinner and a movie. He nervously dug in his pocket for a tiny diamond ring which he offered me, along with his heart. I joyfully and positively accepted. I had always wanted to say "yes" to marriage with such assurance. I knew I wanted to spend my life with him.

I had been attending a nondenominational Christian church since college, but obviously I was not living out what I was being taught when I met Bret and got pregnant. Bret started attending church with me and was as eager for a relationship with God as I was. We both agreed we wanted to take the premarriage class offered at the church, despite our unusual circumstances.

I remember my hand shaking as I called the church office to register for the class. I was so afraid of judgment and condemnation as I asked for the pastor who taught the class. I told him that I was seven months pregnant and wondered if it would be acceptable for us to be in the class. He lovingly reassured me that we were more than welcome in the class. There had been other engaged couples in our situation, and he told me they wanted to help us start our marriage off on the right path. He prayed with me over the phone that day, and we started the class the next week.

Despite our "visible" sin, every one of the ten or twelve couples in the class welcomed us with open arms and made us feel accepted and loved. We began the path of a lifetime together, bringing our newborn daughter, Chelsea, to class with us during the fourth week of a seven-week course. Smiles and coos greeted her as if she belonged there. The love we received in this class was the beginning of a committed walk with God for us both.

On a beautiful August evening, in a garden wedding, Bret and I were married. Three-month-old Chelsea sat in the front row on her grandma's lap. Although we didn't choose the easiest way to start a marriage, I believe that God, through His grace, blessed our little family from the start. He forgave us our sins and opened our eyes.

Chelsea is now almost eight and is a light for God to her family and friends. She is a healthy, happy, beautiful little girl who loves Jesus with all her heart. She already has a complete sense of His love for her and never doubts His presence in her life. This is truly something with which she was born. I know God has great plans for her.

I take no credit for the miracle of Chelsea. It was God's supernatural peace (given to me on my bathroom floor of all places!) that gave me the strength to make the decision I made. In fact, this unplanned pregnancy, which at first appeared to be a crisis, is actually what taught me about God's grace and peace.

Today, Chelsea shares her parents with a precious little sister and a sweet baby brother. I feel blessed to have had this U-turn experience that gave me the knowledge expressed in Romans 8:28, that truly, "In all things God works for the good of those who love him."

LAUGHING WITH GOD ON A BAD HAIR DAY

by Esther Bailey, Phoenix, Arizona

When I started chemotherapy, I thought I was prepared for my loss of hair. I had even quipped to my husband, "Maybe I'll get rid of my dry scalp when my hair comes out."

"It's hardly worth it," Ray replied with a deadpan expression.

From the beginning, I had accepted the news of breast cancer without trauma. Two factors contributed to the sense of peace I experienced throughout each phase of the diagnosis and treatment. A few months earlier, I had been greatly impressed by Dr. Norman Vincent Peale's booklet, "Healing for Loved Ones and for You." The first thing I did when I learned I might have a problem was to reread the faith-building treatise. Any time my faith started to falter, I went back for a refresher course.

Another reason for my upbeat attitude had to do with a statement by my pastor. "Faith that hasn't been tested isn't really faith at all," he said. My life had been quite carefree up to that point. Perhaps it was time for me to learn to deal with adversity.

My surgery went extremely well. They operated on Wednesday, I went home on Thursday, and I attended church on Sunday. I felt surprisingly great!

I elected not to undergo reconstructive surgery because the loss of a breast did not bother me. I simply coined a new slogan: "If you've got it, flaunt it; if you don't, fake it." I was doing okay.

Before starting chemotherapy, I claimed God's promise in Jeremiah 29:11: "I know the plans I have for you, says the LORD, plans for your welfare and not for harm, to give you a future with hope" (NRSV). The verse told me that God would maximize the benefits of chemotherapy and minimize the harmful side effects.

With all that I had going for me, I shouldn't have a problem at all with hair loss, right? After all, if I could handle losing a breast that wouldn't grow back, surely I could deal with a temporary loss of hair.

"Your hair will probably come out two weeks to the day from the first infusion," the nurse had told me.

When I woke up on the morning of the appointed day, my hair was intact. Would it survive a wash? I wondered. As I worked up a lather with the shampoo, my hair began to separate from my scalp. To avoid possibly shedding hair all over the house, I pulled it out by the handfuls. In moments it was gone, and I felt no particular emotion.

Then I looked in the mirror. I was a sorry sight. Looking more like a Martian than an earthling, I quickly donned a turban I had purchased for the occasion. My emotions took a downturn as the day progressed, a situation for which I had not been prepared.

That evening, I lamented the loss of my hair to my husband. For the first time in my battle with cancer, tears began to flow. To me, the turban didn't look much better than my bald head.

"I think you look cute in it," Ray said. When that didn't console me, he added, "I remember seeing Norma Shearer one time in a movie where she wore a turban. She looked pretty and so do you."

Although I appreciated my husband's gallant effort, I still couldn't see it that way. I carried my pity party to bed and didn't sleep well.

My sadness continued the following day. Thumbing through a magazine in the afternoon, an article caught my attention. In dealing with the aging process, the author had looked in the mirror and said, "What's so funny, Lord?"

The scene I pictured in my mind put a different spin on my situation. If God was laughing, why not laugh with Him?

As I looked in the mirror with a smile and sparkling eyes, my self-esteem escalated. I took off the turban and discovered that even Martians look better with a happy face.

Before I started chemotherapy, I had my hair cut short, and I started wearing a wig when I went out in public so people wouldn't notice a drastic change. The wig I purchased at a local salon pretty well matched my hair color and style. I didn't want to wear it all the time, though, because it was uncomfortable and hard to keep up.

Even with a positive attitude, I didn't enjoy wearing a turban or a scarf around the house. When I found a catalog showing lightweight wigs at a nominal cost, I decided to experiment. Measuring instructions indicated I needed a petite size, which turned out to be more comfortable. I ordered a short style in a blond color about three shades lighter than my normal hair.

When I tried on the new wig and styled it, I felt like Cinderella—ready for the ball. "I know blonds have more fun," I told Ray, "because I've been blond for only an hour, and I'm having more fun already."

The next day, I wore my new wig to the hospital for a shot. Looking at me with a question mark, the nurse said, "Bailey?"

"Do you notice anything different?" I asked.

"Yes. The wig. I like it."

The improvement of the new wig over the old one was so remarkable that I ordered two more and scrapped the dowdy-looking one.

Compliments poured in from friends at church. I even received a telephone call from someone who had not been able to speak to me in person. My own hair had never caused that much of a sensation.

A couple of weeks later, an elderly man said to me, "I know you've had lots of comments on your hair, but I want to make one more. It's beautiful!"

I smiled and said, "Thank you." I'm sure God was smiling, too.

So what will happen when my hair grows back in? I don't know. Maybe I'll color it and try to match the style of my wig. Whatever happens, I'll stay plugged in to God's sense of humor, and everything will be all right.

After all, if God can laugh at a bad hair day, who am I not to join in?

A JOURNEY TO MEET THE LORD

By Peggy Whitson, North Aurora, Illinois

It was July in Las Cruces, New Mexico, and I was ten years old. While playing outside, I heard Mom call my name.

"Cissy, would you walk to the baby-sitter's and see if she's able to watch you kids tonight?"

The baby-sitter was only a few blocks away, and the idea of going somewhere, even for an errand, sounded fun. In a generous mood, I asked my younger brothers, Allen and Kinny, if they wanted to go with me. Huge smiles lit up their faces. It was as if I'd given them a gift. Probably not wanting to risk me changing my mind, they ran into the house to grab their shoes.

What a day for a walk! There wasn't enough wind to move a tumbleweed across the road, and the sand burned as it rubbed against my ankles. As the three of us skipped down the sidewalk, laughing, we forgot about the heat—we were having too much fun.

We walked only a short distance when this great idea popped into my head. "Kinny, do you want to see who can walk the fastest?" He accepted my challenge, and as a way to make the race fair, I took two-year-old Allen's hand. About ten minutes into our competition, I turned around to see Kinny ten to fifteen feet behind us. Grinning at the thought of my future victory, I looked ahead again—just in time to see a car jump the curb to the sidewalk. It was going fast and headed right at us. Without even thinking, I jerked Allen and me to the ground of the empty lot next to us.

I knew even before I looked back that Kinny had been hit. I could see his still body lying on the sidewalk. A white picket fence had blocked any chance of escape. Still holding Allen's hand, I ran back to Kinny. His eyes were closed, and his forehead crushed from the tire. I didn't think about what that meant. My mind stopped working, and I couldn't put the pieces together in my head. I wasn't prepared for the probing questions from the reporters and police, seeing Mom's face as I told her what happened, or Kinny's death less than six hours later. Except for the blame I placed on myself because of the accident, I felt numb.

Kinny's death changed me. Through the years, its image played over and over in my mind. Always thinking about what I did—and what I thought I should have done—made the memory of Kinny's tragic death stay vividly clear in my mind. It was a scar on my heart that never went away.

Over twenty years passed before I spoke of Kinny's death, though I relived it daily. Finally, tears fell as the story poured out of me—the hurt seemed fresh, as if his death had happened only days before. My close friend, Len, listened. "Only God can heal the hole that Kinny's death created in you," he told me, and he spoke to me of the Lord.

After more talks with this friend and my husband, Marty, I eventually accepted the Lord into my own life, but the pain of Kinny's untimely death remained a part of me. No matter what I did, I could not fix my heart.

Finally, on one spring day, as I looked at the flowers that sprouted throughout the yard, I felt myself give up. I could fight the pain inside of me no more, and I felt very alone. While driving to the store a little later, the accident enveloped my mind once more. As tears filled my eyes, I cried out, "Lord, I can't take this anymore!"

It was then I heard a quiet voice inside of me say, "You don't have to —I will take it for you." Immediately, a sense of peace came over me, and after twenty-eight years of feeling lost, hope seemed a part of me again.

When I got home that evening, I opened my Bible to read. I looked for no specific Scripture, but my eyes dropped to this verse: "My soul finds rest in God alone; my salvation comes from him. He alone is my rock and my salvation; he is my fortress, I will never be shaken" (Psalm 62:1–2).

In this small passage, I was reminded of what I had forgotten or, perhaps, never knew—the Lord is beside me, and because of His strength, I need never struggle through life's trials on my own. Through God's grace, I was able to let go of the guilt and allow my heart to heal. I needed only to reach for and feel the safety of His arms.

Now when I think of that last walk with my two brothers, it still hurts, but I can smile, too. I view it differently than before. On that hot, summer day so many years ago, it wasn't about who could get to the baby-sitter's first—we were really on a journey to meet the Lord. I thought I would win the race, but I know now that it was Kinny who finished first. I'm catching up, though. My next walk with Kinny won't be in Las Cruces, New Mexico—it'll be at our Lord's home, and we'll be racing down the streets of heaven.

A TRIBUTE TO A "LIFE" HERO

By Michelle Pearson, Leaf River, Illinois

I didn't know Donna very well. I wish I had known her better.

What I did know about her was that she belonged to the same church my family attends. She worked at the school that her young daughters attended. And she was one of the bravest, most courageous people I have ever met.

My first contact with her was at the family day care we had in common. She was my age and just as busy as I was. We both had husbands and children and jobs outside the home and a schedule probably as hectic (if not more so) than any CEO. We never got beyond exchanging pleasantries as we passed each other dropping off or picking up our children.

More than a year ago, I heard that Donna was facing a battle with cancer. And in the months that followed, our church family received regular updates from Donna or her family about her and her health. Sometimes things looked good; other times the news wasn't so bright, but the one continually bright spot through it all was Donna herself. Although I'm sure she wasn't always feeling well, she always looked happy and healthy.

When I was dealing with a painful back problem, she went out of her way to talk to me after church and ask me how I was doing. As I explained my pain, she nodded sympathetically and said, "I know. I get that kind of pain, too. But I think it's my tumor pressing against my spine." She said this as if she were giving me a cookie recipe. I marveled at her candor and acceptance.

When Donna first announced several months ago that her cancer had returned, she said something that will echo in my mind for the rest of my life: "I have no worries." It was at that moment I realized she had something I wanted—an unwavering, unshakable faith in God and His plan for us.

I had wanted to do a feature story on Donna for our local newspaper. I thought her amazing attitude in facing her illness would make a wonderful article. When I asked her about it, though, she said, "Oh, I don't know. I'm really not very good at talking about myself. Besides, I'm terminal. Who would be interested in that?"

If only she had known how many people would be interested in her strength, her courage, her faith. If only she had known how many people, even those who didn't know her well, had been touched and inspired by her. If only she had known how many people would have bought her attitude if there had been a way to bottle it.

Everywhere you look, there are people touted as "heroes." Sports heroes. Movie star heroes. Political or military heroes. They slam-dunk, act, govern, or fight their way to the top, many times without the best of intentions.

Then there are the real heroes, the "life heroes." They are the people who provide us with inspiration, motivation, and encouragement simply by the way they live their lives. They are rare, indeed. How blessed I was to have known one.

CHAPTER EIGHT

Faith and Forgiveness

We live by faith, not by sight.
2 Corinthians 5:7

*"And when you stand praying, if you hold anything
against anyone, forgive him, so that your Father
in heaven may forgive you your sins."*
Mark 11:25

A SIMPLE ACT OF FAITH

by Gerald Eisman, Sarasota, Florida

As I read the announcement of her death, memories flooded back. Her name was Sister Ana Marie, and she was one of the strictest teachers in St. Theresa's Academy, a primary school for good Catholic children and incorrigibles who couldn't function in a public school setting. I guess I was one of the latter.

Considering the reputation I brought along from the public system, I found the easiest way to ease pressures put on me by the Sisters was to volunteer for chores, which I did, often. Except that when I volunteered, it was usually my dad and sometimes my mom that wound up doing the work. I just reaped the rewards.

One hot Friday in early June, as we were packing our books and pads to take home for the weekend, Sister Ana Marie (aka Sister Torquemada) asked, "I was wondering, is there anyone here that might get a parent to drive me to the train station next Saturday? I must be there promptly at 7:00 A.M." Another chance to ingratiate myself and score some more brownie points. My hand shot up. I waved it back and forth while punctuating the action with grunts and a broad grin. "Are you sure your parents won't mind, Mr. Armani?"

"No Ma'am," I said. "My dad will be happy to do it."

"Do what?" my dad exploded when I told him what he'd been volunteered for. "Have you lost your senses? I work seventy hours a week and spend Saturday cleaning and shopping, and you tell Sister that I can take her to the train? That station is twenty-odd miles from here, not counting the distance from our house to St. Theresa's." He fumed at me for a good half hour before he relented and agreed to do it.

At five o'clock on Saturday, I was rudely awakened by Dad. "Up and dressed," he rasped at me. "I want you to know what it feels like to sacrifice your morning off." He pulled the sheet from my body letting the cold morning air touch my warm skin. I yelped, and he smiled. "Very good," he said through clenched teeth. "Very good. The lesson begins."

We picked up Sister Ana Marie "Torquemada" and began the trip to the train station, two towns east of ours. "A very good morning to you, Sister," my dad greeted her, despite what he was feeling.

"If that be God's pleasure," was her terse answer. She took her place in the backseat, placed her one small bag on the seat beside her, and folded her arms across her chest. Staring forward, lips compressed in her usual dour manner, she closed down all paths of communication.

"And where will you be going?" Dad inquired of the good Sister.

"Cleveland," was her succinct response. Out of the corner of my eye, I caught the glare Dad tossed in my direction. His head began to shake back and forth. Boy oh boy, I was in for it when we got home. I was convinced of that. The rest of the trip was made in silence. Dad glowering at the road, me sweating, and Sister staring straight ahead.

When we reached the station, Sister took a seat on a wooden bench at the station house. Dad politely carried her bag over and placed it beside her.

"Have you gotten your ticket?" he asked as politely as he could.

"Not as yet."

"Well, if you will give me your money, I'll purchase it for you."

Sister looked up at Dad. "I have no money."

"No money?" Dad sputtered. "How do you intend to buy a ticket to Cleveland without money?"

"God will purchase my ticket for me," Sister said, confidence embedded in every syllable.

"God? God?" Dad shook his head as if to dislodge an unwanted insect.

"Good luck, Sister," he grunted, then returned to the car, with me trailing after him. He brought the engine to life, jammed the machine into gear with a loud grinding noise, and released the clutch. We lurched ahead. "God's gonna buy her a ticket," he muttered to no one. "Ridiculous!" We drove for several blocks before he looked, or rather, glowered at me. He pulled the car to a stop at the curb. "Did you know about this?"

"No, Sir," I answered honestly. "I sure didn't."

"Do you honestly think anyone will buy her a ticket?"

I hesitated a moment before answering. "I would if I had money," I told him. I reached into my pocket and produced two crumpled one-dollar bills and held them out to him. We looked at each other. "Really.

I would. You told me once, 'Never turn your back on someone less fortunate than you.' Then you said, 'There but for the grace of God, go I.' " We stared at each other some more.

With a suddenness that Dad was noted for, he wrenched the wheel, turned the car around, and headed toward the station. We found Sister Ana Marie seated exactly where we left her. I stood next to the bench while Dad strode to the ticket window. He turned and glared at me again. Sister seemed not to notice.

"Round-trip to Cleveland," I heard him tell the ticket master. He paid for the trip then returned to the bench and did something I never saw him do before. He removed his hat and sat next to Sister as he handed her the ticket.

"I guess you were right about God and the ticket," he said. "Have a safe trip, Sister."

It was a day of wonders. 'Cause then I saw Sister do something I never saw HER do before. She smiled. "I surely thank you, Mr. Armani. You are as good a man as your son is a good boy. God will reward you for this kindness." Sister then resumed her severe look and stared straight ahead.

On the way home, I stole a glance at Dad and caught him with a big grin on his face. He noticed me looking, tousled my hair, and grinned even wider. "God will reward me, eh? Sister is right, you know, but her timing is off. He already rewarded me when He gave me you. You are a good boy."

I was stunned. I was convinced he never noticed me and, based on that childish observation, I'd made a conscious decision to fight him every minute of my life. When I looked into his eyes I saw—he meant it! He meant every word.

Dad passed away a few years after that incident, far too young as far as I was concerned. However, I had discovered an amazing truth. My dad was really a very kind man, and he loved me. Dad's remaining years with me were filled with wonder, and discovery, and understanding.

My eternal thanks to you, Sister Ana Marie, and your simple act of faith. It returned me to my father, or perhaps my father to me, giving us the best years of our life together.

First appeared April 7, 1996—Seek magazine.
Subsequent reprints in April 2000 Wesleyan Advocate
and April 2000 Christian Standard publications.

REMEMBER THE CROSS

by Dianne M. Smith, Fremont, California

I heard the door open and stood as my husband entered the room. "How was the board meeting?" I asked.

"I'm getting off the church board," he said, shaking his head. "I just can't do it anymore."

"Are you sure?"

"Yes," he said firmly.

Our problem with the leadership at church had been slowly escalating—now the dam was breaking. With a heavy heart, I sat down to type the resignation letter he dictated. I felt he had been unfairly discredited and ostracized, but I had hoped he could stand fast and make a difference. True faith and character shine during adversity, but he seemed to be surrounded by those who wanted to snuff out his flame. Quitting the board meant he could do nothing more.

We had helped found the church six years earlier in a shared dream that the Lord brought to life. How could those we worked alongside turn against us?

I finished typing the letter and watched him sign and seal it. I trusted the Lord had a bigger plan that I simply couldn't see. "Well, we still have each other," I said, mustering a smile. His arms enveloped me as we encouraged ourselves to act with kindness toward those who had hurt us.

Church was never the same to us afterward. Rumors flew, and the leadership became defensive, but we tried to remain quiet. "Lord, please help," I prayed. I needed His grace to help me exhibit the fruits of the spirit, especially self-control and patience, when I was tempted to give in to hurt, anger, and disappointment.

After three months, our situation had so deteriorated we spent a day fasting and praying to receive some direction from the Lord. By that evening, we felt His affirmation to leave the fellowship we had loved so deeply.

However, I could not as easily leave my pain as I made my way to the door of a new church. Because it was large, I hoped to heal in anonymity. I couldn't give much, but I needed plenty. Listening to the good-hearted pastor, his soothing words felt like salve on an open sore.

Soon Good Friday arrived, and I went to the special Easter service needing to be uplifted again. As I waited for it to start, music filled the air. At the front of the church, a large wooden cross, held together by ropes, was leaning against the wall.

After some singing and a sermon, the pastor said, "We will close our service tonight with our annual tradition. Each one of us will come and hammer a nail into our wooden cross as a remembrance of what the Lord Jesus Christ did for us on Calvary. We would like the auditorium to be quiet during this time, and when you have finished, you may leave."

Two men solemnly laid the cross down on the altar next to some hammers and a couple of bowls filled with carpenter nails, each tied with a red ribbon. My hands began to sweat and my eyes watered. The imagery was too vivid for me. How could I hammer a nail into that cross? I was sitting in a comfortable culture two thousand years away from that dreadful day when the Savior was sacrificed. If I had been there, I would have stopped anyone from crucifying my Lord!

Or would I?

It dawned on me that those who put Jesus to death were not the only ones responsible for the act. Each sinful human being was responsible because it was for their sins Christ had died. I was just as guilty as those who actually did the deed.

Finally, it was my turn. Someone handed me a hammer, and I took a red-ribboned nail from a bowl. The large cross was now covered with nails, but there was still room for mine. I raised the hammer, and it landed on the nailhead with a thud. I thought of the pain Jesus must have experienced as each blow had pierced Him. Tears streamed from my eyes as I forced myself to hit the nail. . .hit the nail. . .hit the nail.

Then a new thought occurred to me. Not only was my sin nailed to the cross, but also the sins of those who had hurt my husband and me. Jesus had taken the judgment, ostracism, and jealous anger others had directed at us and nailed them to the cross, too. He died for all humankind, including those who had mistreated us. If He could love so forgivingly, would He expect anything less from me? When compared to the cross, my overwhelming sense of betrayal suddenly paled into insignificance. Truly, my bitterness had to be replaced with forgiveness. For my own spiritual health, I needed to let go of the past and move on.

I handed the hammer to the next person and averted my red-rimmed eyes. The experience had been intensely personal. My God had touched my soul.

THE CROSS

by Matthew James, Tucson, Arizona

At the time, I was still a student with only three months left before I would receive my certification as an EMT. Up until this point, it had been all books and slides, practicing CPR on dummies, and bandaging each other in the field outside of the classroom. None of us had any real-life experience yet, but that would soon change. We each had to work several twenty-four-hour shifts in an emergency room before we could be certified.

For my first assignment, I chose a small, rural hospital not too far from where I lived in Phoenix. I wanted something easy at first. Then, after I got my feet wet a little, I could plunge headfirst into the inner-city emergency rooms where the real action was. Here, there would probably be the typical upset stomachs, hurt wrists, and maybe a broken bone or two.

My first day went as I had expected. I took care of a few cuts and a minor traffic accident. People came in hurt, and because of my help, they went out feeling better.

I wasn't used to staying up for twenty-four hours straight and was quite tired by the time my shift was officially over at 11:00 P.M. I dropped a pair of quarters into the soda machine and headed out to my car, praying I wouldn't fall asleep on the long drive home.

Then it happened. An old, beat-up car screeched into the ambulance bay just as I stepped outside. Smoke rose as the car crunched into the concrete divider, the engine still on. The horn started blaring and never stopped. First, I saw the bullet holes in the windshield, and then the driver, slumped over the wheel with a passenger next to him. Blood was everywhere.

I ran inside, telling the nurse to call a code as I grabbed a pair of gloves. In the midst of all the commotion, I ended up on the chest of the passenger, doing chest compression while he was wheeled down the hallway to an ER room. It didn't look good. He was a young Hispanic boy, eleven years old, shot once in the neck and once in the face.

In the operating room, I stepped back as the doctors desperately worked on him. His heart stopped beating several times, and it was clear they were becoming more and more certain he wasn't going to make it.

I was unable to stay and watch as this boy died, so I left the room and went next door to visit the other person we pulled from the car. The man turned out to be the young boy's father. He had been shot, as well, but in the shoulder. He was already awake and stabilized.

"My son, how is my son?" he cried, over and over, but the doctor and nurses in this room didn't know. Covered with his son's blood, I knew. I knew his son probably wasn't going to make it—and I didn't know what to say. As I approached him, his eyes met mine. Reading the despair they must have shown, he began to weep. Suddenly, I was next to him, my hand on his shoulder. With his free hand, he grabbed my wrist. His grip was like iron, stronger than I would have thought possible.

"In my car, there's a cross hanging on the rearview mirror. It's been blessed," he said.

"You want me to bring it to you?" I asked.

"No. I want you to give it to my son. Please, I beg you, please get it and place it in my son's hand."

I didn't know if it was a good idea, or even if I would be allowed to do it, but somehow I was going to grant his wish. Suddenly, I knew that I had to grant his wish, and on legs that weren't my own, I quickly headed outside, sidestepped a police officer, and grabbed the large, Victorian-style cross. I ran back in as the protests of the police officer rang behind me.

They were shocking the boy's chest when I returned, but it definitely looked hopeless. There was no way this young boy was going to survive.

Wordlessly, the doctor allowed me to place the cross in his hand, and I stepped back as they tried to bring him around one more time. Nothing.

As I stood there, staring at the lovely cross cradled in that small helpless hand, I will never forget the next few moments, not for the rest of my life. Just as I saw those small young fingers curl tightly around the cross, the monitor started sounding a steady Blip. Blip. Blip.

The doctors and nurses paused with astonishment. Then they pounced on him again, working quickly to stabilize him. They didn't know how it had happened, and he would take a long time recovering, but he would live. It was a true miracle, and I watched it happen.

I couldn't wait to rush and tell his father the good news. As I ran into the room, he looked up at me and smiled, as though he already knew. "I told you it was blessed," the boy's father said, closing his eyes toward heaven and mouthing a silent prayer of thanks. A police officer was talking to him and asked what was going on. "They saved the boy," I said. "He's going to make it—he's going to make it."

Thirty hours after I had started working, I finally got to go home. I was more tired than I had ever been in my entire life, but somehow I felt better and stronger than ever. Outside, the soda I had purchased was still where it had rolled when I dropped it. I picked it up and kept it. I still have it to this day.

Sometimes at night when I close my eyes, I see those small fingers tightening their grip on that cross. Others may doubt whether the cross made a real difference or not. But I never will. No, I never will.

Published in Light and Life *magazine, 10/93,* Parenting Treasures, *Fall 1995, and* God's Vitamin C for the Spirit, *3/96*

THE BIG THINGS. . .LIKE LEGOS

by Jan Northington, Los Osos, California

"I'm ready to just move on, if you are. . . . I love you," my husband whispered in my ear. He slipped his arm around my shoulder as I leaned against the kitchen counter.

The "I'm sorry" I heard was empty, though. It was like the "I'm sorrys" I made the children say. . .just words. I wanted to be able to say "I love you," but I couldn't do it. I wanted to continue the discussion, finish making my point, and feel as though he had truly heard me. If he wasn't willing to do that, then I wasn't willing to "just move on."

From experience I knew this would pass. In a week, I would wonder why I made such a big deal over such a little thing. Then I would wonder how I ended up with the most wonderful husband on earth. At the moment, however, my thoughts were not running along that path by a long shot.

How could he have shut me off like that? I knew he was tired, but, while I cried, spilling my heart and hurts out to him, he actually rolled over and went to sleep. It seemed like the ultimate insult.

My thoughts were interrupted by Daniel shouting in the children's room. "He took my Legos without asking!" he yelled.

"He wasn't using them, and I wanted to build a house," four-year-old Philip cried.

"But, Mom. They're my new toy," said Daniel. "I don't want him to lose any pieces. And, besides, he never even said 'please.' "

"Oh, Daniel, please let him use the Legos," I pleaded from the doorway. I really didn't need any more conflict this morning.

"No! I don't feel like sharing. They're mine, and I want them!" With that, Daniel began picking up all the Legos on the floor and snatched the pieces from his brother's hands.

I seated Daniel on his bed. Hugging his stiff little arms in mine, I said softly, "Remember the book we were reading last night? Do you remember the words we asked, 'What would Jesus do?' There are times Jesus wants us to give, and even forgive when we don't feel like it. He must have a big smile when we do what He wants even if it's hard for us. I bet you could share your stuffed rabbit all week, 'cause it's not that important to you. But your Legos are a different story, aren't they?"

"Yeah, Mom," Daniel said. "A BIG different story."

"Okay. So, Daniel. What do you think Jesus would do?"

Without any hesitation he replied, "He'd forgive Philip and let him use the Legos. He'd probably even help him build the house." Then he moved off the bed and picked up the case holding his Legos. Walking toward the door, he said, "I'll be right back. I need to ask Jesus to help me change my heart. This one is too hard to do by myself."

Out of the mouths of babes. His words moved me unlike any before. It was a humbling experience to realize that I needed the example of a child to remind me that "this one was just too hard to do by myself."

My tears dotted the bedspread as I prayed. "Oh, Lord, it's too hard to 'just move on' when I want to get even. It's too hard when I don't think I've received a proper apology, and I still feel misunderstood and unappreciated. Lord, if You only understood how I felt."

I had no sooner prayed those words when I realized that of course the Lord knew how I felt! More than anyone in the world, He knew what it was like to feel misunderstood and unappreciated. Didn't He want a proper apology from Peter, or to get even with Judas? Even as He hung on the cross, Jesus forgave the undeserving thief. If Christ could forgive them, and if He could forgive me, how could I not forgive my husband?

"Lord, forgive my selfishness. I need You to help me forgive. Put Your love back into my heart. Amen."

Moments later, Daniel was spilling Legos in front of his brother. "Philip, you can use my Legos all day if you want."

What truly changed Daniel's heart that morning? Of course I'd like to believe he had the same kind of conversation that I'd had with the Lord. Maybe the unexpected arrival of neighborhood friends also contributed, but perhaps that was another way that God helped Daniel work things out, too.

Suddenly, I had a trail of children tramping through my kitchen to the backyard. My husband looked at me sheepishly as he reached for my hand. "Well, Honey, it looks like you're going to have your hands full. Good thing I have to go work today. . .doesn't look like you need another 'kid' around here!"

Did I just hear an apology? I wondered. Maybe, maybe not. But my previously cold and unyielding heart was suddenly warmed.

"I do love you," I said, as I reached to give him a hug. "And, thanks to a little boy, I'm ready to just move on."

WHEN YOU KNOW WHERE YOU ARE HEADED

by John Roberts, Sterling, Colorado

This morning I conducted my third memorial service in the last nine days.

All three people were delightful Christians. It was truly a privilege to be their pastor and conduct their memorial services. In fact, I would go so far as to say these three funerals were actually good, in so far as funerals can be.

These were good funerals because all three people were truly ready to "go." All three were looking forward to heaven. They could hardly wait to see Jesus. My last visit with each of them had the same ring of confidence. They knew, all three of them, where they were headed. It was not simply a matter of having grown weary of being ill and just wanting to "get it over with." No, each of them had a positive and confident expectation that they were about to enter the heavenly presence of God. They were looking forward to it. They were ready to go home. And they were sure of it.

So, how do you get ready to go home? How can you be sure of it?

Other people say that being sure you're going to heaven involves going to church. While participating in a local church is incredibly important and gives you all kinds of benefits, it does not automatically give you the assurance of eternity in heaven. Someone put it this way: "Going to church won't make you a Christian any more than going to McDonald's will make you a hamburger." The analogy is a bit odd, but the point is well taken. Church is important, however, don't think that just showing up there will get you into heaven.

Some people say that being good is the key. Since heaven is a good place, they reason, the way to get to heaven is to be good. The problem with that thought is that heaven isn't just a "good" place. It's a perfect place. Getting there requires not just goodness, but perfection. And since nobody is perfect, well. . .that poses a problem.

These three precious souls who knew they were going to heaven were sure because of one thing: They trusted Jesus for their salvation. They had faith. They didn't trust their good deeds, though they had many.

They didn't trust their church attendance, though they had loved to come to church until infirmity prevented it. They didn't trust their background, their parents' faith, or their church membership. They just trusted Jesus. As the Scriptures say, "God accounted their faith as righteousness," and He declared them fit for eternity in His perfect heaven.

Faith in the grace of God. That's what it takes. Sounds almost too simple, doesn't it?

My last visit with one of the three contained a particularly faith-filled moment. Referring to the painful process of passing from this life to the next, I said, "This is a rough road you're traveling these days, isn't it?"

My dying friend said in reply, "You know, Pastor, any road is okay when you know where you're headed."

THE FIG TREE

by Gerry Di Gesu, West Chatham, Massachusetts

I yanked and tore at the large weed which would not let go of its hold in the earth. Finally, I got it halfway out, but it was so stubborn I was exhausted from the struggle and quit trying. My father had died two weeks earlier. It was the first week of November, and I was clearing out his beloved backyard garden. I thought of leaving the dead plants and unharvested, rotting vegetables until spring, but Mom asked if I could find time to "clean up the garden." She couldn't bear the constant reminder of Dad each time she looked out her kitchen window.

Mom came out of the house to check on my progress. "What happened to Daddy's fig tree? It looks as if the frost has heaved it out of the ground." She gently touched the "weed" I had been struggling to pull out a few minutes earlier. I hadn't known it was Dad's fig tree. It looked like a weed. Dad's friend had given it to him two years before. My father had nursed it and checked its progress daily because he wanted a fig tree like his father had when Dad was growing up. It had grown only a few inches. "Wait until next year," he would say, laughing whenever we teased him about it.

"The kids were probably digging out here, Mom," I choked, knowing I could never tell her how I had struggled to pull it out. I felt sick to my stomach. The dirt around it was loose, so I patted it back around the exposed roots. "We'll see how it is in the spring." I took Mom inside for a cup of tea. Feeling sick and guilty, I couldn't continue my work.

I never finished the garden that fall. Through the winter, every time I visited Mom, my eyes were drawn to that solitary stick in the middle of the garden. Unspoken guilt and shame engulfed me. I knew it was dead. And I had killed it.

The following spring, when Mom sold her home, I returned to finish cleaning up the garden. I couldn't leave the mess for the new owners, knowing Dad would want it to look neat and well kept. It was overrun with weeds, but at least they hid the tree from view.

Furiously, I ripped and tugged at the strong, healthy weeds. Although the sun shone brightly, I felt as cold as stone. I was saying good-bye to my dad, my yard, my childhood. I reached to pull out the last row of brush when I realized the fig tree was suddenly right in front of me. The tiny stick was covered with leaves, and new shoots reached up from the ground.

Tears rolled down my cheeks as I stroked the leaves. I could feel the core of bitterness inside me slowly dissolve and be replaced by a warm feeling of acceptance and hope. Dad was here with me in his garden. I carefully dug out the tree and wrapped it in burlap to transplant it into my garden.

That was twenty-three years ago. Today, I picked the first fig of the season and knew Dad was with me as I savored the sweetness of the fruit, just as I had felt him with me that spring day. The renewal of warmth and hope in my heart that day arose out of the word that had sprung into my mind—resurrection. God had given new life to this stick I had yanked from the ground and left for dead that winter. I knew He had done the same for Dad. It is His great promise to us all.

Previously published in the Pleasantville News & Views,
June 2000

EVERYBODY KNOWS EVERYBODY

by Lea MacDonald, Tichborne, Ontario, Canada

Today was a special day, the type of day which restores a faith of sorts. And in that faith I found a lesson, taught to me by my six-year-old son, Brandon.

I watched him at the kitchen table carefully packing his lunch bag. I was going to take him along with me to work. As he put it, "I'm going to be a worker-man."

We arrived at a small bungalow in the suburbs of Kingston. Our job was to install indoor-outdoor carpet on the porch and steps.

I rang the doorbell. I could hear the dead bolt being released, then the handle-lock and security chain. The door swung slowly open revealing an old, thin man. He looked ill. His white hair covered his head in patches. The powder blue shirt hung from his shoulders as though on a hanger—his belt, several sizes too big.

I smiled, asking if he was Mr. Burch.

"Yes. Are you here to do the porch and steps?"

"Yes, Sir."

"Okay. I will leave this door open."

"Okay, I will get to work."

"Do you have a fridge?'" blurted Brandon. The old man looked down at Brandon who extended his lunch.

"Yes, I do. Do you know where to find a fridge?"

"Yes, I do," said Brandon walking past the man. "It's in the kitchen."

I was about to suggest to Brandon that he was being bold by walking in before being invited, but before I could, the old man held his finger to his lips gesturing it was okay.

"He'll be okay. He can't get into anything at all. Does he really help you?"

I nodded yes. Brandon returned asking, in his most elflike voice, "Do you have a coloring book?"

Again, I was about to suggest to Brandon that he was perhaps being bold. I extended my hand beckoning him outside. The old man grasped my hand feebly. He looked at Brandon.

"Your father tells me you help him."

"Yes. I'm a worker-man," Brandon replied with pride.

I looked down adding, "Apparently his job today is to keep the customer busy."

The old man looked at Brandon releasing my hand, a faint smile appearing.

"Maybe you could do some work inside and show me how to color?"

With a most serious look, Brandon asked, "Dad, will you be okay?"

"Will Mr. Burch be okay?" I answered.

"We will be fine. We will be right here at the table. Come help me get out the book, worker-man."

As I worked, I could hear Brandon comment, "You have colored in this book. You are a good colorer."

"No, I didn't color these pictures. My grandchildren did."

"What are grandchildren?" Brandon asked curiously.

"They are my children's children. I am a grandfather."

"What's a grandfather?"

"Well, when you grow up and get married and have children of your own, your dad will be a grandpa. Then, your mother will be a grandma. They will be grandparents. Do you understand?"

Brandon paused. "Yes, Grandpa."

"Oh, I don't think I'm your grandpa," the old man suggested.

Brandon rubbed his hair from his eyes. Studying the crayons, he selected one and continued to color.

Brandon said, "Everybody knows everybody you know?"

"Well, I'm not sure they do. Why do you say that?" The old man looked curiously at Brandon who was diligently coloring.

"We all 'comed' from God. He made us all. We are all family."

"Yes, God made everything," the old man confirmed.

"I know," said Brandon in a lighthearted voice. "He told me."

"He told you?" The old man was clearly curious.

"Yes, He did. He lives up there." Brandon pointed to the ceiling looking up with reverence. "I 'b-member' being there and talking to Him."

"What did He say to you?" The old man placed his crayon on the table focusing on Brandon.

"He said, 'we are all family.'" Brandon paused then added logically, "So you're my grandpa."

The old man looked to me through the screen door. He smiled. I was embarrassed when he saw me watching them. He told Brandon to keep coloring; he was going to check on the job.

The old man made his way slowly to the door. Opening it, he stepped onto the porch.

"How's it going?" he asked.

"It's going okay," I said. "I won't be long." The old man smiled slightly.

"Does the boy have a grandfather?"

I paused. "No, he doesn't. They were gone when he was born. He has a Nana, you know, a grandmother, but she is frail and not well."

"I understand. I have cancer. I'm not long for this earth either."

"I'm sorry to hear that, Mr. Burch. I lost my mother to cancer."

He looked at me with tired, smiling eyes. "Every boy needs a grandfather," he said softly.

I agreed, adding, "It's just not in the cards for Brandon."

The old man looked back to Brandon who was coloring vigorously. "How often do you come to town, Son?"

"Me?" I asked.

"Yes."

"I come in almost every day."

The old man looked back to me. "Perhaps you could bring Brandon by from time to time, when you're in the area, that is, for thirty minutes or so. What do you think?"

I looked in at Brandon. He had stopped coloring and was listening to us. "Could we, Dad? We are friends. We can have lunch together."

"Well, if it's okay with Mr. Burch."

The old man opened the door, returning to the table. Brandon slid from his chair and walked to the fridge. "It's lunchtime, Grandpa. I got enough for both of us." Brandon returned to the table. He removed the contents from the paper bag. "Do you have a knife?" asked Brandon.

The old man started to get up.

"I can find it. Tell me where to look," instructed Brandon.

"The butter knives are next to the corner of the counter, in the drawer."

"Found it!"

Brandon returned to the table. He unwrapped his muffin. With the care of a diamond-cutter, he cleaved two perfect portions. Brandon placed one portion on the plastic the muffin was wrapped in. He pushed it toward Mr. Burch.

"This is yours." He carefully unwrapped the sandwich next. "This is yours, too. We have to eat the 'samich' first. Mom says."

"Okay," replied Mr. Burch.

"Do you like juice, Brandon?"

"Yep, apple juice."

Mr. Burch walked slowly to the fridge. He removed a can of apple juice and poured two small glasses. He placed one in front of Brandon.

"This is yours."

"Thank you, Grandpa."

Brandon punctuated his eating with questions to Mr. Burch, and fits of coloring.

"Do you play hockey, Brandon?"

"Yep," said Brandon, studying the end of his sandwich before biting into it. "Dad took me, Tyler, and Adam in the wintertime."

"Years ago," Mr. Burch started, "I used to play for a Senior-A-team. I was almost ready to play for the NHL, but I was never called up. I did play with a man that was called up, though. He was a fine player. Bill Moore was his name."

My heart leapt to my throat. "Tutter Moore?" I asked through the screen.

The old man was startled. He looked at me. "Yes. He was called up to Boston. You've heard of him?"

"Yes," I said, my voice cracking. "You're eating lunch with his grandson."

The old man looked back to Brandon. He stared for a few moments. Brandon looked innocently at Mr. Burch.

"Yes. . .I see it now. He looks very much like Tutter. And the Nana, is Lillian?"

"Yes," I replied.

The old man clasped Brandon's hand.

"Brandon, I owe you an apology. You were right, and I was wrong. Everybody 'does' know everybody."

And that was the day my son got himself a grandpa, and I got myself a lesson in faith that yes, we are all a part of God's family.

First appeared in: Chocolates for a Woman's Heart,
Simon & Schuster, 1998

LESSON FOR A LIFETIME

by Sheila Hudson, Athens, Georgia

"If they steal it, they steal it," Tim, my trusting husband, said as he went off to shower and get ready for dinner.

Our moving van was locked tight under a security light in the motel parking lot. I attributed my anxiety to exhaustion after hours of driving, punctuated by children's questions and my tears. We were leaving Cincinnati, where we'd had lots of friends and a church that meant much to our family. Bittersweet emotions accompanied us as Tim drove the van, and we followed in the car.

When we stopped in Kentucky for gas, Tim and the girls decided we should celebrate our anniversary, an occasion we had barely noticed. We had fourteen years of marriage to celebrate, plus we were moving home to Georgia, to our family, and an exciting ministry on the campus of the university.

The next morning, Tim dressed early and went to check on the truck. As I was braiding J. J.'s hair, he burst into the room, saying he couldn't find the van. "What do you mean, you can't find it?" I said. "How can you lose a twenty-four-foot moving van?" The words tumbled out of my mouth, and I wanted to recall them immediately as I saw the color drain from his face.

Missy began to cry. She knew from his tone that Daddy wasn't teasing. The seriousness of the situation began to sink in. The hours passed in a blur. The police came and asked a lot of questions. We telephoned the van company, our family, and various insurance companies. We returned to our room after a valiant effort to eat breakfast and started to make a list of the moving truck's contents.

All the while, a giant cold fist grew larger and larger in the pit of my stomach. Reality was settling in. When my brain began functioning, the panic started. What would we do? How could we survive? We had no savings—how could we replace anything?

Tim suggested that we pray. I didn't feel like praying, and I suspect he really didn't, either. Nevertheless, we joined hands and prayed humbly and simply. Amid sniffles and sobs, we asked for our things to be returned. We praised God that no one was injured and that we had each other—our real treasure. Only the passing traffic broke the morning silence as we waited.

That afternoon, we received a call from the police. They had recovered our truck on a back road. Our hopes soared! When we arrived at the abandoned van, we found only Tim's desk and a few cartons of books. Only later did we realize that Tim had just what he needed to get started in his new ministry. More resources would follow. I couldn't contain my tears as I picked up love letters strewn over the truck bed. This violation of my privacy was more than I could bear. I searched through the boxes of books and papers for our daughters' baby books and my wedding album, but they weren't there. Who would do something like this? Who would want to take things that had no real value other than sentiment?

It's been fifteen years, and each time I recount this story, I marvel at how friends, acquaintances, family, and strangers responded. In an outpouring of love, we received more than $16,000 in cash, plus clothes, household goods, pantry items, toys, bicycles, appliances, and tons of cards and letters.

The theft of our moving van is a benchmark for us. We speak of events as "before the theft" or "after the theft." It is and will always be a significant event in our family's history, but it isn't a negative one. In many ways, it was a "blessed theft," for in the removal of the weight of worldly possessions, we learned the lesson of a lifetime—forgiveness.

SWEET JESUS AND THE ICE STORM

by Maxine Wright, Bremen, Georgia

Winter arrived in Atlanta this weekend. We had an ice storm, and with it came all the problems that usually attend such events. The most notable difficulty was the loss of electricity. Our home was only without power for a few hours, though. My daughter and her children were not so lucky, so they came over to stay with me.

Even though we had lights and all, the children were very excited. One flake of snow in the South will energize kids more than batteries do the Energizer Bunny. It was really hard to keep them in the house. We ended up having a wonderful, if exhausting, day.

I was tucking my granddaughter Jessica into bed when we started to talk about angels. They were on her mind. We had just watched the television program *Touched by an Angel*. She believed in them, she told me, with all seriousness. "Well, I do, too," I said to her. Then she related to me what had happened to her the night before, when the power went out in her house. She said, "I woke up and it was really dark in my room. I started to go to Mommy, but I couldn't see anything. So, I looked up and said, 'Jesus, I need Your hand to take me to my mommy.' And Jesus took my hand and took me to Mommy." Through misty eyes, I managed to say that was sweet of Jesus. She offhandedly said, "Oh, Mimi. That's just how Jesus is; He's a very sweet man."

I thought about what Jessica had told me all that night. It wouldn't leave me. I began to think about the areas of my life where I can't "see" anything. I am in the autumn of my life, and I know I will soon be facing my winter years. I watch my mother struggle from time to time and wonder how I will face this unknown in my time. I worry about being a burden to my daughters. What will happen if I'm left alone?

Reflecting on this, I thought of all the unknowns in every stage of life, and how much time is wasted worrying. When we're young, we wonder and worry about what the future holds for us. When we get older, our concerns center around how to live with what the past has left us, and then what the future will hold for us. Life is full of unknowns and uncertainties every day.

Then along comes a five-year-old child to remind us that we should never worry about the unknown. All we have to do is reach up and ask Jesus to take our hand. Life would be so much simpler if we could all have that kind of faith and trust.

After all, Jesus is a very sweet man.

WITHOUT QUESTION

by Marlene Capelle, Sherican, Colorado

Not long ago, a coworker of mine came to work late. She said that traffic was backed up for blocks because of a momma duck and her eleven little ducklings. They seemed to be on their way to the river, six blocks away. During rush hour traffic, those six blocks might just as well have been a million miles away.

My coworker said it was truly amazing, sitting in rush hour traffic patiently waiting for the small family to cross the street. There were no horns honking, no screaming or finger-pointing, even though the cars at the end of the line would have had trouble seeing what was holding them up.

A little later, my walking buddy and I were getting ready to go for our daily walk. I suggested we go see if the ducks made it to the river. The odds of finding the ducks were slim, but we decided to look anyway. My buddy suggested we walk through the park, which we rarely do.

In order to get to the park, we had to cross three busy streets. We shared our belief that the chance of those ducks having made it to the river was pretty slim. We thought about abandoning the whole idea because we would rather think the ducks made it than to see somewhere in the middle of the road a gruesome display that they had not.

As we got to the other side of the park, we saw an SUV stopped in the road and a lady on a bike next to him. It looked like two friends who'd run into each other and picked a most unusual place to stop and chat. Then, right in front of us, we saw momma duck jump off the street and into the grass. One by one, all her ducklings followed behind. The man in the SUV and the lady on the bike had been stopping traffic so they would not hit the ducks.

We ran across the street and followed the ducks down to the river. The ducklings were so little all we could see of them was the tall grass waving as they plowed through it. I think the momma duck knew all along what she was doing, but the babies were following without question or knowing where they were going. She had to lead them across dangerous streets through an unfriendly environment to their place of safety. If we could only all have that much faith and perseverance!

And think of what a life we could all have if we showed as much patience with each other as was shown that day. There was no road rage or anger as people who were usually in a hurry stopped to wait for Momma and her ducklings to reach the river.

And once there, after an hour and a half of running on hot pavement, the babies rested for less than a minute before they began following their momma once again. . .upstream!

I felt so blessed seeing this miracle; and yes, I do believe it was a miracle, even if not on the scale of the saints.

Sometimes, God allows us to see His work in the "little miracles" that occur each day. You only have to have faith and keep your heart open to see them.

TRIBUTE TO AN OLD WOMAN

by Marlene Depler, Longmont, Colorado

I must have been seven or eight years old when I first met her. In fact, I do not recall a first meeting. We had recently moved from a small town in Kansas to Bandon, Oregon, in order for my father to take this position. She was just there, one of the members in the church at which my father was the new minister. For me, a somewhat shy and insecure young girl, this was a wonderful adventure. Living near the ocean was alluring to someone whose roots for generations had been in the Midwest. I had no way of knowing just how fondly I would later recall these years or this woman. Everyone in our little congregation just called her "Grandma Loomis." I think her first name was Maude. She had neither husband nor children, although I vaguely have the impression that she had been married at one time. She was probably in her sixties, if you can base age on the perceptions of a child.

Grandma Loomis had coarse gray hair pulled back loosely into a bun of no particular style. Her face was angular and weathered. No one would characterize her as being beautiful. Her hands were rough and stiff, and her knuckles were knobby and knurled. From today's vantage point, I am quite sure she had arthritis. As a child, I just didn't know about such things. Her clothes were unfashionable with the faint smell of goats. There was no doubt in anyone's mind that she was a bit peculiar and eccentric.

Grandma Loomis lived several miles out in the country and up in the hills, on Bear Creek Road. Her three-story, tumbledown house sat on the side of a hill, looking down over the road. She confined herself to living in only two rooms, a kitchen and a bedroom. They were cluttered, with no particular sense of order or beauty. Just outside the back door was a small porch stacked high with wood. A clothesline stood parallel to the short walk that ran from the back porch to the dirt drive. Directly across the drive, behind the house, were the goat pens and a ramshackle semblance of a barn or shed that was home to about six to eight goats. The air was filled with constant bleating and scented with the combination of manure and animal fur. It seemed to me that these goats were Grandma's life.

What was it about this outwardly unappealing woman that I would remember her forty years later? I recall with delight her invitation to any and all of the children in the church to visit her home for a day, a weekend, or a week. Her only stipulation was that we come in twos. I have no idea how many times I visited her home. I think that I usually went with my sister Barbara or a friend named Debbie. Once, I even rode the school bus out to her place after school.

I loved driving out Bear Creek Road to this unsightly, unlikely haven of sorts. To roam the hillsides, attempt to milk the goats, and explore all the empty rooms of this old house was all I needed to have a delightful time. Given our childish imaginations, our play knew no limits. We were allowed to sleep anywhere we wanted in that house. We usually slept in the bedrooms on the second floor. One time, she let us make a tent of blankets over the clothesline and sleep on cots underneath our marvelous architectural structure.

My favorite supper was pancakes served with brown sugar and whipped cream from the goats' milk. The warm pancakes would partially melt the sweet brown granules and the clouds of whipped cream. Delicious! I thought it was a meal fit for a queen!

At night, she would let her hair fall down from her bun, sit upon her bed, and read. Books and magazines were randomly piled in stacks around her bed. I specifically remember her reading from a book titled *Little Britches*. Besides the wonderful trips to her house, there was one other thing that stands out in my mind. Grandma Loomis took me to my first ballet. I believe it was just a performance at the local high school. I do not even know who else went with us—perhaps my older sister, Barbara. What I do remember are the beautiful, fairylike dancers. I was completely mesmerized as they twirled and spun about the dance floor on their toes. For weeks after this, I tried to walk and dance on my toes. I never saw another ballet until I was an adult. How was it that this woman had any interest in "cultured" things like ballet? There are many things I never knew about Grandma Loomis and now wish that I could ask her.

Our family moved back to the Midwest after my fifth-grade year. I never saw her again. That was forty years ago. I am quite certain that she is no longer living. I am sure her shoes no longer leave prints in the mud between the house and the goat pen, but her "heart print" has been indelibly stamped on me. If I am ever in Bandon again, I will try to find Bear Creek Road and see if that old house is still standing.

Although I seriously doubt that it still physically exists, it still stands in my heart with her in it. Grandma Loomis, you never knew what you meant to me. Your faith was one of quiet and unsung action, not profound words or deeds. I am filled with immense gratitude.

Thank you! I can only hope that I leave as many "heart prints" as you did, and that my example of faith will be so enduring.

CHAPTER NINE

Prayer

*"Therefore I tell you, whatever you ask for in prayer,
believe that you have received it, and it will be yours."*
Mark 11:24

Published in Heart-stirring Stories of Romance,
Broadman & Holman, 2000

ON A MOUNTAINTOP IN NORWAY

By Charlotte Adelsperger, Overland Park, Kansas

In 1961, I attended the University of Oslo International Summer School in Norway. Fresh out of college, I was learning all about Norwegian culture to teach my fourth-graders in the States.

One weekend my travel friend, Karin Lindahl, and I took a field trip via train from Oslo to Bergen. We loved the historic coastal town of Bergen with its bustling open-air markets. But I shall never forget our second day there. We rode the funicular, or mountain cable car, to the top of Mount Floyen, one of the seven mountains surrounding the city. We were captivated by the awesome view of the town, the harbor, and fjords. While Karin went into a shop, I followed a path down to a quiet spot overlooking Bergen. Those moments have stayed with me all these years.

That night, I wrote in my diary. July 21, 1961:

Today on Floyen, I came to a lovely place where I saw rich moss among the trees. I spent time in silent prayer. I opened my whole self to God and asked Him to guide my life as a Christian single person and teacher. As I prayed, I turned over to God my deepest desire, which was to find the husband right for me. May I always remember the serenity and power on the mountain overlooking Bergen. Today was a day of dedication.

After returning to the States, I dated several men, but none seemed to be "the one." My experiences in a number of church singles' groups were dismal dead ends. After three years of discouraging results, I took a final risk in faith and tried one more singles' event at a church. There I met Bob Adelsperger, recently back from air force service on Okinawa.

Bob was my bridge partner at one of the group's card game nights. Now there was a man with qualities! We dated, fell in love, and were married in June 1965. Of course, I told Bob all about my prayer for a husband on that mountain in Norway. Even our two children, Karen and John, heard the Bergen story any number of times.

When Bob and I planned a trip to Europe for 1998, I insisted we include Norway. We traveled the same scenic train route to Bergen. As we took the funicular to the top of Mount Floyen on a sunny June afternoon, I could feel my heart begin to race.

At the summit, Bob and I strolled hand in hand, wide-eyed as we looked down on colorful Bergen. "You were right. It's beautiful!" Bob said.

"Come this way," I urged, tugging his hand. "I'm taking you to the spot where I prayed for you. It may take a few minutes to find it, considering that was thirty-seven years ago!" But there it was, lovely view and all. And thick moss still covered the ground. Bob and I were all smiles as a Norwegian snapped our picture. We hugged.

"I thank God for you," I whispered. Then we kissed, and the camera clicked again.

Published in The Lookout—*May 9, 1999*

WHO'S THE MAMA NOW?

by Sandra Campbell, Garden City, Michigan

I took my mom shopping today. Once a week, we plan a day to buy groceries, go to doctor appointments, pick up her medicine, or just window-shop and have lunch. It is our precious time together.

But today, at the end of our busy day, I spent as much time communing with my heavenly Father as I did conversing with my mom. I found myself driving away from her apartment and asking myself a melancholy question, "Who's the mama now?"

I was born the last of her six children and now, forty-five years later, I am still her "baby girl." I don't reminisce a lot about my younger years, but occasionally sweet memories come back to me in bits and pieces.

It seems just yesterday that Mama held my hand so I wouldn't get lost. Today, I held Mom's hand to help balance her unsteady feet. *Dear Lord, help me not to hurry her along just because I have so much else to do.*

Yesterday, Mama would remind me to always dress warmly for this cold Michigan weather. Today, I gently scolded her because she forgot her hat and gloves. *Father, help her to know my only concern is for her continued good health.*

Yesterday, Mama made sure I had green and yellow vegetables with every dinner. Today, I had to make her buy some at the market even though she protested vigorously. "Nothing tastes good anymore!" she lamented. *Dear Lord, help me take time every day to be sure she is eating right, even when she doesn't want to be bothered.*

Yesterday, my short, stubby legs ran to keep up with her at the grocery store. Today, I waited while she meandered slowly up and down each aisle. *Please help me not to show my impatience with an irritated voice or tired eyes.*

Yesterday, Mama would calm my fears when I had to go to the doctor. Today, I tried to reassure her as we waited in yet another new office. *Oh God, please let this doctor find the cause and solution for these bad spells.*

Only yesterday, Mama would sit up with me at night to talk away my "boyfriend blues." Tonight, I sat beside her bed attempting to talk her through yet another worrisome attack. *Jesus, help Mom to learn to claim Your Word that teaches us to be anxious about nothing* (Philippians 4:6–7). *Let my example show her that Your peace comes through prayer.*

Yesterday, Mama would leave a night-light on for me, so I wouldn't be afraid in the dark. Tonight, I left it on for her, near my phone number, for the very same reason. *Lord, may Mom know that Your presence is with her always. You are only a prayer away.*

Just yesterday, my small, skinny arms flung around her neck to give big hello kisses. Tonight, she reached up to hug me. I gently bent down to give a good-bye kiss. "I love you, Honey," she said. "I love you, too, Mom, very much!" *Thank You, Lord, for such a precious mom. Help me be as good a mama to her as she has been to me.*

She is eighty-five years old now. In these, her sunset years, may she be able to rest in knowing that I am now caring for her needs. *And Lord Jesus, thank You that I can draw from Your strength to relieve the daily pressures that our changing roles may bring. After all, You willingly accepted the ultimate role-reversal when You left the glory of heaven to take on the form of a Servant* (Philippians 2:5–8).

As she continues to rely more on me, may I learn to depend more and more upon You.

A LESSON ON PRAYER

by Cheryl A. Paden, Fremont, Nebraska

"These two molars will have to be pulled," the orthodontist said. I listened carefully to his explanation of the latest plans for my son Isaac's teeth. I was acutely aware of the look of fear on Isaac's face at the mention of pulling teeth. I knew he didn't want to go through that again. However, I made the appointment with the dentist. In two weeks, the teeth would come out.

Every day Isaac begged not to have the teeth removed. He came up with all sorts of other options. Having gone through the same thing as a child myself, I strongly sympathized with him. It was necessary, though, and I could see no way out of it for him.

As we drove to the dentist's office on the day of the dreaded appointment, I glanced into the rearview mirror. My son was in the backseat with his head bowed and his hands folded in prayer. He must have sensed me looking at him. "I'm praying to not have my teeth pulled," he explained to me.

I was heartsick. I knew how disappointed he would be. Concern that his faith in prayer would now be lessened troubled me. I had no words of comfort, so I just drove.

In the dentist's office, the nurse took Isaac back to the procedure room. I sat in the waiting room with a heavy heart, knowing how frightened he was feeling.

In a few minutes, Dr. Mike came out to me. "I really don't know why these two teeth need to be removed. I'd like to call your orthodontist and discuss it with him." I was stunned. Sure enough, one phone call to the orthodontist confirmed it. The teeth could be left to fall out naturally.

I left the office with a very happy little boy. I could only shake my head in amazement. How had I forgotten the basic truth that God listens and answers even our simplest prayers?

That day, we both learned a lesson about the power of prayer. One learned with the faith of a child and one through doubt. Next time, I'll try to have the faith of a child. And I won't miss another opportunity to pray with my son.

Published in Purpose *7/6/99;* Spirit *7/99;*
Reprint in the Standard *6/17/2001*

THE WRONG ROAD

by Gilda V. Bryant, Amarillo, Texas

My husband, Robert, and I had been visiting with his family in Midland, Texas, and were driving home to southeastern New Mexico. Pregnant with our first child, I wanted to arrive before dark. It was only a two-hour drive, one we'd made many times, through a flat landscape of mesquite trees, pumpjacks pulling oil from the earth, and endless barbed wire fences. An occasional skinny, long-legged jackrabbit broke the monotony with its zigzagging burst of energy.

Then we saw the road sign. We were traveling in the wrong direction! How did we manage to do that? We had the westerly sun to guide us and a map, yet we had taken the wrong road. We thought we knew the area roads and found it hard to believe that we had failed to find the right one. How could we miss the familiar highway we had traveled so many times before?

"I'm sorry, Hon. I really don't know how we missed it. I'll turn west on the next farm-to-market road." Robert smiled reassuringly at me. "We should intersect the highway from there. We'll get you home before dark."

We continued through more of the same flat pastures and spied a lean coyote. There was the ever familiar mesquite, dry grass, and a few skinny, white-faced Hereford cows. The pungent aroma of an agitated skunk wove its way into the car. Clumps of prickly pear cactus rose from the prairie like weird, deformed hands. But there was no sign of human habitation. There was just the vast emptiness of desert. We felt like we were the last people on earth. Then, up ahead, we saw a car parked on the side of the road.

As we approached, we could see a young woman, in an attractive dress and high heels, reaching in the trunk, struggling to lift the heavy, dirty spare tire from its nesting place. Her young son wore chinos and a blue dress shirt with a bow tie. His hands were black from his wrestling match with the spare. An adolescent girl stood at the car's side. The rear right tire was as flat as the west Texas terrain around us. We parked behind them and got out to give a hand.

Breathless and disheveled, the woman said, "Thank you for stopping. I've never done this before. I had no idea how heavy this tire would be." After lifting the spare out of the trunk, Robert went to work removing the flat. As he worked, he noticed that all the tires on the car were rather worn.

"You from around here?" he asked.

"We live in the next town over, about ninety miles," she answered. "We were just coming back from church with my folks when this happened."

"Well, when you get back home, you should have your husband take a look at your tires," Robert advised. "You should probably replace them. This is no country to get stuck in like this."

She colored slightly, and an awkward silence ensued. Finally, she said, "Thanks, I'm just recently divorced, and I guess I'm not used to taking care of everything myself yet. I'll take care of the tires right away."

With help from the young son, who was obviously acting as the "man of the family," Robert finished changing the tire. "There you go," he said, wiping his hands. "That'll get you home at least. Just don't forget to have the rest of them checked."

"I won't. I promise. And thank you so much," she said. As we shook hands to say good-bye, she held on to ours for just a second and said quietly, "You know, I prayed for you to come and help us." Robert and I just smiled.

"Glad we were here, then," my husband said. "We'll follow you for a ways to make sure you're okay. Our turnoff isn't for a bit yet."

They were fine. And with a final honk of the horn and a wave, we left them on their own as we turned onto our own road home.

We didn't say much on the rest of the drive, watching the familiar landscape speed by. We were both lost in thought. Was a mother's heartfelt prayer the reason we missed a highway we had always found before? How else could our meandering route be explained? I believe that God used us to be His servants to provide help and safety to strangers on a long, lonely Texas road. A peacefulness settled into my heart as I thought how our heavenly Father takes care of His children—how He answers prayers in ways we might never expect.

Another prayer was answered that day, too. We arrived home as the sun was sinking into the horizon, just before dark.

Published in Guideposts *12/2000*

A SIMPLE PRAYER

by Kathryn Lay, Arlington, Texas

"Please let me see a frog tonight. In Jesus' name, amen."

I hugged my four-year-old daughter good-night and tucked her into bed with her favorite books to look at. Her prayer was simple and cute, something from a book of kids' prayers. We had been talking about frogs and lizards and turtles that day, three of her favorite creatures.

"When will the frog come?" she asked.

I smiled. "Well, Michelle, I haven't seen any frogs yet this year; we'll just have to wait and see." I felt bad that she would be disappointed.

"God can do anything," she announced. "Just like my daddy."

A lump filled my throat. She trusted in her earthly father and her heavenly Father. Difficult times had made me doubt God's love for me;

how I longed for my daughter's kind of unconditional trust and belief.

I went into the kitchen to do the dishes. With hands sunk in hot, soapy water, I closed my eyes and prayed. "I know it's a silly request, God. But, there's something about the way she truly believes You'll answer her prayer. Do You hear her? Do You hear me?"

My husband returned home late from his volunteer work at church with the "English as a Second Language" class for refugees. Michelle had been asleep an hour. Richard and I talked over our day and how the class went that night. I shared Michelle's prayer with him and we both smiled.

"Oops, laundry," I said, jumping up to move the wet clothes from the washer to the dryer. I turned on the garage light and was startled by movement near the open door that led to the backyard.

Our dog barked at the corner, stopping to sniff at something. I took a careful step forward, ready to run if one of our giant, fast-moving waterbugs should suddenly head my way. Near the back door sat a large, bug-eyed, brown frog.

"Outside," I ordered the dog. After a momentary chase with the frog being two hops ahead, I held the bulging, squirming creature in my hands and carried my prize into the house.

"Hey, look," I said, holding it out to my husband. "I think Tippy was about to have a late-night snack of frog legs."

"Wow, it's too bad Michelle's not awake," he said.

How could I have forgotten? My mouth nearly hit the floor when I remembered her prayer—and then my own.

"Quick," I said, "wake her up."

My surprised husband stared at me as if I'd done one too many loads of laundry. Under most circumstances, after a very long day with our active child and an even longer evening of convincing her to go to bed, I rarely encouraged awakening our little sleeping beauty. But this was different.

She needed to see this frog.

She held the frog and petted it, more sleepy than interested, and not the least bit surprised that her prayer had been answered.

But I was overwhelmed at the quick response to her simple prayer . . .and to mine as I'd prayed over soapy water and dirty dishes. What a loving Father, to see the importance of such a small child's request, a chance for her to see the power of an earnest prayer.

My faith took its own leap that night as I set the frog free in our front yard, watching him jump away. "Yes, Michelle, you are absolutely right," I said aloud. "God can do anything." Sometimes, my daughter teaches me more than I teach her.

WHEN FAITH CONQUERED FEAR

By Jocelyn Rogers
As told to Esther M. Bailey

Sitting beside my husband in church, I tried to concentrate on the worship service. I sang the words of the hymn, but my mind replayed the doctor's words that dashed our hopes. From the beginning of our eight-year marriage, Marvin and I had yearned for a child. The doctor treating us for infertility had recently said, "I'm afraid we've run out of options."

With little prospect of becoming natural parents, we had already started the adoption process. It was too soon to predict the outcome of our effort.

I glanced down at the church bulletin to check the page number of the next hymn. My eyes centered on upcoming events. I drew in a quick breath. Marvin leaned toward me and whispered, "What's wrong?"

Unable to speak, I pointed to the announcement in the bulletin: Baby Dedication next Sunday. Marvin's eyes registered pain that matched my own, but he reached for my hand. His tenderness provided the strength to endure the rest of the service.

On the way home from church, Marvin said, "Why don't we drive up to Phoenix for church next Sunday?"

I seized the opportunity to escape what, for me, would inevitably be a painful experience. The last time I attended a baby dedication, I had cried until there were no tears left.

"Yes, let's," I said. It would be good to get away, and I could see some of my friends, as well. Growing up in Tucson, I had made friends throughout Arizona while attending youth camps and other church-related functions.

Even before I married, I had a terrible fear that I might never become a mother. As the firstborn of a mother with Rh-negative blood and a father with Rh-positive blood, I remained an only child. Memory of my childhood always centered on the periods of grief when two babies were stillborn. Later, the joy resulting from the birth of a live baby lasted only four days.

When I was seven, Mrs. Binkley and her baby came to live with us while her husband was in the military. I was a little mother to the baby we called Binky. Each day, I rushed home from school to "my baby." The slightest whimper from the child sent me running. Tenderly holding him, I crooned, "There, there, Binky, don't cry." When he clutched my finger with his little hand and smiled, happiness rippled through my body. I was born to be a mother.

Before Binky's first birthday, I heard the devastating news. Mr. Binkley was coming home. I would lose my baby.

While Mrs. Binkley packed to leave, I moped around the house. When she told us good-bye, I timidly asked, "Will I ever see Binky again?"

With her baby cradled in her arms, she smiled and said, "Of course. We won't be living that far away. You can come and see us any time."

Fate shattered my hope of continuing the relationship. Shortly after the family moved, Binky died. The rooming house where they moved had been sprayed with insecticide, and enough of the residue remained to poison the child. It was as though I had lost my own child.

At the Phoenix church on the following Sunday, the sight of friendly, familiar faces helped blot out the anxieties I lived with. I was feeling comfortable until a couple I had known in the past approached me to show off their new baby daughter. My heart flipped. How could I extend to them my best wishes when tears threatened to surface?

I cleared my throat and willed my voice to hide the pain I felt. "Congratulations, I wish you every happiness," I said.

"We're going to dedicate her to the Lord this morning," the young mother said.

Lord, help me! my heart cried as I struggled for composure. Quickly, I admonished myself: *Don't panic! Think positively about the recent application for adoption.* I excused myself as graciously as I could and made my way to a pew near the back of the church.

When Marvin joined me, I told him about the dedication. "Will you be all right?" he asked anxiously.

I nodded, determined to put on a good front.

After the benediction, I mingled with my friends while Marvin stood at the back of the church.

A longtime friend, a godly woman affectionately known as Mom Pulsipher, greeted my husband. Sensing his wounded spirit, she said, "What's the trouble, Son?"

"We came here because they were having a baby dedication at Tucson; then they had one here, too. We feel bad because we can't have a baby."

The kindly woman gazed at my husband with her sparkling blue eyes that radiated compassion. "Bring Jocelyn here," she said.

As Marvin and I knelt before a small bench in the back of the church, Mom Pulsipher placed her saintly hands on our heads and prayed a simple prayer. Many people had prayed with us and for us. We had lived with constant prayer in our hearts for many years. This time, however, something was different.

Never before had my faith been so inspired. It was as though a door had opened wide, and a fresh breeze poured over my soul. I suddenly understood I did not need to solve my own problem. I could give my desire for a child to God and allow Him to handle it in His own time and in His own way. In one moment, faith conquered my fear. The anxiety that had plagued me for years drained from my body.

God's timing was perfect. Two months later, I learned I was pregnant. While waiting for the birth of Loretta Lee Rogers, I gained greater understanding of the Virgin Mary's words: "My soul doth magnify the Lord" (Luke 1:46 KJV).

Although Loretta remained an only child, she fulfilled our yearning for parenthood. We watched her grow up to love the Lord and marry Kyle Cooper, a youth pastor. Today, she is widely known as Lauren Rogers on ABC radio and television. On January 21, 1999, God gave us a bonus with the birth of our grandson, Carson Wade Cooper.

Throughout the years, I have experienced many difficult times, including the recent death of my husband. Sometimes I react with anxiety. Then I recall Mom Pulsipher's prayer that turned my fear to faith.

Past experience reminds me that the God I serve is still bigger than any of my problems and is always worthy of my trust.

WALKING ON WATER

by Peggie Coletti Bohanon, Springfield, Missouri

Women don't walk on water—and I don't really, of course. But God has a wonderful sense of humor, and through His providential plans for my life, and even through my own feelings of uncertainty, inadequacy, and downright fright, I have learned I can walk on water with His strength. I can do the impossible with His help and direction.

One evening, after a promising interview with a wonderful Christian company and an offer of a great ministry position, I faced a decision. Could I do it? *Of course not,* I thought. No way could I be an editor and an administrator and whatever else was involved. I had neither the education nor the expertise—or so whispered the inner negative voice who at times whispers to us all. But I did consent to think about it, pray about it, and give the company a decision the next day.

Heading back to my hotel room, I could not sleep. Thoughts wandered around in my weary brain as I wanted so much to know God's will. It would mean some changes (and change has always been scary for me), some turnarounds in my lifestyle (and who, at my "unmentionable" age likes new directions!), and a commitment to a "real job" (as though homemaking is not a "real job"!). So I prayed. I mean, I really prayed. "Lord, is this the direction You want me to take? I am willing—but Lord, it is so big, and I am soo scared!" But God, who loves to turn us around in our tracks, has a plan. He decided that the middle of the night was a good time to reveal it, and so in my late-night confusion, I found myself being drawn to His Word—to a familiar story from childhood. You guessed it—Peter walking on the water!

When God speaks to me—either through people, circumstances,

or His Word—He seems to enjoy getting my attention in creative ways that no mortal would ever think of doing. My life is full of funny stories about God's divine sense of humor. He often chooses Scriptures, unique ones, as a very special "signpost" of His will and direction. I was about to learn, once again, that I could trust Him with the turnarounds of my life, that He was my master navigator.

But back to Peter—I searched through my Bible to find the exact passage. The visual picture grew stronger and stronger in my mind and heart. I could "see" with spiritual eyes the story come alive. Peter, stepping out of the boat—but not quite. One foot in, one foot out, and of course, scared to death, like me! I saw the rolling, raging waves. I saw Jesus, in white garment, standing with hand outstretched, saying to Peter, "Come!" The picture in my mind, while not a vision, was so real to my heart that I knew God was speaking.

And suddenly, I knew He wasn't just speaking to Peter. He was speaking to me! "Come, Peggie, get out of that boat; you, too, can do what you think is impossible. You can walk on the water—not in your own strength, but because I am calling you." God was directing my course—He would be with me; He would help me do what I felt so inadequate to perform on my own. I knew in my heart what my answer would be the next day. I closed the Bible and went to sleep for whatever was left of the night.

The next morning, my husband and I visited a church, my heart still full of the experience of the night before. A guest speaker took as his text, "Work out your salvation with fear and trembling, for it is God who works in you to will and to act according to his good purpose" (Philippians 2:12–13). My heart nearly burst; my eyes filled with tears. I knew God once again was telling this worried, in-the-way woman to "walk on the water."

That afternoon, when asked if I would accept the position, I smiled and replied, "With fear and trembling, yes, I will." Am I happy with the "new direction" my life has taken? You'd better believe it. Have there been adjustments? You had better believe that, too—some days I forget to do the laundry (not such a bad thing to forget, eh?). I have had to learn new ways and means of getting it all done. God has set my feet on a new, untraveled path—one with many twists and turns, ups and downs. Yet, as I continue to heed His voice, I find it is a direction more glorious than one I could have ever dreamed of taking on my own. His plan is purposeful—and it is perfect!

And has God been faithful? Has He ever been faithful! He has helped beyond measure; He has anointed me to do the work which He has called me to do. I am the "walk-on-water-woman," not because of me, but because of a wonderful Lord, Who, in the middle of the night, extended His hand across the waves to one very insecure woman and said, "Come!" His Word still works—I have proved it so!

INTO GOD'S HANDS

By Kathy Semon, Rice Lake, Wisconsin

After trying for three years, I was finally pregnant with our first child. I should have been overjoyed at the prospect. Instead, I found myself filled with a deep sadness. My grandmother, who was very dear to me, was dying from emphysema. It tore my heart out to know she was suffering, and because of my fragile pregnancy, I would not be able to go and see her.

Day after day, I would pray to God for a miracle to spare her life. I was not ready to give her up and pleaded with Him to make her better so I would not lose her. After some deep soul-searching and prayer, I finally realized what happened to my grandmother was really up to God, not me. I then began to pray for His wishes and was able to put my grandmother's life into His caring hands. It was one of the hardest things I have ever done, but God blessed me for it.

I will never forget the day that changed my life forever. A day that changed forever how I would look at God's awesome power to turn sadness into joy and tears into laughter. I remember sitting on my couch to rest, when suddenly a deep urgency to pray for my grandmother overtook me. With tears streaming down my face I prayed; "God, please let my grandma know how much I love her, let her know how much I wish I could be there with her!" I went about the rest of my day marveling at the new direction my life had taken after that prayer, a direction of wonderful peace.

Later that same evening, my mother called with an update on Grandma's condition. There was usually very little to say since Grandma was so weak and rarely talked or even moved. But today had been different. Mother told me the strangest thing had happened that day. During her visit, Grandma looked up at her and said, "Tell Kathy to come over here by me for a minute. I need to tell her how much I love her." Mom explained I was not there, but she would make sure to pass the message on to me.

I was speechless. At first, I felt so honored that of all the people in Grandma's life, she had been thinking of me and singled me out to tell me she loved me. Then it struck me like a true "bolt from heaven." Mom had been visiting with Grandma about the same time I had been crying and praying for God to let her know how much I loved her. God had answered my prayer!

If I had ever doubted the power of prayer before that, I most certainly do not now. God changed my life that day and turned it around in a way I will never be able to explain. As it says in Isaiah 26:3–4, "Thou wilt keep him in perfect peace, whose mind is stayed on thee: because he trusteth in thee. Trust ye in the LORD for ever: for in the LORD JEHOVAH is everlasting strength" (KJV).

My U-turn was at last understanding that we serve a God Who can not only move mountains but can also touch the hearts of those we love!

IN HIS TIME

by Nancy Gibbs, Cordele, Georgia

My husband was a pastor serving in a small country church. As the pastor's wife, I supported the mission activities and taught the ladies' Sunday school class. This wasn't how it had started though. At a very young age, I began reading and writing stories for my parents and grandparents. By the age of fourteen, I knew my calling was to become a writer.

However, at eighteen, I became a mother of twin sons, which took up a great deal of my time. Five years later, our baby girl was born. For the next eighteen years, I gave my all to my family, while serving God in whatever church we were in at the time. Somehow though, it didn't seem to be enough.

While watching a televised crusade in our living room one night, I felt God's presence right there beside me. As the lyrics of "Just As I Am" were being sung, I paced my living-room floor. Even though I had been a Christian for many years, I never felt as though I was doing everything God would have me do with my life. I knew somewhere and sometime God would show me something else He wanted me to do for Him. It was during the crusade that night that His direction was revealed to me. His Spirit engulfed my soul that evening like it had never done before.

"God is speaking to me," I told my husband and pastor. "There is something else God wants me to do with my life," I said, as I wiped away tears. "I have no idea how to begin, but I know it has something to do with writing." I prayed for hours, after the telecast. I cried out to God and begged Him to show me how to start my new mission.

A few days passed. My sons convinced me on-line was the place to be. The day I signed on for the first time, I found the perfect place to begin my writing adventure. I wrote many stories about Jesus and His everlasting love for the world. I began winning contests, but more importantly, I began winning souls for God.

"Writing is a difficult business to break into," many writers told me. "You will need an agent," others said. Even though I knew these words were probably true, I was convinced, with God's help and my determination, I would become successful in His time. After all, I already had the greatest agent of all on my side! I felt He wouldn't have allowed me to get this far without continuing to help me along the way.

In only a few months, I started writing a weekly religion column for my local newspaper. With every issue, more souls were won, many lives were being changed. Seeing my words in print and having some of my other stories published in various books and periodicals affirmed to me that I was doing what God would have me do. For the first time in my life, I felt complete. I knew beyond a shadow of a doubt

God was dictating His words to me. I diligently typed while He gently spoke to my heart. I was happier and more content than I had ever been. My prayer time each day increased as my relationship with God grew stronger. With an unwavering faith, I continued to write. In less than one year after the crusade, I was working as a freelance writer in the Christian market and loving every minute of it.

My husband and I continue to serve in our wonderful little church, and I still enjoy teaching my senior ladies' Sunday school class. God has empowered me to accomplish many things for Him. I am so grateful for that beautiful night while sitting in front of the television set—the night that brought a U-turn into my life.

For all those many years, the words and the desire to write were inside me. After my children were grown, the time came for me to begin my writing ministry. In His time, I discovered all things are possible, if we only pray, believe, and put our trust in Him. For as we read in Romans 8:28: "And we know that all things work together for good to those who love God, to those who are the called according to His purpose" (NKJV).

CHAPTER TEN

New Direction U-Turn

Therefore, if anyone is in Christ, he is a new creation;
the old has gone, the new has come!
2 Corinthians 5:17

Oh God of second chances and new beginnings,
here I am. Again.
Nancy Spiegelberg, Vermilion, Ohio

Previously published in Seek, *December 14, 1997*

A DECEMBER STORY

by Claudia C. Breland, Maple Valley, Washington

Early in December of 1991, I was driving home from my little auto repair shop in Fall City, a small town in Washington State. Every day I drove to and from work on Highway 18, which wound among the evergreen forests in the Cascade foothills. Several times each week, I would see people stopped by the side of the road with car trouble, and I almost always stopped to help.

Coming down the highway from Tiger Summit, I spotted an old 1968 Pontiac pulled over on the shoulder, with its hood up. It looked as if it should have gone to the salvage yard years ago. I pulled in behind it, and walking up to the two disheveled men standing there peering into the motor, I asked, "You guys need some help?"

After a few minutes, it was obvious that the two of them were both high on drugs or drunk (or both) and wouldn't know a battery cable if it jumped out at them. After checking all the obvious trouble spots, I straightened up and told them, "I can't figure out what's wrong with this heap, so there's only one thing left to do."

"Wha's that?" asked one of them.

"We need to pray!" Ignoring their dropped jaws and incredulous expressions, I sternly told them to shut their eyes and bow their heads. "I'm going to lay hands on this motor and pray for it."

Snickering, they did as they were told, and I proceeded to pray, giving it all I had. It was a thundering, powerful prayer, thanking God for His many gifts, and ending with "In the name of Jesus, I command this car to start!" I got into the front seat, turned the key, and the old Pontiac came to life, purring like a kitten. Getting out again, I said matter-of-factly, "Well, you're all set now. You'd better stop somewhere and have a cup of coffee. You need something to sober you up some."

Sobered by the experience, the driver asked in a hushed and incredulous voice, "How can I pay you?"

I said, "I tell everybody I help the same thing. You can pay me back by helping someone else who's stopped by the side of the road." I said good-bye and continued on my way, murmuring a brief prayer for their safety and stifling my doubts about helping somebody so inebriated.

Four years later, on December 21, 1995, I left work feeling sorry and depressed. I had given up my own auto repair shop in Fall City and was now working at a shop in Seattle. I'd worked at three different shops in the last ten months and was no stranger to the unemployment office. While stopping for construction as I was driving south on I-5, my motor suddenly putt-putted and came to an abrupt stop. Glancing down at the gas gauge, I groaned. I'd been so busy this week, I never even thought about getting gas. Traffic had started moving again, and there were impatient honks from the waiting drivers.

Getting out of the car, I walked back to the driver directly behind me. The other man climbed down from his truck and came forward. He was clean shaven and energetic and asked heartily, "Are you having problems? Anything I can do to help?"

"Awww, I ran out of gas," I told him in a disgusted tone of voice. "This week I've been so busy I never thought to look at the gas gauge, and I ran out just sitting here."

He nodded understandingly and suggested, "Why don't we push your car over to the shoulder, so we can let traffic get by. I've got a five-gallon can of gas in the back of my truck."

The two of us pushed my little Subaru over to the shoulder, and he pulled in behind me. As he began pouring gas into my tank, we started talking. I told him, "I don't have any money with me, not a dime, but if you'll give me your name and address I can send you a check."

The other man shook his head. "I always tell people the best way they can pay me is to help somebody else."

I chuckled, "That's what I tell people, too—in fact, I remember once I prayed over a car, and it started!"

The other man suddenly straightened up and looked at me intently, then a wondrous smile spread from ear to ear. "Was that on Highway 18, about four years ago?" When I nodded, he said in amazement, quietly, "That was me!" He put the gas cap back on and said, "Look, why don't we pull off at the next exit. I have a story to tell you."

After we'd both pulled into a parking lot, the other man got out of his truck, introduced himself, and started talking. "First of all, I can't tell you how many times I have racked my brain, trying to remember what you looked like. Many, many times I've talked over that incident with my friend. All we could remember was you praying over that old junk heap and making it start!"

His excitement mounted as he continued, "When I got home that night, I couldn't sleep a wink. After I told my brother what happened, he told me that I should take it as a sign from God that He loved me and wanted me to turn my life over to Him. So I started going to AA meetings and got clean and sober for the first time in over twenty years. My brother invited me to an Easter cantata at his church. He promised there'd be no preaching, just music. Well, they didn't have to preach; the words of the songs reached out and grabbed me by the heart. That night, I gave my life to the Lord and accepted Him as Savior."

I was moved by this man's openness as he continued, "My friend and I decided to go into business together as general contractors, and we're doing very well. I don't have any physical problems despite being an alcoholic for twenty years, and I'm engaged to be married in June! Your prayer changed my life!"

As I listened to his testimony, my heart felt a lot lighter. I said a silent thank You to God, for allowing me to hear the rest of the story. In turn, I told him about some of the things that had happened in my life in the last four years. We visited as though we were lifelong friends.

"Oh, one more thing," I said as we exchanged business cards. I had decided that he deserved to hear the rest of the story, too. "You remember how I insisted that you and your buddy both close your eyes when I prayed over your car?" He nodded. I grinned and said, "In looking your engine over, I saw that the coil was not bolted down as it should have been. So while I was praying, I just reached over and plugged it in."

RIVER RIDE

by Harry Vann Phillips, Germany

As a young man from a single-parent home who had grown up on the wrong side of the tracks, I spent my freshman year of college skipping more classes than I attended and being involved with things counterproductive to getting good grades. I wanted to have fun. I did not use good judgment that year and wound up with the minimum grade point average needed to return for the fall semester. It was with that same attitude that I left my hometown to spend the summer of 1979 working in Naturita, Colorado.

In Naturita, I was hired onto a drilling rig as a roughneck where I worked twelve hours a day, seven days a week, drilling seven-foot diameter air shafts into uranium mines. Time off was scarce. The work was dirty, hard, and dangerous, but it paid well. The people I worked with were tough, hardworking types with a penchant for playing just as hard as they worked.

In the middle of one of our jobs, our rig broke down. Since replacement parts were not readily available, it would take a few days to get the repairs made. Our boss told us to cut back our work hours for a few days until the rig was back in operation. At the end of one of those short workdays, our work crew decided to go swimming in a nearby stream.

It was a hot day in late May. Swimming in a clear mountain stream promised to be a nice break from the rigors of working on the drilling rig. We all knew a spot we thought would make a good swimming hole. Once there, we jumped out of the pickup truck and quickly took off our shirts and shoes. After a few minutes of splashing each other, we decided to body-float downstream and get out at a point before the stream emptied into the San Miguel River.

It started out great. The stream did all the work, carrying us single-file through deep pools and shallows with small rocks grabbing at the seats of our pants. It was very serene and relaxing as we laughed and talked while floating past some very spectacular scenery. The idea of floating in the San Miguel River began to seem like a good idea. We had no idea of what we were about to get into. The tranquil environment made us totally oblivious to the danger waiting for us.

What happened next was terrifying. A few meters upstream from where our gently flowing stream entered the San Miguel River, the current began to pick up speed. What had been a lazy, fun-filled experience suddenly exploded into a high-speed life or death struggle between three men and the rushing current of the San Miguel. The river was flowing very fast from the meltwater coming off the snow packs high in the mountains. The river water was also much colder than the water in the slow-moving stream.

As the current swiftly pushed us to the middle of the river, we struggled to swim out of the main current toward the close bank on our left. My boss was able to quickly make it to the water's edge and scrambled out of the clutches of the raging torrent. I saw him climb the river's bank as the current pulled me past him into deeper and faster-moving water. The second guy from our crew was nowhere to be seen.

Huge swells of fast-moving water were directly in front of me. I knew it was going to take every ounce of energy I had to get myself to the river's edge. As I struggled in vain against the current, it was all I could do to keep my head above water. My body was caught in the torrent. Pure adrenaline kept my arms and legs pumping furiously just to keep my head above water.

I was being swept along like a rag doll just a few short feet from the bank. I thought if I could just keep my head above water, the current would get me close enough to grab a tree limb or a root in order to pull myself out of the water. At that point, I thought the worst was over, and I would be able to escape from the angry San Miguel. I was wrong though. The harder I tried to grab hold of a root or branch, the faster the river seemed to carry me along.

As I raced toward a bend in the river with the bank on my right, I kept reaching for tree limbs and branches just above my head. Suddenly, my extended body slammed into a boulder that must have been the size of a Volkswagen and was just below the surface of the water. The force of the impact completely knocked the wind out of me and flipped me upside down as the river continued to push me along. There was no way for me to tell where the surface was as I was twisted and pulled mercilessly by the roiling water of the San Miguel. With my lungs begging for air, I could not fight my way to the surface. The river had complete control of me.

The lack of oxygen and pain from the impact with the boulder were combining to put me into shock. Then, as suddenly as I went under, the current shot me to the surface. When I broke the surface, gasping for air, I found myself once again on the opposite side of the river.

The river's current swept me close to the bank, now on my left. The twigs at the end of the tree branches hung like tiny fingers over the water as the torrent carried me farther downstream. The twigs raced through my hands as I desperately tried to grasp something to hold on to. The harder I tried to grab one of those fragile twigs, the more my strength was drained from me.

I was exhausted and almost completely drained of energy. I could no longer reach for the fragile twigs hanging just inches above my head, and swimming was unthinkable. It was all I could do to keep my head above water. To make matters even worse, the current was pulling me toward rapids with white caps, which meant lots of submerged rocks and certain death. I was too weak to keep up the fight for much longer.

With my strength almost gone, I began to believe I was going to die. There was nothing more I could do. It was at that moment I began to pray. I am not exactly sure what I prayed for. All I remember saying was, "Please, God, save me. I do not want to die. I will never do anything wrong again. Please forgive me for all the wrongs I have done." I kept praying to our heavenly Father asking Him to save me, but I prepared myself for death as I was swept closer to the rapids. I was now too weak to even move my arms. I knew I could not escape the river. No one could escape the river at that point!

No one, that is, except for the Lord God Almighty. It was then that a miracle occurred. In what I was sure were my last moments on the face of this earth, I spotted a boulder jutting out of the water just a few meters downstream and immediately in front of me. If only I could make my way to the boulder, I would be saved. And just as miraculously as the boulder appeared, the current carried me to its base where I grabbed it and hung on for dear life. I hugged that boulder with every ounce of energy left in my body. It was the perfect size for me to hang onto. After a few moments, I crawled up atop that mighty rock.

Miraculously, the third guy from our crew, Randy, reached the safety of that rock, too. Safely on top of our rock and out of harm's way, I thanked the Lord for saving me and promised Him my life. I prayed and prayed giving thanks to Father God over and over. I stayed on the rock long enough to regain my strength and then climbed up the riverbank to the road going back into Naturita. I just walked in a daze not even noticing the seat of my jeans was missing.

I spent the rest of the summer working on the drilling rig and enjoying the beauty of western Colorado. Needless to say, I did not do any more body-floating. By the middle of August, I was on my way back home with a new attitude toward life.

When I returned to college in September, my grades improved, and the following spring semester I made the dean's list. I achieved the dean's list twice more before graduating. After graduation, I received a commission as an officer in the United States Army. Over the course of my career, I achieved the rank of Lieutenant Colonel.

I owe my very life to the Lord. I try to repay my debt to our Father in heaven every day. When I share my love of God with others, I always think of the time when He proved that His love for me is as solid as a rock. I tell them that He built His Church on a rock, and that a rock also became the foundation of my own faith in a very tangible way.

A better object lesson I cannot imagine.

FROM BELEAGUERED TO BLESSED

by Linda Nathan, Maple Falls, Washington

"Don't bother me! I am working!" I snapped at my son Eric. When he wasn't pestering me for hugs, he would hang over a chair two inches from my desk, analyzing every dot and comma, offering sage advice gained in his fifteen years of wisdom. I knew he would be irritated with me for awhile but, after all, I had to work, didn't I? Grumpy, I tried to return to my computer.

"Honey, I need more socks." My husband's clarion call shattered my carefully reordered thoughts. "Aren't you going to do wash?"

I sighed, setting down the manuscript I had been trying to edit. This was a far cry from the organized work life I had previously led, and certainly not what I'd had in mind when I had prayed for my own home business. Now that I was no longer an "official" working mom in the marketplace, my family considered me fair game for their attention.

Exhausted by ten years in the legal profession, longing for more time to write and spend time with my family, as well as suffering from chronic health problems, I had prayed for a change. And God had answered my heartfelt call.

Two months before our scheduled move from Oregon to Bellingham, Washington, He began supplying everything I needed: computer equipment, supplies, even a business name—Logos Word Designs. With such a response to my prayers, I was confident He would also provide a third bedroom in our new location so that I could enjoy an office of my own.

Well, God blessed our move and gave us a lovely apartment all right, but He forgot the third bedroom. Now, I sought His inspiration scrunched behind a makeshift plastic shield, protecting my printer from the kitchen sink. Behind me, the dining table pressed up against my chair, reminding me of the laundry piled on it, while under my feet cascaded baskets of filing. I remembered how, camera in hand, my last employer used to prowl law firms, recording employees' shameful disorder for posterity. How he would love zeroing in on me now!

God! I complained silently, *Why did You do this to me? How can I possibly work like this?* My prayers were fervent, panicky cries for greater efficiency and a change of situation. I struggled to maintain that pleasant fiction known as professionalism that I had enjoyed at the office. But keeping an active devotional life, following a strict work schedule, fixing meals and cleaning house, and being everything to everyone was just too much.

As this unrealistic scenario took its toll, it began to dawn on me that perhaps I was my own problem. In the pressures created by our small apartment, the interactions of our strong-willed family, and my driving aspirations, all of my sharp "professional" edges showed—an asset in an office setting perhaps, but a disaster at home. The very traits that had made me such good legal support made life a nightmare when applied to my family life!

I had developed valuable abilities—jewels that I knew the Lord intended for use in His service. I was discovering, however, that I had developed some other qualities along the way, too—ones He didn't want in His service! Hidden within the positive qualities of discipline, perseverance, and efficiency, lurked self-righteousness, driving ambition, guilt, and a critical, controlling spirit. Caught up in the feverish whirl of work and ministry, I had not been part of my family life the way I had wanted to be. As I began to understand that God had designed this situation for my own good, I prayed for guidance.

The Lord began by inviting me to enjoy long, leisurely mornings before plunging into work—and even then to "plunge" with care. It was difficult. At first, the guilt was awful. Leisure. Wasn't that doing nothing? Quiet walks in the woods. . .long talks with God. . .idle reading. . .sewing, dreaming, resting. Things I had not done in a long time.

This gracious new setting gave me a new perspective, opening up a whole new world for me. Into this unfamiliar quiet poured the revelation of what an immense treasure my family is and how isolated I felt by my drivenness. Now I saw that He was using the loving disorder of my home life to help me (hopefully) grow kinder and gentler, enjoy life more, and come out of that driving, self-imposed isolation.

It took nearly a year before I could finally begin asking myself some vital questions about my life, such as: So what? Who cares? and Who notices? I am doing what I love. My health is slowly improving. The place is basically orderly (sometimes), and I do most of my work on the phone or alone anyway. We may not be rich, but I am free. In a few years my big, friendly son will be eighteen and on his own. He won't pester me to play games anymore or leave his shoes and socks in the middle of the rug or give me (I have to admit it) good suggestions on my work.

And, after nearly thirty years of marriage, life with my husband is blessed and rich. All of a sudden, the remaining years are few and precious—surely not meant to be squandered in selfish ambition and life-negating order.

Looking back, I can finally thank God for His exasperating answer to my prayer for a third bedroom. The sharp jewels of my talents are far more attractive in a gentle setting.

Uh—excuse me. Eric just came in. Think we will go play some chess.

MY BUDDY JULES

by Paul Madison, Williamstown, New Jersey

I had only known Jules for about three months. He had already been working for a year at the luxurious high-rise apartment building on what is known as the Main Line of Philadelphia. Although he had spent most of his thirty-two years in poverty, which would harden most people, there was something kind about him. He was quick with a joke or something silly that would bring laughter to the rest of us on the maintenance staff.

He had this one special talent of driving you crazy with his singing at the most inappropriate times. You would be struggling with a repair job, and he would start his crooning. The trouble was that he would pick the only line from the song that he knew and sing it over and over again. After hearing this ten times in a two-minute stretch, it was common to say, "If you sing that one more time, I'm gonna caulk your mouth shut," and Jules would say something to the effect of, "What, you don't like that song?" Most of us would just reply, "The song's okay, but you keep singing the same thing over and over; can't you sing something else? You're driving me up the wall." Jules would clear his throat and ask, "How's 'bout this one?" And then he would sing the same lyrics yet again. You would just put your head down and laugh.

The day that I will remember for the rest of my life as the working of the Lord, Jules and I were working on the fourth floor where the study room and our shop are located. The study room was for the many undergrads that lived in the building or for anyone who just wanted to get away and read the paper in peace. It included an area with all kinds of vending machines. As I walked past the study room, I saw a young fellow of about twelve who looked as though he was buying a soda. I continued toward the shop to get Jules because I needed his help.

As Jules and I approached the study room, I decided to get a drink. While I was putting money into the machine, I saw Jules's hand reach over toward one of the vending machines, reach down and grab something, and hurriedly put whatever he had grabbed into his pocket.

"Okay, Pardner, what did you find?"

"Nothing, Man. You can't find what you own."

"Wait a minute here, what are you talking about, Jules? What did you find?" Jules pulled out two crumpled-up twenty-dollar bills, and he was grinning from ear to ear.

Then I remembered the boy that had been near the machine only about five minutes earlier. "I think I know who that belongs to, Jules." The grin left Jules's face, replaced by a look of anger that I had never seen from him.

"Yeah, you know who it belongs to. ME! I found it and it's mine now." Jules wadded up the money and stuffed it back in his pocket. I started to explain to him about the young guy I had seen a moment ago, but he cut me off. "Let me tell you something. I had my bike stolen from me this week. I used that bike 'cause I don't have a car or a license. I live in a shack where the roaches and the mice are threatening to call the Board of Health. I had a crackhead up there the other day, and she didn't even want to stay. So you think I'm worried about some rich kid that lives in this building getting his money back? It's probably his video game money or his allowance. I'm thirty-two years old, and I ain't got forty dollars to lose, let alone give it back to somebody I don't even know. So just forget it. It's mine now."

I was a bit taken back by this tirade. I hadn't seen this anger or bitterness from Jules in the time I thought us to be friends. We started to leave the room when in walked the young fellow I assumed had lost the money. He had an anxious look on his face when he asked, "Excuse me, but I lost some money in here. Did you see it?" Jules had a cold look on his face as he said, "No, we didn't see no money. You should be more careful." I caught Jules's eyes as we started to walk out the door.

Once we were out of earshot, I had to ask him, "Since you know who that money belongs to now, do you feel like the owner or do you feel like a thief?" We both looked back into the study room and watched as the young man tried in vain to look behind the machines. This time when we saw his face, he was wiping tears from his eyes.

Jules shrugged his shoulders and said "Too bad for him."

Now I was angry as I walked away from Jules. Angry with someone that I thought was a friend and more angry with myself for not doing the right thing. Jules would have surely lost his job if I had spoken up after he denied having the money. I walked into the shop and kicked some of the wood and debris that was always scattered around the floor. I looked at the half-filled paint cans and thought I would love to go over and knock them all over the shop. Just as I was about to sit down on a milk crate, our manager, Mike, walked in and said, "I've got to get ahold of Jules."

My heart jumped, fearing that the young man had put two and two together and come up with me or Jules as the culprit. "What do you want to see him for, Mike?" Mike shook his head in disgust.

"I want to see if that knucklehead wants one of those two bikes out on my patio." Being the building manager, Mike lived on premises and had two relatively new bikes that his kids never rode. "I just want to get rid of them before they get any more rust on them and they're worthless."

Well, I thought to myself, how do you like that? Jules takes some kid's money, then someone replaces the bike that was stolen from him. I wanted to tell Mike to give the bike to somebody more deserving when Jules appeared in the doorway. "Well, I hope you're happy."

"What do you mean, Jules?" I asked.

"I just hope you're happy. I gave that dumb kid his money back." Mike looked on puzzled.

"What kid? What money?" he asked. I felt a moment of relief from my own guilt.

"Nothing, Mike. Jules found this kid's money, and he was teasing about not giving it back."

Mike just looked at Jules and said in mock anger, "I'm giving you one of the bikes out on the balcony. But if you ever sing that stupid song again, I'm taking it back."

Jules looked at me and said, "Thanks, Man."

"Thanks for what?"

"For telling Mike I needed a bike 'cause mine got stolen."

Before I could get the words out, Mike yelled at Jules. "He didn't tell me nothing about no bike. I saw that piece of junk you had when I took you home the other day and figured if anyone needed a bike, you did." Jules thanked Mike as Mike closed the door yelling, "Yeah, whatever."

I couldn't wait to find out what brought on the change of heart. "So what made you do it? Did that kid threaten you?"

Jules just smiled. "Nah. I just thought about my life and how hard it's been. I know He doesn't make deals, but I thought maybe if I did something nice for somebody, God would do something nice for me. And I just remembered how I felt when I went downstairs to get my bike, and it was gone. Then I realized that there's a way to change the things in my life, and the start is changing myself. I also want to thank you for helping me."

"Thank me? For what?"

"You made me think of the Lord."

I was taken aback again. "I made you think of the Lord?"

"By you acting as my conscience, you made me remember the more important things. And keeping that money would have set me back. I've been doing a lot of prayin', and sometimes I think it's worthless.

But I've come a long way in the last few months." Jules went on to tell me that he had been hooked on drugs, and he was unreliable to his friends and family. He had started praying a while back, and he had seen a change in his life, but it was slow and small.

As much as I wanted to take the credit, I realized that God had stepped in and answered Jules's prayers.

"Sorry, Jules. I'd like to take the credit, but I can't. There is something in you that deserves the credit. I think the sacrifice you made by giving that money back to help dry that kid's tears will be rewarded someday." I'd forgotten about the bike.

"Rewarded, huh? That bike is the first installment!" We both laughed and went to lunch.

That was six years ago. There is something special in Jules now, too. It is the light he brings whenever he is around. He gives praise to God every day. I only wish I could be half the person he has come to be. On that day six years ago, he taught this self-righteous person that giving, when you are in need yourself, is the way to all good things. And I guess that is what it's all about, isn't it? That is what Christ did for us. Christ was in need, and He still gave His very life for us.

A lesson that should remind us daily how to give of ourselves.

OUT OF THE DEPTHS

by Bernis Elverum, Faribault, Minnesota

"How beautiful! How fantastic!" These were my words as I viewed the ocean for the very first time. "Quite different from the prairies, isn't it?" remarked my cousin Ina. "It sure is," I said with awe, "even the smell is different—salty and wet."

Ina and I were both fifteen, and though we had both been born in Saskatchewan, Canada, our lives had been very different. She grew up in southern California, four blocks away from the ocean. I had been raised in Minnesota and had never seen the ocean until this day. We were on our way with her parents to their home, where I would spend the winter of 1930 with them. A winter that would change my life.

In our home in Minnesota, church attendance was a top priority. When I left on my trip, one of the things Mother had told me was, "Don't forget to go to church."

My aunt tried to help me fulfill this promise. However, the church we attended in California was very different from the one I was accustomed to at home. The church at home was a small building with a small, but friendly, congregation. The pastor and his family were close friends of our family, and I knew the entire congregation. I enjoyed the order of the services and knew all of the songs we sang. I enjoyed going to church. I felt close to God, and I read my Bible and prayed daily.

The church I attended with my aunt was huge, with hundreds of people I did not know. The order of the service was strange, and the songs were unfamiliar. One day, I told my aunt I did not want to go back to that church. Ina chimed in, "I don't want to go either."

"What will your mother say?" my aunt asked. "I doubt if she would like this church either," I replied, knowing in my heart that even if she didn't like it, she would still have attended faithfully.

Instead of seeking out a new church, we simply stopped going. We added Sunday morning as another day we could go to the beach. I began reading my Bible less and less and soon forgot all about it. How quickly I forgot my foundation.

I enjoyed the ocean immensely. I did not know how to swim, but it was such fun having the breakers splash against my back and swirl around me. One day, I was feeling particularly brave and went out beyond the breakers. I was jumping up and down with delight along the great swells of water. I was having a wonderful time until I noticed that when I came back down from a jump, I could barely touch the ocean floor. I also felt a tug on my legs and feet. *What is happening to me?* I thought. It was as though the sand was sifting out from under my toes. I suddenly realized I was being pulled out into the ocean depths. I was paralyzed with fear and in my panic could not even scream for help. I was going to drown.

In this extreme situation, I returned to prayer and begged God to help me return to the shore. Although I had ceased attending church, had ceased reading my Scriptures, and had neglected my daily prayer, God had not forgotten me. He gave me a burst of tremendous strength in my arms and legs, giving me the ability to make it back to the breakers, which helped propel me back to the shore. Weak and shaking, I flopped on the sand, barely believing I was safe. I knew how close I had come to leaving this world, and it had truly frightened me.

I could hear Ina scolding, "What were you thinking, going way out there when you can't even swim?" I did not have the strength to answer her. I was too busy talking to God. *Dear God, I am so sorry. You are so good. Forgive me and thank You, thank You, thank You for rescuing me.*

That evening, I returned to my Bible, to the foundation of my life, and vowed never again to exchange it for worldly pleasures. As I read in my Bible, "Out of the depths have I cried unto thee, O LORD" (Psalm 130:1 KJV), and then, "God is our refuge and strength, a very present help in trouble" (Psalm 46:1 KJV), I said aloud, "Oh, Lord, I sure experienced that today. Thank You. Thank You. Thank You."

COMING IN TO THE LIGHT

by Nicole Winters, Milford, Iowa

I was fifteen years old when I was diagnosed with a cancerous tumor in my leg. At that time in my life, I wasn't aware of God on a daily basis. I believed in God, but I had no idea of all the wonderful things He was capable of doing in a person's life.

I went through the first eight months of chemotherapy and three months of radiation without really comprehending what was happening to me. I just wanted it to be over with. To me, it all seemed like a big nuisance, rather than a life-threatening disease. I was not able to go to school, nor did I even want to. I was bald and wore a wig. I had lost touch with all of my friends, and I pushed away all of my family. I was alone and depressed.

Despite what the doctors, nurses, and even my mother said, I stopped undergoing chemotherapy. I had only four treatments left but felt empty inside and could not find the strength to go on. I ran away from home, so I would not have to go back to the hospital. I couldn't stand the thought of going through another treatment of chemotherapy. I was pale, skinny, and sickly looking; I did not recognize myself anymore. The depression got worse, and I became suicidal. I didn't care about myself, or even my life. Yet after numerous suicide attempts and two overdoses, I was still alive.

Then one day, my life was changed. I was watching TV and someone who was also going through a serious disease said, "God will not give me more than I can handle." I had never heard that before. At that time, I was not very familiar with the Bible. Suddenly, it was like walking into a pitch black room and flipping a switch, filling it with light. Something clicked inside me, just that fast, and I knew then I was not alone. I knew that God was with me and always had been. He had been there the whole time but was waiting for me to realize it. I had never felt such peace in my life.

The realization that I could not do it all on my own became so clear to me. Just like asking someone for directions when you are lost, I asked God to help me do what I needed to do to get better—in my body, heart, and mind. I began reading the Bible for help. Through His Word, He showed me how to handle life and to be grateful for everything I have, in spite of the difficulties my illness brought. God gave me the strength to return home and complete my treatments. I felt His presence every step of the way from that point on.

There was a time when I thought cancer was the worst thing that had ever happened to me. Now I see it as a blessing in disguise. It helped me to open my heart and find the Lord, and now I have become much stronger with His help. I could not have done it alone. I would not be here today if not for this sudden U-turn in my life.

Every day I am aware of His presence. Talking with Him, praying, and reading the Bible help me throughout the day. It strengthens me to know that, even when I was going the wrong way, God never forgot about me. He was always there taking me out of the darkness and into the light. When things get hard and I don't know what to do, I remember to let go and allow God to guide me. Surrendering myself to the Lord and placing my life in His hands was the best thing I have ever done. I am so grateful that He showed me the way. I pray I can live my life in such a way as to show others His merciful healing and hope. He truly can heal our bodies and our souls. He has shown me love, understanding, patience, and forgiveness. And it has made all the difference in the way I live my entire life.

CHAPTER ELEVEN

Thankfulness

Be joyful always; pray continually;
give thanks in all circumstances,
for this is God's will for you in Christ Jesus.
1 Thessalonians 5:16–18

"MAKE A WISH, MOMMY"

by Susan Fahncke, Kaysville, Utah

The next day was my twenty-eighth birthday, and I was depressed. I was used to celebrating it with the friends I had moved away from. I was used to presents and phone calls, none of which I would be receiving this time. Divorced, raising two children alone, and too poor to even afford a telephone, I was going through the most dark and depressing time in my life. I hadn't lived in Utah very long and was still trying to adjust to the snow. This particular January was one of the most brutal in years.

The snow outside was literally thigh-high, and it was a daily struggle to leave the house, adding to my isolation. My son Nicholas was in kindergarten, and I was a junior at nearby Weber State University. I had taken the quarter off because my five month old, Maya, had been very ill, so I had no real social life. Depression became so second nature that I didn't even remember the happy, laughing person I used to be.

Tucking the children into bed that night, I was in a cloud of hopelessness. My little Nick wrapped his chubby six-year-old arms around my neck and said, "Tomorrow's your birthday, Mommy! I can't wait!" His blue eyes sparkled with an anticipation that mystified me.

Kissing his sweet rosy cheeks, I hoped that he didn't expect a birthday party to magically appear, like it does on his birthday. Life is so simple when you're six.

The next morning, I awoke before the children and began making breakfast. Hearing noises in our tiny living room, I assumed Nick was up and waited for him to come in to eat. Then I could hear Nick talking to Maya. He was sternly telling her to make Mommy smile today.

It suddenly hit me. Being so wrapped up in my misery, I didn't see how it affected my children. Even my little boy sensed I wasn't happy and was doing his best to do something about it. Tears of shame at my selfishness washed down my face. I knelt down in our little kitchen and asked for the strength to somehow find happiness again. I asked God to show me some beauty in my life. I asked Him to help me see, really see, the blessings I did have.

Putting a smile on my face, I marched myself into the living room to hug my children. There sat Nick on the floor, Maya on her blanket next to him, and in front of them was a pile of presents. A birthday party for three.

I looked at the pile of presents. Then my disbelieving eyes went back to my son. His face was gleeful at my shock. "I surprised you, Mommy, didn't I? Happy birthday!" He grinned his toothless, adorable grin.

Stunned, I knelt down next to him and, with tears in my eyes, I asked him how in the world he had possibly found a way to get me presents. He reminded me of our trip to "All A Dollar." I remembered him telling me he was spending the allowance he had been saving for ages. I had laughed at his bulging pockets and remembered thinking that he walked like John Wayne, his pants loaded down with his life's savings. I had almost chided him for spending everything he had so carefully saved, but thought better of it and did my shopping while he did his.

Looking again at the beautiful pile of presents in front of me, I couldn't believe that my small, darling son had spent everything he had in his crayon bank on ME, his mom. What kind of kid goes without the toys he wanted so that he could buy his MOM a pile of presents?

There, I heard a voice in my heart say, *I am showing you your blessings. How could you ever doubt them?* My prayers were being answered. No one was more blessed, and no one had more to be thankful for than I did. I had been so selfish and petty to feel unhappy with my life.

With tears flowing, I gently hugged my son and daughter and told them how blessed I was. At Nick's eager prompting, I carefully opened each present. A bracelet. A necklace. Another bracelet. Nail polish. Another bracelet. My favorite candy bars. Another bracelet. The thoughtful gifts, each wrapped in gift bags and wrapping paper purchased with a six year old's allowance were the most perfect I've ever received.

The final gift was his personal favorite. A wax birthday cake with the words "I love you" painted in fake frosting across the top. "You have to have a birthday cake, Mom," my oh-so-wise little one informed me. "It's the most beautiful cake I've ever seen," I told him, and it was.

I was so wrapped up in my own problems that I couldn't even see that the greatest joys, blessings, and sources of laughter that I would ever know were right there in front of me. My small son, with his enormous child-sized heart taught me this great lesson.

Then he sang "Happy Birthday" to me in his sweet little-boy voice that melted my heart and brought on more tears. "Make a wish, Mommy," he insisted.

I looked into my little boy's shining blue eyes and couldn't think of a single thing I would wish for. "I've already got my wish," I whispered through the tears. "I have you."

THE BAD DAY

by Karon Goodman, Oxford, Alabama

It was going to be a bad day. I could tell. The morning started out that way and only grew worse when I lost my temper with my son over yet another schedule change he didn't tell me about.

I started going through the "poor me" list in my mind as we drove to school. *Why,* I fumed, *does life have to be so full of problems that seem to multiply like unmatched socks?*

Then I heard an unexplained beeping from somewhere in the car. Just one more irritation to go along with the rest of my day. The next second, the radio quit and the tachometer fell to zero. I realized the harder I pushed the accelerator, the less it responded. Well, I thought, I had been fairly unpleasant to my family lately, even before the argument with my son. I figured this was my latest punishment. God's little "slap on the wrist" for being so hard to get along with the past few days. My son sat silently next to me, as if to say, "See?"

I had no choice but to continue on to the school because there was nowhere to pull over on the road we were on. As I made the right-hand turn before the last hill, the one that makes Pike's Peak look like a speed bump, I just prayed we'd make it to the summit. Normally, it's a second-gear hill, but this drive wasn't even close to normal. I slammed it into first and floored the accelerator. It was just God, me, and my still silent son.

All I could hear was my own voice praying and the putt-putt-putt from the engine as it protested the climb. The Bible verse that came to mind was the final part of Matthew 28:20: "And surely I am with you always, to the very end of the age." *I hope that includes to the top of this hill,* I thought. And as we crawled up that horrendous hill, I swear the vision in my mind was unmistakably the hand of God pushing us gently to the top, the smile of a patient, protective parent on His face. Miraculously, we made it. The engine's final wheeze coincided with my pull on the emergency brake as I parked the car. We could have gone no farther. But then, we didn't have to. My son jumped out, disappearing into the front door of the school.

I called my husband at work to describe the problem. I told him that I could probably find someone to drive me home if he couldn't come to get me. "Okay, Honey," he said. "Just leave it, and we'll get it this afternoon."

We don't live near the school like many of the students do, so whoever drove me home would likely have to go out of her way, unless I could find Gayle. She went right past our place. I rarely saw her in the mornings, but that day she was there as soon as I looked up for help. She was happy to give me a lift.

Later, when the adrenaline had stopped flowing like the Mississippi, I thought about the events of the morning. Was it really a bad day? Not at all. It was a very good day.

Life just isn't always perfect. We all fight with our kids sometimes. Car trouble is a universal nightmare. Inconveniences and setbacks are part of life. It isn't always some sort of heaven-sent punishment when things go badly.

God doesn't always need earthquakes or tornadoes, terminal illnesses or financial disasters to remind us that He's there. He can use the most simple, everyday irritations that routinely prey upon us all to put His hand behind us and give us a little push to remind us that He's there.

When put in perspective, I could see that God wasn't choosing to punish me for my foul temperament and disgruntled state of mind. He was loving me into changing them. He does that a lot, for all of us.

I would have a chance to apologize to my son for my outburst—and I would.

The car's problem could be diagnosed and fixed. We made it to a safe place, with no injuries or need for police officers to direct traffic. My husband considered only the mechanical facts of repairing the car. My son was just glad he wasn't late for school. My friend never gave a second thought to driving me home.

If they missed the significance of the experience, then maybe it was only meant for me. And I got it. Thank God.

BATHROOM BLESSING

by Malinda Fillingim, Roanoke Rapids, North Carolina

Whatever else can be said of me, I cry well. In the four months that my daughter Hope was in the hospital with an undiagnosed problem, crying became a habit. I tried to be really strong for her sake. I bravely sat with her, held her hand, and reassured her that everything was going to be okay, even when I really wasn't so sure myself how things would turn out.

One afternoon, when I was completely worn out and needing a break, my husband volunteered to sit with Hope. I needed a quiet place to go and pray. I needed a place where I could break down, and no one would notice. The only place I could find was the large bathroom off the lobby. There, I locked the bathroom stall door and began to cry.

Loud sobs echoed throughout the tile-floored room. I blew my nose on the remaining shreds of toilet paper, flushing the toilet so the sound would drown out my weeping. After a few minutes, feet began to appear, one pair after another, under my locked door. Voices began to stir.

"Are you okay in there?" a woman asked. Another woman slid a cold paper towel under my door. "Whatever is wrong, Honey, I am going to pray for you. It'll be okay." A teenager told me I could have her unopened can of soda and rolled it to me. I thanked her and drank it, soothing my sore throat. Two women offered to wait for me outside in the hall and share a prayer with me. Another young woman with two small children told me she was sorry for whatever was wrong. Many people shared words of comfort. One person even sang "Amazing Grace" to me!

My bathroom stall became a holy place where sorrow was shared by strangers who comforted me sight unseen. Except for feet, of course, I smiled to myself.

I finished my crying. The tears had cleansed my soul, and strangers had buoyed my spirit. As I walked back to Hope's room, a woman came up to me, asking me how I was feeling. When I asked how she knew me, she laughed and said, "I recognized your shoes!" Looking down, I recognized hers, too. We hugged and exchanged stories.

Returning to Hope's room, I looked at our situation with new faith and with the reassurance that I was not alone. God had spoken to me through the kindness of strangers.

A bathroom stall may not have a lot of room, but it is plenty big enough for God to work wonders and help one's perspective on life take a U-turn.

Published in The Phoenix *12/2000*

WINTER BUBBLES

by Eunice Loecher, Woodruff, Wisconsin

"Grandma, can we blow bubbles now?" Taylor asked, tugging on my sleeve. Turning to look at my four-year-old granddaughter, every part of me wanted to shout, "No!" She would ask why. What reason would I give?

"It's winter in Wisconsin. The temperature is fifteen degrees below zero outside. Grandpa died last week, and I don't feel like doing anything"?

I decided it would be easier to blow bubbles than try to explain. We bundled up in our coats and gloves, before carrying the large economy-size bottle of bubble solution out onto the deck. Taylor carried six different-sized bubble blowers.

Her first bubble emerged in a swirl of pink, blue, and yellow color. It floated slowly, then suddenly shattered like glass.

"Wow, Grandma, what happened?" Taylor asked. We had blown bubbles together many times, but nothing like that had ever happened before.

"The air is so cold today that the bubble froze and turned into ice," I explained. "That's why it didn't pop the way they usually do."

Taylor was delighted and blew bubble after bubble, until we were surrounded by a floating rainbow of colored crystal balls. Suddenly, my world was filled with the laughter of a four year old on a cold, winter afternoon.

Briefly, tears filled my eyes. Frozen bubbles might be a small thing to some people but not to me. There had been no moments of joy for a long time. Cancer, with its pain, suffering, and death had filled my life for months.

Jesus said, "Let the children come to me, and do not hinder them, for the kingdom of heaven belongs to such as these" (Matthew 19:14). Thankfully, I had not listened to my own excuses that afternoon. Blowing winter bubbles with my granddaughter became the most important thing to do that day. In her innocence, Taylor had taken me by the hand and shown me that life could once again hold moments of joy and beauty. Times that make life worth living.

A DENTIST MADE ME A FIGHTER PILOT

by Lowell "Duke" Embs, San Antonio, Texas

Two weeks before I graduated from the University of Illinois, the Korean War started. As soon as I got home from school, I went to the navy recruiting office in downtown Chicago. The place was packed, so I stood in line holding my birth certificate, college transcript, and social security card.

When I got to the head of the line, a guy with several stripes on the sleeve of his white jumper looked at me from behind a desk.

I paused and said, "I want to be a navy fighter pilot."

"Go out that door, turn left, and go to the first door on the right."

His eyes said "Move," so I did. The first door on the right opened easily, to a very large room containing at least two hundred guys my age in various stages of undress. For the next six hours, I became like them, answering more questions about my physical condition than I ever had before.

About 5:00 P.M., those of us who remained were told to come back the next day for more tests. These turned out to be IQ, psychological, and psychiatric evaluations.

At the end of those exercises, we were told we'd be notified whether we passed, and if we did when to report to Pensacola, Florida, for fighter pilot training.

I was ecstatic when I learned I had passed, and each day that I waited for my orders grew longer than the last. My only comfort was the attention I received from the gals in town when I would tell them I was going to be a navy fighter pilot.

Five months after being accepted, while still awaiting my orders to Pensacola, I developed a toothache. Off to the family dentist. His office was a second-floor walk-up in an old building in Blue Island, a downscale suburb of south Chicago. Dr. Cibock didn't make appointments. You just showed up, signed in on a legal pad, and waited your turn. The space wasn't air-conditioned, and the doctor didn't use Novocain, so it was best to have a tooth problem in the colder months.

When I was finally seated in the dental chair with mouth open, Dr. Cibock said, "What's the problem?"

"This tooth hurts," I said, pointing to a lower molar. "I've gotta get it fixed before I go."

"Yep, you have some other cavities, too; where are you going?"

"Waiting to go to Pensacola to be a navy fighter pilot," I proudly said.

"Well then, we'll just fix this one, and let the navy take care of the rest after you report in."

"Okay by me," I said.

And that's the way we parted. I was five dollars lighter but pleased my dentist was willing to hand me off to Uncle Sam for future care.

Four months later, my orders arrived. They read something like: Report to Naval Air Station Glenview, Ill, Building 21201 at 0800 on 1 June 1951, for processing to Naval Air Station Pensacola, Florida, as a Naval Air Cadet (NAVCAD).

Whoopee! In the navy at last. . .well, almost.

The first thing that began after we all assembled was clothing removal—much like we'd experienced nine months previously. When I reminded one of the medics we'd already been down this road, he replied, "That was then; this is now." And the look that accompanied his statement clearly meant back talk was not allowed.

So, I went along in silence until I was seated in the dental chair. The dentist was a full navy captain, probably about fifty. He poked, prodded, and pushed, finally saying, "Sorry, Son, we can't take you in this man's navy."

"You can't what?" I said leaping from the chair. "What do you mean?"

"We have strict medical prerequisites. You have too many cavities. You don't qualify for the NAVCAD program."

My world fell apart. I was ready to try anything as I pleaded, "Listen, Doctor, Sir, ever since I was accepted nine months ago, I've told every pretty girl who'd listen I was going to fly the navy's fastest and newest jets. If you don't let me in, I'll be destroyed. I'll never be able to show my face at home. . .never."

"Sorry, Embs, you have too many cavities."

"I'll get them fixed," I practically begged.

"A dentist would have to stay up all night."

"I know one who will."

"What's his name?"

"Dr. Cibock."

"Really?"

"Please Doctor, Sir, I've gotta get to Pensacola."

"Okay, meet me here tomorrow morning at eight with those teeth fixed, and you can go."

It was 4:45 P.M. Next door was a building that said Ships Store. I ran inside and headed straight to the cash register where I traded two dollar bills for twenty dimes. Out of the corner of my eye, I spotted a telephone booth. Inside hung a phone book for the North Chicago suburbs, both white and yellow pages.

"Okay, God, You're on—help me out here," I prayed, as I flipped to D for dentists and started calling.

My pitch was simple, "I need an appointment RIGHT NOW, to get some cavities filled so I can go to Pensacola, Florida, in the morning to learn to be a navy fighter pilot."

I got laughed at, hung up on, and apologized to—but on the fourteenth call, I hit pay dirt. The dentist had been in the navy and told me to get to his office as soon as I could!

I called a cab, and twenty minutes later he pulled up. The dentist had a Glenview address, so we were at his office in less than ten minutes. The fare was five dollars.

The dentist smiled as I bolted in. I grinned back. His assistant had left for the day, so it was just the two of us. Fortunately for me, and how I thanked God for it, he had the latest in equipment, high speed drills, water circulating devices, and the best thing of all—Novocain.

For three solid hours, he drilled and filled. When it was over, he told me he'd repaired seventeen surfaces. At three bucks a crack, that came to $51.

The cab fare back to NAS Glenview was another five, leaving me with $37 from the $100 I'd started with that morning. I found my room in the B.O.Q. where we were billeted for the night and set my travel alarm for 6:00 A.M. My aching jaw didn't impair my sleep, and the next thing I heard was the buzz of my clock.

At 7:30, I was waiting for the navy dental office to open. When it did, I went in and sat erect in the waiting room. The doctor arrived and gave me a half nod.

Soon my name was called, and I went where the enlisted man pointed. The doctor with four stripes stood beside the chair; I sat down and he said, "Open up."

I did.

"Well I'll be," he said with a smile. "Go catch the train with the rest of your pals and good luck, Son."

Later that night, as I listened to the sounds of the rails, I thought of the dentist who, quite literally, saved my career. Without his help, my entire life would have been different. I owed my future to an unselfish man, and I silently thanked the good Lord for sending me the dentist who had what it took to make me a navy fighter pilot—a warm heart, a sense of giving, power tools, and Novocain.

WAKE UP CALL

by Philip Steele, Chelsea, Michigan

"Open up in there," I heard the policeman say as he banged on my bathroom door. Just like in the movies, the next statement was, "Open up or we'll break down the door and drag you out!" Only this wasn't the movies, and I was the one hiding in a bathroom with several kegs of beer. It had started out as a simple college party with my five house buddies and me. We had provided kegs of beer which we let anyone drink, even if they were underage. People were drinking and dancing to the loud music, and everyone was having a good time. To us, it was just some fun. We never realized the consequences of our actions until it was too late.

I opened the door, not knowing what was to happen to me, and fought back my tears. They asked for my ID, and I provided it. They asked me why I had hidden, since I was twenty-one. I responded that I had gotten scared when someone had yelled that the police were there. When they asked me if I lived here, I lied and said I didn't, so they let me leave.

I did not want to deal with any of it. I just wanted to get away from everything and think for awhile. I wandered the streets, afraid to return, but knowing my friends and I would have to pay for our actions. We had been totally irresponsible. We should never have allowed underage kids to drink and party at our house.

That night I started talking to God like I had never done before. I believed in God, but I suddenly realized I was never really a true Christian. I knew this was God's way of getting my attention. He was letting me know He was not happy about where my life was heading. I promised Him that if He helped me with this situation that I would follow His way and do whatever He wanted me to do with my life. I plea-bargained with God for my freedom.

When I finally decided to return home, I found that a warrant had been issued for my arrest. If I didn't turn myself in, the police would bring me in. Knowing there was nothing left to do, I went to the police station. They questioned me about the night, and I told them everything. Thankfully, no one had gotten hurt, but there were some very young kids who were very drunk, and things could have taken a far more serious turn.

The police gave me a ticket and told me to appear for my arraignment within ten days, or I would go to jail. As it was, the charges against me could result in six months' jail time. I shuddered to think what that could do to my life, my education, my future career, and to the life of my family. I went to my arraignment a few days later, only to find out that I would have to return a month later for an actual trial.

I was scared to death.

For that month, I prayed and studied the Bible more than I ever had. I went to church services more often and listened to the preacher and tried to apply his lessons to my life. For the first time in my life, I felt close to God. I felt able to go to Him with all my troubles and knew He would help me out. I wondered why it had taken this situation to open my eyes. I knew that God was on my side, and that was all the help I really needed. But I also knew that I would still have to face the consequences for my previous actions.

Praise the Lord, my lawyer was able to plea-bargain a possible $1,000 fine and six months in jail down to $500 and six months' probation with no permanent record. I read it over and knew that God had helped me out. God alone had made this possible. I now know how Barabbas must have felt when he heard that he was being set free, even after all that he had done.

After that, I dedicated my life to God the best I could. Before that event, I wasn't a real Christian and only went through the motions of serving God. I said I loved the Lord, but I didn't really have love for Him in my heart. After that event, my actions changed. I started loving God from my heart and following His Word, becoming a true Christian.

God does allow U-turns, and I am living proof. I was on a road that was leading to jail, but I allowed God to work in my life and direct it, and not only did I graduate college with a master's degree, but I am doing what He wants me to do, and I have never been happier or more thankful!

NO MORNING IS JUST LIKE ANOTHER

by LaRose Karr, Sterling, Colorado

The morning started just like every morning. The alarm clock went off at 6:35; I hit the snooze alarm for ten more minutes while I tried to get my mind started. At 6:45 when the alarm sounded again, I hit the snooze alarm once again. This time my mind was awake, but I needed time to open my eyes and focus on the room. This is my morning routine.

Finally, a few moments before 7:00, I get up and walk from one end of the house to the other for the bathroom routine. I brush my teeth, wash my face, and turn on the curling iron. This is my morning routine; I seldom alter it in any way. I go back to the bedroom and make the bed. Never can I let a morning go without making the bed. I do this day after day after day.

Then I cross through the kitchen, living room, and hall to wake up my children. They barely stir beneath the covers, sometimes moaning if I choose to sing while waking them up. We then get dressed and get in the car.

On the morning of this story, I dropped off two kids at the middle school and my oldest daughter at the high school. As I'd had no breakfast at home, I began to think about where I would get a morning snack. The 7-11 is my favorite place to stop. You never know who you might see getting their coffee and donuts.

It was a morning just like any other.

As I opened the door to my office, I was quickly reminded that in the blink of an eye our lives can change. Another death had occurred within the body of the congregation. A church member had gone on, the second one this week. As I heard the details and the story of his life, I read the sadness on the pastor's face and sense it in his soul. Death is something that always takes us by surprise, even when it is expected.

I wake up, hit the snooze button, take kids to school, all the while unaware that just across town a family may be grieving for the loss of a mother, or a wife may be crying for her husband. It makes me understand more fully that life is a gift. We must live it with every intention of doing what we can to minister to others, to touch another life in whatever way we can.

For who knows, tomorrow we may be the ones who have gone on. It happens in the blink of an eye.

ALLISON'S CONCLUDING THOUGHTS

Excuse me, please. I can't leave without asking one most important question. Do you have a personal relationship with the eternal God? I'm not talking about "getting a religion." I'm talking about "getting a relationship." You may have read every word of this book and yet never experienced the peace, strength, and hope that our authors have shared with you here.

I spent decades of my life looking for fulfillment in all the wrong places. Today, I have peace, strength, and hope because there was a time in my life when I accepted Jesus as my personal Savior. That is what I mean by getting a "relationship," not a "religion."

The way is simple. It only takes three steps.

1. Admit that you are a sinner: "For all have sinned, and come short of the glory of God." Romans 3:23 KJV

2. Believe that Jesus is God the Son and He paid the wages of your sin: "For the wages of sin is death [eternal separation from God]; but the gift of God is eternal life through Jesus Christ our Lord." Romans 6:23 KJV

3. Call upon God: "If thou shalt confess with thy mouth the Lord Jesus, and shalt believe in thine heart that God hath raised him from the dead, thou shalt be saved." Romans 10:9 KJV

Our web site has a "Statement of Faith" page that you might find interesting and comforting. On that page you will find helpful (and hopeful) links to other spiritually uplifting web pages. Please visit it at: http://www.godallowsuturns.com.

Salvation is a very personal thing. It is between you and God. I cannot have faith for you; no one can. The decision is yours alone. Please know that this wonderful gift of hope and healing is available to you. You need only reach out and ask for it. It is never too late to make a U-turn toward God. . .no matter where you have been or what you have done. Please know that I am praying for you.

> God's Peace and Protection Always,
> Allison Gappa Bottke

Future Volumes of
GOD ALLOWS U-TURNS

The stories you have read in this volume were submitted by readers just like you. From the very start of this inspiring book series, it has been our goal to encourage people from around the world to submit their slice-of-life true short stories for publication.

God Allows U-Turns stories must touch the emotions and stir the heart. We are asking for well-written, personal, inspirational pieces showing how faith in God can inspire, encourage, heal, and give hope. We are looking for human-interest stories with a spiritual application, affirming ways in which Christian faith is expressed in everyday life.

Because of the huge response to our call for submissions for volume one, we plan to publish additional volumes in the U-Turns series every year.

Your true story can be from 500–2,000 words and must be told with drama, description, and dialogue. Our writers' guidelines are featured on our web site, and we encourage you to read them carefully. Or send us a SASE for a copy of the guidelines.

GOD ALLOWS U-TURNS
P.O. Box 717
Faribault, MN 55021-0717
E-mail: editor@godallowsuturns.com
web site: http://www.godallowsuturns.com

Fees are paid for stories we publish, and we will be sure to credit you for your submission. Remember, our web site is filled with up-to-date information about the book project. Additionally, you might want to take advantage of signing up to be on our free "Hotline Update" list for Internet users. Visit us soon at: http://www.godallowsuturns.com.

NOTE: We prefer stories to be submitted via our web site, although "snail mail" submissions are acceptable.

SHARING THE SUCCESS

The Holy Bible is quite clear in teaching us how we are to live our lives. One of the most profound lessons is that of "giving." Scripture refers to this often, and never has the need to share with others been so great.

"Give, and it will be given to you. A good measure, pressed down, shaken together and running over, will be poured into your lap. For with the measure you use, it will be measured to you." —Luke 6:38

In keeping with the lessons taught us by the Lord our God, we are pleased to have the opportunity to donate a portion of the net profits of every *God Allows U-Turns* book to a nonprofit Christian charity.

We have selected the following to receive a portion of the proceeds from the book you are holding in your hands now.

REST MINISTRIES

A nonprofit Christian organization dedicated to serving people who live with chronic illness or pain by providing spiritual, emotional, relational, and practical support through a variety of programs and resources, including national HopeKeeper groups and an interactive web site. Rest Ministries also seeks to bring an awareness and a change in action throughout churches in the U.S., in regard to how people who live with chronic illness or pain are served, and teaching churches effective ministry tools in outreaching to this population. Call 888-751-REST (7378). Or visit the web site at www.restministries.org.

ABOUT OUR EDITORS

ALLISON GAPPA BOTTKE lives in southern Minnesota on a twenty-five-acre hobby farm with her entrepreneur husband, Kevin. She is a relatively "new" Christian, coming to the fold in 1990 as a result of a dramatic life "U-turn." The driving force behind the God Allows U-Turns Project, she has a growing passion to share with others the healing and hope offered by the Lord Jesus Christ. Allison has a wonderful ability to inspire and encourage audiences with her down-to-earth speaking style as she relates her personal testimony of how God orchestrated a dramatic U-turn in her life. For further information about Allison, visit her information page on the book's web site: http://www.godallowsuturns.com/aboutauthor.htm or http://www.godallowsuturns.com/modeling.htm.

CHERYLL MARIE HUTCHINGS was born in Ohio as Cheryll Marie Gappa and has resided for the past eleven years on the outskirts of Medina, Ohio. She and her family live in a rambling ranch home on twenty-three acres. Minutes from "civilization," yet secluded enough to enjoy the area wildlife that ambles through her own backyard in abundance, she enjoys bird feeding and watching. Her husband of twenty-four years, Robert W. Hutchings (Bob), is maintenance superintendent at Johnson Controls in Oberlin, Ohio. Her nineteen-year-old son, Aaron, plays the guitar and hopes one day to write Oscar-winning music for the big screen. Her sixteen-year-old son, Scott, plays the trumpet and may decide to continue in music, work in the theater, or become a master chef. Currently, Cheryll works for the Brunswick Community Recreation Center.

ELLEN SEIBEL joined the U-Turns team as a coeditor in the spring of 2000. Although an Easterner by birth, Minnesota has been her home for the last decade. After living in Los Angeles, California, for nearly fifteen years, Minnesota was a welcome respite from traffic, smog, and concrete. At the moment, she and her family live at a college preparatory boarding school where she functions as a dorm parent in the boys' dormitory. Her life is centered around her own two sons, but she also has the privilege of being the surrogate "mom" to other boys on campus. Ellen is active in her church community as a volunteer, singer in the choir, and soloist.

ABOUT OUR WEB SITE

We first announced God Allows U-Turns on the World Wide Web in February of 2000. The Lord used this avenue of communication to reach across all borders; geographic as well as racial, political, denominational, and social. Stories began to come to us via our web site, first by the dozens, then hundreds, and now thousands.

While our web site is specific to the God Allows U-Turns book series, you will find we also offer important links to other major Christian web sites, links we encourage you to visit. Additionally, we have placed a "Statement of Faith" page on our site to clearly establish our beliefs.

The global opportunities a web site provides are mind-boggling, but we need your help to make the kind of impact we know is possible. Please visit our web site and forward it to your family and friends. Virtually everyone has a story to tell, and future volumes will enable those stories to be told. We are accepting true short stories NOW for future volumes. Visit our "Future Volumes" page on our web site to find out more.

Remember, our web site is filled with up-to-date information about the book project. You will be able to access tour and book-signing calendars on the site, as well as read stories from the current volume. Additionally, you might want to take advantage of signing up for our free "Hotline Update" list for Internet users. Our free yahoogroups.com list can be accessed via our web site. It's easy to join. Don't miss out on current news and reviews.

Visit us soon at: http://www.godallowsuturns.com.

AUTHOR/CONTRIBUTORS

All of the stories in this volume of *God Allows U-Turns* were submitted by readers like you. We are blessed to have had this opportunity to glimpse into their lives, if only for a moment, and we thank them for sharing their faith with us. We have included information about each contributor below. In some cases, we have added contact information at their request.

PETER ADOTEY ADDO of Greensboro, North Carolina, is a retired minister of the Western North Carolina Conference of the United Methodist Church. Born and raised in Ghana, West Africa, he has had a long and varied career as a poet, short-story writer, folklorist, college chaplain, and botanist.

CHARLOTTE ADELSPERGER lives in Overland Park, Kansas. She is coauthor of *Through the Generations: The Unique Call of Motherhood.* She has authored two other books and has written for more than seventy different publications such as *LifeWise* and *Woman's World.* She is also a popular speaker. She can be contacted at 11629 Riley, Overland Park, Kansas, 66210, or by telephone at 913-345-1678.

CINDY APPEL from St. Louis, Missouri, is a wife, mother, and freelance writer whose work has appeared in over twenty-five publications. Her first novel is scheduled for release in 2001. She writes a weekly column on-line for the *Fort Worth Star-Telegram,* which you can reach via her homepage: cynthianna@postnet.com.

TAMMERA AYERS of St. Marys, Ohio, has a B.A. in Social Work but is currently a stay-at-home mom for her three children. She is active in the children's ministry at the church she and her family attend.

ESTHER BAILEY lives in Phoenix, Arizona, with her husband, Ray, where they attend North Hills Church. She is a freelance writer with more than eight hundred published credits and is coauthor of two books: *Designed for Excellence,* and *When Roosters Crow.*

PAT TOORNMAN BALES still lives in Brighton, Colorado, with her three sons. They live on the same farm of which she writes in her story. Her oldest son will be attending medical school in 2001, with thanks to some of his experiences with the sheep he has raised. Pat teaches school and writes books and short stories in her free time.

CORY BALL resides in Phoenix, Arizona. He is a remarkable young man who has struggled through many difficulties. As the survivor of a drive-by shooting that left him a triple amputee, he now lives independently. Today he can say that he is thankful for the incident that led him to take refuge in Christ.

TRACY BOHANNON of Riverview, Florida, is twenty-seven years old. She has been married for five and one-half years. The proud mother of a four-year-old son, she is also a foster mom to two children. She has been the foster mother to six other beautiful children.

PEGGY COLETTI BOHANON lives in Springfield, Missouri, with her husband, Dr. Joseph Bohanon, and two teen sons. She is on the ministry staff of Gospel Communications Network, Muskegon, Michigan, and serves as executive director of the *Internet for Christians* newsletter. She is also Webmaster and originator of the popular Christian Internet site, "Peggie's Place" (www.peggiesplace.com).

ALLISON GAPPA BOTTKE makes her home in Faribault, Minnesota, where she and her entrepreneurial husband live on a twenty-five-acre farm. The God Allows U-Turns project has been ten years in development. (www.godallowsuturns.com)

LANITA BRADLEY BOYD is a freelance writer living in Ft. Thomas, Kentucky. In her writing, she draws upon many years of teaching public school, her work in various church ministries, and interviews and articles of interest. She can be reached at info@sboyd.com.

CLAUDIA BRELAND lives in Maple Valley, Washington, with her husband and two children. Currently a librarian with the King County Library System near Seattle, Claudia has been writing inspirational essays for five years.

GILDA V. BRYANT is a freelance writer living in Amarillo, Texas. She continues to drive on the back roads.

STEPHANIE WELCHER BUCKLEY of Edmond, Oklahoma, is an inspirational writer and speaker. She hosts *State of Change,* a Christian program on KTOK, the highest-rated talk radio station in Oklahoma City. Weekly "State of Change" newspaper columns are syndicated through Oklahoma. To reach her, write to: P.O. Box 1502, Edmond, Oklahoma, 73034; or www.stateofchange.net.

DARLYN BUSH of Abbeyville, Louisiana, is a latecomer to the literary world, who, in spite of the dire warnings from professionals, has pursued her passion. Knowing that she could give spiritual guidance to people in need, she has written her heart out. She is thankful to God for the joy that her writing has given to both her and her readers.

SANDRA J. CAMPBELL is a freelance writer in Garden City, Michigan. She has three grown sons and a wonderful husband of twenty-six years. Her eighty-five-year-old mother still enjoys independent living in her own apartment.

MARLENE CAPELLE resides in Sheridan, Colorado. She is a published author of poems and short stories. At the moment, she is working on novel-length stories.

CANDACE CARTEEN lives in Portland, Oregon, and is a technical writer by profession. She and her husband, George, have one son, Keefer.

JOAN CLAYTON and her husband, Emmitt, live in Portales, New Mexico. She has written six books and has had over 350 articles published. She is currently the Religion columnist for her local newspaper.

JAN COLEMAN from Auburn, California, is an author and speaker. She encourages from Joel 2:25: "God will restore the years the locust has eaten." He replaces our ruined dreams in the most unexpected ways. Look for her book on this theme from Broadman & Holman, spring 2002. She can be reached at jwriter@foothill.net.

HEATHER COLLINS-HAMILTON now lives in Collierville, Tennessee. She encourages anyone involved in an abusive relationship to seek professional help. She advocates responsible intervention by anyone who may know people who are trapped in the cycle of domestic violence.

CHARLENE COOK of Murfreesboro, Tennessee, has been married for thirty years and has two grown sons. She says she has done everything from being a cop to a cook! She has been seeking the Lord since she was a teenager.

JACQUE E. DAY lives in Chicago, Illinois. Her work appears in various newspapers and small presses, and she holds the Linda Haldeman Award for Fiction. She is also a producer for the Discovery Health Channel series, *Chicago's Lifeline.*

MARLENE DEPLER lives in Longmont, Colorado, with her husband, Ray. She is a mother, grandmother, writer, and freelance editor. Marlene enjoys gardening, traveling, and reading.

GERRY DI GESU lives on Cape Cod, in Massachusetts, where she says the gift of nature gives her great peace and helps bring balance and perspective to her writing. She says, "I have always been able to find God's promise of new life during the sad seasons of my own growth."

DAWN AND ALEXANDER EDWARDS live in a suburb of Chicago with their two-year-old son, Julius, who is the light of their lives. Dawn is a full-time mom and a freelance writer. Alex is an insurance executive.

GERALD EISMAN of Sarasota, Florida, is a member of the healthcare field. A student of human nature, his stories reflect people at their best.

BERNIS ELVERUM lives in Faribault, Minnesota. After spending the winter of 1930 in California, Bernis returned to Canada and attended Prairie Bible College. In 1939 she moved to Minnesota. After fifteen years of mission work in northern Minnesota, Bernis took nurse's training. For the next twenty-three years she worked in hospitals. She moved to Faribault in 1967.

LOWELL "DUKE" EMBS lives in San Antonio, Texas. Before becoming a navy fighter pilot, he graduated from the University of Illinois in 1950. Following his release from active duty, he entered the life insurance business, where he stayed for twenty-six years. During that time, he gathered material for his first book, *Committed,* published in 1995.

SUSAN FAHNCKE of Kaysville, Utah, is a freelance writer and runs her own web site. She has stories published in numerous books and magazines. To learn more about Susan and sign up for her free daily inspirational e-mail list, visit www.2theheart.com, or e-mail her at Susan@2theheart.com.

MALINDA FILLINGIM of Roanoke Rapids, North Carolina, is an ordained Baptist minister. She finds great joy in being the mother of Hope and Hannah and the wife of David. "Blessings can be found wherever there is love—even rest areas!"

NANCY GIBBS lives in Cordele, Georgia, and is a weekly religion columnist. She is a contributing writer for Honor Books and Guideposts Books and has been published in numerous magazines and devotional guides. She is a pastor's wife and the mother of three grown children.

KARON GOODMAN lives in Oxford, Alabama, with her family. She has written for many print and on-line publications including *Woman's Day, Bride Again, Writer's Digest, Petersen's Bowhunting, Momscape,* and more. Her gift book, *Everyday Angels,* was published by Barbour Publishing, Inc., fall 2000.

CATHY HERHOLDT lives in Bothell, Washington, with her husband, Bret, and three children, Chelsea, Reilly, and Nicolas. She is a part-time writer/copy editor at a local newspaper and enjoys quilting and cooking.

CARLIN HERTZ lives in Fort Washington, Maryland. He is married to Jonata Johnson-

Hertz, and they have a two-year-old son, Carlin, Jr. Carlin, Sr., is working on his first novel.

JOEL HOLTZ lives in Vadnais Heights, Minnesota. He is a radio producer and avid reader. He and his lovely wife, Rita, hope to retire in beautiful central Oregon someday.

SHANNA HOSKISON of Pecan Gap, Texas, has been married to her husband, Terry, for twenty years. They have two daughters, Terrica (eighteen) and Tirzah (ten months). Shanna's passion is to put into words the Lord's blessings in her life.

MICHELE HOWE of LaSalle, Michigan, has published over five hundred articles. She reviews for *Publishers Weekly, CBA Marketplace,* and *CCM Magazine.* Michele is also the author of *Going It Alone: Meeting the Challenges of Being a Single Mom* and *Bible Stories, Food and Fun.*

SHEILA HUDSON lives in Athens, Georgia. She is the founder of Bright Ideas and is featured in *Chocolates for a Woman's Heart, Chocolate for a Teen's Soul, Chocolate for a Woman's Blessing, Taking Education Higher, God's Vitamin C for a Man's Soul.* You can contact her at 161 Woodstone Dr., Athens, GA 30605, 706-546-5085, or sheila@naccm.org.

MATTHEW JAMES lives in Tucson, Arizona, with his wife and two children. He has been writing for ten years.

AMY JENKINS resides in Wauwatosa, Wisconsin, with her husband, children, and pets. She is a freelance writer and speaker, published in local and national magazines. She has authored two seminars and is writing a series of articles entitled "Boomin: Inside the Biggest Generation."

SARA JORDAN lives in Canton, Ohio. She has been published in Billy Graham's *Decision* magazine, *Lighthouse Digest,* and as a staff writer for *Connection: The Good News Magazine.* Her short stories have appeared in *Thema, 3.5 Plus,* and *Nota Bene* literary magazines. She and her husband are in the process of adopting a daughter.

LA ROSE KARR lives in Sterling, Colorado, with her husband and their four children. She is a church secretary who enjoys people, travel, and storytelling. She believes her writing is a gift from God and gives Him all the glory. She can be reached at rosiebay@kci.net.

LINDA KNIGHT lives in Woodslee, Ontario. She is an inspirational writer. Her published credits include hundreds of greeting card verses, as well as plaques, mugs, shirts, calendars, anthologies, adult and children's devotionals, and magazine articles.

KATHRYN LAY of Arlington, Texas, lives with her husband and daughter. She is a freelance writer whose work has appeared in *Home Life, Woman's Day, Guideposts, Chicken Soup for the Mother's Soul,* and more.

EUNICE LOECHER lives in Woodruff, Wisconsin. She is a recent widow. Her days are filled with the joy of raising her grandchildren and keeping up with her eighty-eight-year-old mother. She enjoys writing and celebrating the gifts the Lord brings into her life each day.

MARTHA LARCHE LUSK is a native Texan who lives in Dallas. She is the author of four books. Her work has appeared in more than fifty publications. She was first published, at the age of ten, in a children's Sunday school magazine.

LEA MACDONALD of Tichborne, Ontario, is a retired manager of applications development for an aerospace company. He is currently writing a book called *A Simpler Place in Time*. "Everybody Knows Everybody" is one story from his book, which takes a warm and nostalgic look at humanity.

PAUL MADISON lives in Williamstown, New Jersey. He is an avid sports fan. At forty-six years of age, he realized that the world is too perfect to have been created by a disorganized big bang. Paul is still amazed at His creation.

MICHELLE MATT lives in Sanford, Maine, with her husband and their five children. She has been published in a variety of markets and has won several writing contests from the State of Maine Writers Conferences.

CHARLES MCKINSTRY of Roanoke, Virginia, began writing in 1990 at the age of sixty-eight when he retired from a Cancer Rehab House which he comanaged with his wife, Mary. Since then he has written twenty true stories and twenty-five fictional stories.

LINDA NATHAN of Maple Falls, Washington, has been speaking, teaching, and writing from an evangelical perspective since 1980. She is editor of a large monthly Pacific Northwest news magazine, a former editor of Christian Coalition's Washington State newsletter, and has had her own writing business since 1992.

JAN NORTHINGTON lives in Los Osos, California. She is a CLASS graduate and Certified Personality Trainer. She is the author of the book *Separated and Waiting*, and has written numerous articles for the Christian marketplace. Jan is married to H. A. and has four children.

CHERYL NORWOOD lives in Canton, Georgia, just north of Atlanta, with her husband, Mike, in a small World War II bungalow. She has been published in several other anthologies and is currently working on a book project of her own.

CHERYL PADEN of Fremont, Nebraska, is married and has three sons. She worked for twenty-three years as an R.N., retiring to become a freelance writer and lay speaker in the United Methodist Church.

LINDA PARKER lives in Windermere, Florida, with her two daughters and her three cats. She is a Magna Cum Laude graduate of the University of Kentucky. Her current book, *The Son of the Kalahari*, is scheduled for distribution in the spring of 2002.

MICHELLE PEARSON lives in Leaf River, Illinois. She is a freelance writer whose personal relationship with Christ began when she met her husband, Jeff. They and their children live on a fourth-generation family farm in northern Illinois.

LIEUTENANT COLONEL HARRY VANN PHILLIPS resides in Rauenberg, Germany, with his wife, Mary, and their two sons, Sean and Eric. His aspiration is to be a Christian writer.

MARILYN PHILLIPS of Bedford, Texas, is a former teacher. She has written three books: *A Cheerleader for Life, God Speaks to Cheerleaders,* and *Cheering for Eternity.* Her articles have been published in *Guideposts, Parent Life, Home Life,* and *Living with Teenagers.* Marilyn and Nolan have two grown children, Bryant and Rebecca.

ROSE PLIHCIK lives in Gilbert, Arizona, although she was born and raised in northeast Connecticut. She is a published author. She moved to Arizona in 1996. Her husband died in 1998. Recently, she moved closer to family members, and she works part-time in a Christian bookstore.

MICHAEL T. POWERS resides in Janesville, Wisconsin, with his bride, Kristi, and their two boys. He is a motivational speaker, business owner, high school girls' coach, and author of the book: *Straight from the Heart.* See his Internet magazine and inspirational web site at: http://www.MichaelTPowers.com. E-mail: Thunder27@AOL.com.

VIVIAN PRESTON now lives in Barberton, Ohio, although she was born in Buffalo, New York. For seventeen years she worked in the Children's Department of the Barberton Public Library. She is published in both the secular and the religious markets. She also writes a weekly column for the local paper.

HARRY RANDLES lives in Hot Springs Village, Arizona. Born in upstate New York in 1919, he "flew the Hump" in World War II. Later, the GI Bill provided his education. Since earning a Ph.D., his career has been in education: public schools, Syracuse University, and Vanderbilt. Now retired, he spends his time reading and writing.

DOROTHY RIEKE lives in Julian, Nebraska. She taught school for forty-four years. She is a devout, born-again Christian. She is married to Kenneth, and they have a wonderful daughter, Cindy.

PASTOR JOHN ROBERTS lives in Sterling, Colorado, where he is senior pastor at First Baptist Church in Sterling. He also writes a weekly religious column for the local newspaper. He and his wife, Debbie, have two talented children: Laura, age nineteen; and David, age seventeen.

KATHY SEMON resides in Rice Lake, Wisconsin, with her husband, Jon, and son Michael. Kathy is employed as an educational interpreter for the deaf and hard of hearing. When not working, she enjoys reading, singing, and spending time with her family.

DIANNE SMITH lives in Fremont, California.

LAURA SMITH resides in Roswell, Georgia, but grew up in Columbus, Ohio. She graduated with a B.S. in Business from Miami University in Oxford, Ohio. After leasing corporate real estate for ten years, she retired from corporate America to be a stay-at-home mom and to pursue her passion for writing.

NANCY SPIEGELBERG of Vermilion, Ohio, is the author of poems in many books, magazines, and anthologies. She is a mother and grandmother and is a former R.N. She is also a former staff worker for Youth With A Mission (YWAM). She enjoys playing the piano and organ, and photography. She also creates poem graphics for www.godthoughts.com. Due to multiple sclerosis, she resides at an assisted living facility.

GIL STADLEY lives in Paynesville, Minnesota. He is a retired military member who spent twelve years in Japan where he met the subject of his story. His wife is from Japan, and they visit Japan every second year.

PHILLIP STEELE lives in Chelsea, Michigan. He comes from a small town and has always wanted to write. "With God's help, I know I can accomplish my dream and glorify Him at the same time."

RONDA STURGILL lives in Shalimar, Florida. A paraplegic since a horseback riding accident in 1972, Ronda is a Christian speaker who encourages her audiences to look beyond their circumstances to experience God's grace. Married to Tim Sturgill, a

USAF chaplain, they have one eighteen-year-old son, Toby.

LYNN ROATEN TERRELL lives in Wichita, Kansas. She has been published around the world for thirty years and has numerous awards for her humorous and inspirational stories and poetry. She and Amos, an engineer, have two children, Lori and Ken. She runs IdeasInProduction.com from their historic home in Wichita.

JANICE THOMPSON of Spring, Texas, is a homeschooling mother of four daughters. She also teaches classes in creative writing and drama at Christian Arts Academy, a Houston area School of the Arts. She and her husband have a vital interest in teens and youth ministry.

ELIZABETH TURNER is from Oakville, Ontario, Canada. As a wife, mother, and ICU nurse, Elizabeth uses her writing for personal growth.

MARY ELLA VAUSE lives in Blanco, Texas. Her writings grow from love of life and Jesus. She is a wife, parent, teacher, nurse, writer, volunteer, and Webmaster. She taught preschool through university, was a school nurse, then a family nurse practitioner for over twenty years. She is the mother of five and grandmother of seven.

JOHN P. WALKER lives in New Cumberland, Pennsylvania. He worked as a radio announcer before answering God's call to ministry. He pastors the West Shore Brethren in Christ Church near Harrisburg, Pennsylvania. John lives with his wife, Bonnie, and daughters, Charity and Stephanie. His passions include writing, photography, and skydiving.

PEGGY WHITSON lives in the Chicago area with her husband, Marty. She is a freelance writer who specializes in short stories and articles but is also in the process of working on a novel. She can be reached via e-mail at jyotis@aol.com.

CANDICE WILBER lives in Longmont, Colorado. She is a full-time music teacher and young-adult novelist. She lives with her husband, Patrick, and their two pet hermit crabs.

NICOLE WINTERS lives in Milford, Iowa. She is twenty-one years old. She was in England for six months as a nanny. Currently, she is a nanny in Iowa, where she is closer to her family. She usually spends her spare time writing, which she has done ever since she could read and write.

MAXINE S. WRIGHT lives in Bremen, Georgia, with Larry, her husband of thirty-five years. They have two daughters and four grandchildren. Maxine enjoys taking pieces of her life and writing about the lessons she has learned through the years. She hopes that something she has learned will encourage others.

D. L. YOUNG resides in the scenic city of Chattanooga, Tennessee, with her husband, daughter, and two precious kitties. Her work has appeared in *Touch* and *Black Velvet* magazines. She is currently working on her first book about two teenaged girls in search of angels. She believes our main purpose on earth is to take care of each other.

WE WANT TO HEAR FROM YOU!

Win FREE copies of

Using this volume of *God Allows U-Turns,* please select your favorite story for each of the categories below. You may enter your selections on our web site: www.godallowsuturns.com or mail them to us (using this page or a photocopy of it) at:

Allison Gappa Bottke
The God Allows U-Turns Project
My Favorite Story Contest–01
P.O. Box 717
Faribault, MN 55021-0717

From those readers who respond with their comments, we will choose a winner at random every month for one year. Winners will receive five complimentary copies of *God Allows U-Turns* to give to family and friends. The winner's selections, comments, and photo (if available) will be posted on the *God Allows U-Turns* web site each month. The deadline for submitting feedback for this volume is June 30, 2002. The first winner will be posted one month after the book's release date (July 2001).

CATEGORIES:
1. Most inspiring story
2. Most humorous story
3. The 4-hanky story
4. Most thought-provoking story
5. Most hopeful story
6. Most representative of God working in everyday life